The three amigos

Spanish and Latin American Filmmakers

Series editors:
Núria Triana Toribio, University of Manchester
Andy Willis, University of Salford

Spanish and Latin American Filmmakers offers a focus on new filmmakers; reclaims previously neglected filmmakers; and considers established figures from new and different perspectives. Each volume places its subject in a variety of critical and production contexts.
 The series sees filmmakers as more than just auteurs, thus offering an insight into the work and contexts of producers, writers, actors, production companies and studios. The studies in this series take into account the recent changes in Spanish and Latin American film studies, such as the new emphasis on popular cinema, and the influence of cultural studies in the analysis of films and of the film cultures produced within the Spanish-speaking industries.

Already published

The cinema of Álex de la Iglesia Peter Buse, Núria Triana Toribio and Andy Willis

Daniel Calparsoro Ann Davies

Alejandro Amenábar Barry Jordan

The cinema of Iciar Bollaín Isabel Santaolalla

Julio Medem Rob Stone

Emilio Fernandez: pictures in the margins Dolores Tierney

The three amigos

The transnational filmmaking of Guillermo del Toro, Alejandro González Iñárritu, and Alfonso Cuarón

Deborah Shaw

Manchester University Press

Copyright © Deborah Shaw 2013

The right of Deborah Shaw to be identified as the author of this work has been asserted by her in accordance with the Copyright, Designs and Patents Act 1988.

Published by Manchester University Press
Altrincham Street, Manchester M1 7JA, UK
www.manchesteruniversitypress.co.uk

British Library Cataloguing-in-Publication Data is available

Library of Congress Cataloging-in-Publication Data is available

ISBN 978 0 7190 9759 1 *paperback*

First published by Manchester University Press in hardback 2013

This paperback edition first published 2015

The publisher has no responsibility for the persistence or accuracy of URLs for any external or third-party internet websites referred to in this book, and does not guarantee that any content on such websites is, or will remain, accurate or appropriate.

Printed by Lightning Source

This book is dedicated to Mitch and Theo with love.

Contents

List of figures	page ix
Acknowledgements	xi
Introduction	1

Part I. Guillermo del Toro: the alchemist
1 *Cronos*: introducing Guillermo del Toro 19
2 Generating an authorial presence with *Hellboy II: The Golden Army* 45
3 *El laberinto del fauno*: breaking through the barriers of filmmaking 67

Part II. Alejandro González Iñárritu: independent filmmaker
4 Crashing into the international film market with *Amores perros* 95
5 *21 Grams*: an American independent film made by Mexicans 114
6 *Babel* and the global Hollywood gaze 135

Part III. Alfonso Cuarón: a study of auteurism in flux
7 Alfonso Cuarón's first films in Mexico and the USA 159
8 Cuarón finds his own path: *Y tu mamá también* 176
9 *Children of Men*: the limits of radicalism 201

Conclusion 225

Filmography 231
Bibliography 246
Index 261

List of figures

2.1 The King of Bethmoora (*Hellboy II*, Guillermo del Toro, 2008; Dark Horse Entertainment, Lawrence Gordon Productions, Relativity Media, Universal Pictures)   page 62
2.2 The King of Bethmoora (*El laberinto del fauno*, Guillermo del Toro, 2006; Estudios Picasso, Tequila Gang, Esperanto Filmoj, Sententia Entertainment, Telecinco)   62
2.3 Prince Nuada enters the underworld of the elves in exile (*Hellboy II*)   64
2.4 Ofelia enters the underworld (*El laberinto del fauno*)   64
3.1 The post-torture scene (*El laberinto del fauno*)   75
3.2 Ofelia is reborn as Princess Moanna (*El laberinto del fauno*)   76
3.3 Professor Pomona Sprout (Miriam Margolyes) holds up the mandrake (*Harry Potter and the Chamber of Secrets*, C. Columbus, 2002; 1492 Pictures, Heyday Films, Miracle Productions)   82
3.4 Ofelia looks at the mandrake (*El laberinto del fauno*)   82
4.1 A close-up of Octavio (Gael García Bernal) at the dogfight (*Amores perros*, Alejandro González Iñárritu, 2000; Altavista Films, Zeta Film)   101
4.2 A long shot from the point of view of El Chivo (Emilio Echevarría) as he stalks his next victim (*Amores perros*)   102
5.1 Jack tells his wife about the accident (*21 Grams*, Alejandro González Iñárritu, 2003; This Is That Productions, Y Productions, Mediana Productions)   128

5.2	Cristina in the nightclub where she goes to score some drugs (*21 Grams*)	130
5.3	Jack attempts suicide in jail (*21 Grams*)	131
5.4	Cristina and Paul in the rain (*21 Grams*)	132
6.1	Moroccan women are viewed from the bus (*Babel*, Alejandro González Iñárritu, 2006; Media Rights Capital, Paramount Vantage, Anonymous Content, Central Films, Zeta Film)	144
6.2	The camera focuses on Susan in the tour bus (*Babel*)	144
6.3	Chieko at the club (*Babel*)	150
7.1	Clarisa (Claudia Ramírez), the air hostess (*Sólo con tu pareja*, Alfonso Cuarón, 1991; Fondo de Fomento a la Calidad Cinematográfica, Instituto Mexicano de Cinematografía, Sólo Películas)	162
7.2	Gloria (Isabel Benet), Tomás's boss and occasional lover (*Sólo con tu pareja*)	162
7.3	Gloria waits for Tomás in Dr Mateos's apartment (*Sólo con tu pareja*)	166
7.4	Sara Crewe's (Liesel Matthews) room is magically transformed (*A Little Princess*, Alfonso Cuarón, 1995; Warner Bros Pictures, Mark Johnson Productions, Baltimore Pictures)	172
8.1	The car is dwarfed by the landscape (*Y tu mamá también*, Alfonso Cuarón, 2001; Anhelo Producciones, Besame Mucho Pictures)	189
8.2	Julio, Tenoch, and Luisa in the car (*Y tu mamá también*)	192
8.3	Luisa with Mabel and family (*Y tu mamá también*)	194
9.1	A member of Homeland Security keeps guard over imprisoned Foogies (*Children of Men*, Alfonso Cuarón, 2006; Universal Pictures, Strike Entertainment, Hit and Run Productions)	209
9.2	Miriam is captured by security forces (*Children of Men*)	210
9.3	Theo and Kee make their way through the Muslim uprising (*Children of Men*)	210

Acknowledgements

I would like to thank friends and colleagues in the academic community who helped in various ways, from sending me work prior to publication, to reading drafts, and suggesting sources. These include Luisela Alvaray, Jose Arroyo, Marimar Azcona, Sayantani DasGupta, Ann Davies, Celestino Deleyto, Stephanie Dennison, Rosalind Galt, Katie Grant, Miriam Haddu, Sue Harper, Paul McDonald, Laura Podalsky, and Dolores Tierney. Thanks also to Núria Triana Toribio and Andy Willis, the series editors, for their support and advice, and to Ralph Footring for his meticulous copy-editing.

Others have also helped along the way, and I'd like to thank Droo Padhiar, Amy Davies, Julia Kleiousi, and Linda Mason, and my colleagues at Portsmouth University for their support: Ruth Doughty, Reka Buckley, and Christine Etherington-Wright. My students deserve my thanks too for indulging my ideas on many of the films in this book. I would also like to acknowledge my gratitude to Lincoln Geraghty, Justin Smith and Graham Spencer for their support for research at Portsmouth. Thanks as always to my special mum, Lesley, and to my mum-in-law, Nana Pat.

The manuscript was delivered on time thanks to The Centre for Cultural and Creative Research at the University of Portsmouth, which provided teaching relief. Thanks are also due to Saer Maty Ba for making sure the students were in good hands when I was on study leave.

Versions of the material contained in chapter 6 have been published as '*Babel* and the Global Hollywood Gaze' in the journal *Situations: Project of the Radical Imagination*, special issue, *Global Cinema* (2011), 4(1), 11–31. Selections of material in chapter 8 have been published as '(Trans)National Images and Cinematic Spaces: The Cases of Alfonso

Cuarón's *Y tu mamá también* (2001) and Carlos Reygadas' *Japón* (2002)', in *Iberoamericana* (2011), 11(44), 117–134. I am grateful to the publishers for their permission to reproduce the material.

Introduction

Introducing the directors

Guillermo del Toro, Alejandro González Iñárritu, and Alfonso Cuarón are the best-known Mexican directors internationally, yet none of them has directed a film in Mexico since Cuarón's *Y tu mamá también*, made in 2001.[1] All three have made films in the USA; del Toro and Iñárritu have directed films in Spain, while Cuarón has mainly worked in the USA and the UK. These facts tell us a great deal about the nature of the film industry today: the lack of substantial funding for Mexican productions; the sites of economic power; and the global ambitions of the directors themselves. After their first low-budget Mexican feature films *Cronos* (del Toro, 1993) and *Sólo con tu pareja* (*Love in the Time of Hysteria*) (Cuarón, 1991), and the commercial hit *Amores perros* (Iñárritu, 2000), all three directors initially followed the golden path to the US film industry to further their international careers. Del Toro made the mainstream film *Mimic* (1997), Cuarón directed the children's film *A Little Princess* (1995), while Iñárritu succeeded in immediately establishing his auteurist credentials with the 'independent' film *21 Grams* (2003), starring Benicio del Toro, Naomi Watts, and Sean Penn.

All three have global auteurist ambitions which Mexico, with its limited funding possibilities, has not been able to accommodate.[2] Del Toro and Cuarón have had to balance these ambitions with the demands of the film industry and both have made highly acclaimed films that have combined commercial success with critical praise: the best-known examples of these are *El laberinto del fauno* (*Pan's Labyrinth*) (del Toro, 2006), and *Children of Men* (Cuarón, 2006). They have also directed more mainstream films that have been rather poorly received in critical terms (*Mimic*, del Toro; *Great Expectations*,

Cuarón, 1998). This dual-track career pathway taken by both directors problematises the use of the auteur category traditionally associated with quality art cinema, a category which is a key area of investigation in this book.

Iñárritu has succeeded in having more creative control over all of his films than his two compatriots, whether he is working in Mexico, the USA or Spain. However, he too has knowingly learnt and applied the cinematic languages of a new international style in order to enter the global channels of film production, distribution, and exhibition, and he has followed the expected guidelines of his paymasters. Thus, a key question when exploring the work of Iñárritu is what is meant by independence when working with major (predominantly North American) production companies.

Although del Toro, Iñárritu, and Cuarón have made very different films from each other, in diverse international and industrial contexts, all of which will be outlined in detail in the three parts of the book, the directors have a number of factors in common. When compared with other contemporary Mexican directors, they have had unprecedented international success and have crossed linguistic, national, and generic borders, cutting through traditional divisions created by film markets. They have cultivated auteurist personae through the films they have directed, their roles as producers, and by paratextual means (including DVD commentaries, interviews given in multiple fora, and in some cases special books released to accompany the films).

They have also strategically claimed a collective Mexican identity, and provided support to each other as well as other Mexican filmmakers, despite the fact that most of the films they have directed have been made outside Mexico, and have been reliant on US and European film financing structures. Rather than conceptualising Mexican cinema in opposition to US cinema, and eschewing their Mexican identities once they had crossed the border, they have worked to create a symbiotic relationship between the two. This can be seen in the relationship they have cultivated with their own production company, Cha Cha Cha, and Focus Features, the specialty branch of Universal Pictures. In 2007 the three filmmakers managed to secure a deal with Focus which gives them $100 million for a five-film package, thanks to their reputations.[3]

They have also harnessed a collective identity within Mexico and have used their international status to take on the role of advocates and ambassadors for the national film industry. In March 2007 an event was held at the Mexican Senate to honour their success. At this event, *los tres mosqueteros* (the three musketeers), as they are popularly known in Mexico ('the three amigos' in the USA), called on the Mexican government to do more to foster and protect Mexican cinema (*La Nación*, 2007). Del Toro, who acted as spokesperson for the three, suggested that the North American Free Trade Agreement (NAFTA) be revised in order to apply protectionist measures for Mexican cinema, which would include screen quotas for nationally produced films (*La Nación*, 2007). Their campaigning tour included a meeting with the then newly appointed Mexican President, Felipe Calderón, and the heads of cinema chains (*La Crónica de Hoy*, 2007). The three directors were lobbying for tax initiatives to stimulate filmmaking, more opportunities for the distribution and exhibition of Mexican films, and more involvement in film production from television companies. Thus, while most of their recent films cannot be categorised as Mexican, they remain important figures within Mexican film culture.

Guillermo del Toro

Guillermo del Toro has carved out a name for himself as a director of genre films, and he happily borrows and merges characteristics from fantasy, realism, horror, art cinema, and adventure films to make what has come to be seen as a 'del Toro film', a label that carries over from films made in Mexico, Spain, and the USA. Del Toro has also cultivated his role as a producer, acting in that capacity on a number of high-profile Spanish-language genre films, including *El orfanato* (*The Orphanage*) (Bayona, 2007), *Los ojos de Julia* (*Julia's Eyes*) (Morales, 2010), and *Rudo y cursi* (*Rough and Corny*) (Carlos Cuarón, 2008). He has also been an executive producer and producer for an increasing number of US productions, including *Don't Be Afraid of the Dark* (Nixey, 2010), which he co-wrote, *Kung Fu Panda 2* (Yuh, 2011), and *Puss in Boots* (Miller, 2011).

As a director, del Toro sees no limit to the variety of genres he can incorporate into his films or the number of intertextual references that can be borrowed from these genres, as will be seen in part I of the book. Any eager film critic or film buff who attempts to spot or follow up all of these will end up frustrated at the difficulty of the task (as I quickly discovered). In terms of production contexts, del Toro's corpus can be broadly divided into Spanish-language films – *Cronos*,

El espinazo del diablo (*The Devil's Backbone*, 2001) and *El laberinto* – and big-budget Hollywood projects – *Mimic*, *Blade II* (2002), *Hellboy* (2004), and *Hellboy II: The Golden Army* (2008). This, however, does not follow a neat divide that would allow a critic to separate out two career stages. On the contrary, there has been no chronological logic to the director's working practices and he has managed to combine making Spanish-language films with bigger-budget Hollywood projects. As will be seen in the chapters on *El laberinto* and *Hellboy II*, del Toro talks of both projects in the same breath in interviews and sees them as originating from the same imaginary universe. The creation of a recognisable style that cuts across national and generic borders is also made possible by the fact that he has been able to work with cinematographer Guillermo Navarro, his Mexican compatriot, on all three Spanish-language films, and on the *Hellboy* films. In chapters 2 and 3, I explore similarities between the films generated by the authorial force of del Toro, but also points of divergence occasioned by the very different production contexts.

Del Toro's first film was *Cronos*, which was partly funded by the Mexican Film Institute (Instituto Mexicano de Cinematografía, IMCINE), and partly self-funded. It won a number of national and international awards, which brought the director to the attention of Hollywood. As a result of this attention, he was employed as a director on the mainstream fantasy horror film *Mimic* (1997), produced by Miramax and Dimension Films. This was not, however, a happy experience and the director claims he lost all his battles with the studios regarding the screenplay, but managed partially to assert his style in relation to the look of the film (Wood, 2008).[4] Creative control was restored on his next project, *El espinazo del diablo*, which was made following the offer of finance by El Deseo, the Almodóvar brothers' production company, and co-produced with del Toro's production company, Tequila Gang, and the Mexican company Anhelo Producciones (which had also produced Cuarón's *Y tu mamá también*). As IMCINE had refused to fund del Toro's planned project, he decided to re-contextualise this political ghost story to the Spanish Civil War, not the Mexican Revolution as originally intended (Lázaro-Reboll, 2007: 43).

Few filmmakers have made themselves so at home in such diverse national and industrial contexts as del Toro, and in the chapters on the director I consider how he has weaved his way through small and large Mexican, Spanish, and US production contexts. I also explore his travels through genres, and labels signalling market differentiation such as art cinema and fantasy filmmaking, and consider how notions of high and low culture are intermingled in his texts. I explore the auteurist strategies that he has cultivated and explain what is meant by a 'del Toro film'.

Alejandro González Iñárritu

Del Toro's compatriot Alejandro González Iñárritu has also cultivated auteurist strategies, but to very different effect. Iñárritu has a more coherent corpus and a team with whom he has worked for the first three films: screenwriter Guillermo Arriaga, cinematographer Rodrigo Prieto, production designer Brigitte Broch, and the composer Gustavo Santoalalla. Together they have developed an identifiable style from within the codes of an international film language.[5] In the chapters on the director I pay close attention to the features of this language, and explore the ways that *Amores perros* entered the global market through its reliance on narrative experimentation and stylistic features of intensified continuity (Bordwell, 2002a). These features include rapid editing, fluid camera work and a hand-held camera, and the use of a range of shots, such as extreme close-ups and extreme long shots. This analysis of film form is developed in the chapter on *21 Grams* (2003), as I examine the way in which Iñárritu adopts the language of US independent cinema, with a focus on the narrative structure and the application of a range of colour palettes. Iñárritu and his team's fluency with the codes and conventions of serious, quality global film has allowed his films to be distributed internationally and consumed as art-house inflected independent films, labels and categories that I explore in some depth in part II of the book.

Iñárritu, like del Toro and Cuarón, has worked in a range of national and production contexts. His first film, *Amores perros*, was a successful, privately funded 'national' film that was an international success, and raised both his profile and that of Mexican film. This opened the doors to allow the director to make the 'independent' US feature *21 Grams*, set and filmed in Memphis. Following *21 Grams*, Iñárritu and team made their most ambitious film, *Babel* (2006), located in four countries and featuring six languages.

A text not considered by this book, as it was released after the planning and writing of part II, is Iñárritu's latest production, *Biutiful* (2010), his first film to be made without the input of Arriaga, following a fall-out over questions of creative ownership regarding *Babel*. *Biutiful* can also be read through a transnational framework and reaffirms Iñárritu's status as transnational director. It is a Mexican, Spanish, US (Focus Features) co-production, set and shot in Spain and featuring transnational Spanish star Javier Bardem, and dealing with the hidden lives of immigrants in Barcelona.

Alfonso Cuarón

Alfonso Cuarón has also followed a transnational trajectory, making films in Mexico, the USA, and the UK, and, like del Toro, he has had a varied career, taking on auteurist and studio projects. His first feature was the state-produced Mexican sex comedy *Sólo con tu pareja* (*Love in the Time of Hysteria*, 1991). Although it was not successful on the global scale of *Amores perros*, or indeed his second Mexican film, *Y tu mamá también* (2001), it was part of a series of films that brought middle-class Mexicans back to the cinema, and its domestic popularity afforded him the opportunity to pursue a Hollywood career. Cuarón went on to direct two star-studded features, *A Little Princess* (1995) and *Great Expectations* (1998), both of which were entirely US funded, the former a Warner Bros Pictures production, and the latter financed by independent company Art Linson Productions and major studio Twentieth Century Fox.

While the director has declared himself happier with the creative process of making *A Little Princess* than *Great Expectations* (Krassakopoulos, 2007), neither of these were auteurist projects, in that the director was hired by the companies to bring quality to the products, which he did through a distinctive visual palette and mise-en-scène. Despite the very different industrial context, Cuarón brought a number of artistic ideas he and his cinematographer Emmanuel Lubezki had developed with *Sólo con tu pareja*, notably the use of a green colour palette and opulent, highly decorated interiors and lush exteriors. In the second part of chapter 7, I consider the tensions between the director and production company in the making of *Great Expectations*, and examine the distinctive mise-en-scène and the significance of the artistic choices made in the three films associated with his green period in terms of Cuarón's career trajectory.

It is worthy of note that the style and the focus on the colour green applied in *A Little Princess* and *Great Expectations* were abandoned once Cuarón was able to retain creative control with *Y tu mamá*

Introduction

también and *Children of Men*. Indeed, the return to Mexican filmmaking for *Y tu mamá también* can be seen as an attempt to establish an authorial voice, and a new signature filmic trait is developed, namely the unusually long take often used for tracking shots. Yet, as is the case with del Toro, the search for commercial art cinema acclaim is followed by a commercial blockbuster, and after returning to Mexico to make *Y tu mamá también*, Cuarón located to England to work on the Warner Bros Harry Potter franchise for *Harry Potter and the Prisoner of Azkaban* (2004). This was followed by his most acclaimed work to date, also filmed in England, the Oscar-nominated *Children of Men*, which was both a medium-budget commercial venture funded by Universal Pictures and an auteurist project. The screenplay was co-written by Cuarón, and P. D. James's novel on which it is loosely based was significantly altered to fit the director's vision for the film.

Theoretical approaches

The diverse national, production, and generic contexts in which the directors have worked require new ways of thinking about cinema, resulting in the questioning of a number of traditional ideas. These include challenging the ways both markets and critics have created clear-cut distinctions between mainstream commercial and independent art cinema, and the ways they have conceptualised US, Latin American, and European cinema as discrete entities. The work of the three directors (each in its own way) blurs generic and national boundaries and creates new hybrid formations. The most fruitful theoretical approaches that can be applied to analyse working practices and texts centre on new readings of auteurism and transnational film theories.

As stated above, the types of film that the three directors have made have been so diverse that no simple application of the 'auteur' label is possible across the board. Iñárritu has been the most careful to ensure creative control over his films, and has worked only with 'indie' production companies, albeit in the case of Focus Features one affiliated to the major studio Universal Pictures. Both del Toro and Cuarón have directed auteurist films and both have been directors-for-hire who have incorporated their own visual style into a text over which they have not felt control. The diverse paths taken by the filmmakers mean that it is not particularly productive to make 'for and against' type arguments in relation to whether del Toro, Iñárritu, and Cuarón can be seen as auteurs, as this can be a subjective view that changes from one critic to the next. It is more fruitful to explore the ways texts themselves are constructed as auteurist, and the relationship between these and the markets at which they are aimed. Related to this is the way that each director uses texts and paratexts to enhance his auteur status and the reasons for this. How, for instance, does del Toro make auteurist claims for a Hollywood blockbuster, based on comics drawn and written by Mike Mignola? This is the central question addressed chapter 2, on *Hellboy II: The Golden Army*.

Auteurism is intimately connected to theories on the transnational in film, and is central to the travels of the three directors and their films. The directors have put much energy into cultivating this status (charted throughout this book), as it is has provided them with passports to filmmaking in national contexts beyond Mexico; Mexican finances, whether secured privately or through the state, could not provide the resources to accommodate their filmmaking ambitions and visions. The shift in the geographical locations in which the directors are working leads to new ways of understanding the auteur category for those working within Latin American film. As Marvin D'Lugo (2003a: 110) observes, a number of Latin American directors, such as Arturo Ripstein in Mexico, Fernando Solanas in Argentina, and Tomás Gutiérrez Alea in Cuba, became 'authorial icons', who took on a representational role in terms of their national cultures. As D'Lugo affirms (2003a: 110):

> In each case, their well-established reputations as oppositional, anti-status quo, resistance figures had become refigured as national auteurs, principally through international film festivals which privileged the authorial as an expression of the national.

Del Toro, Iñárritu, and Cuarón demonstrate a shift away from this position held by a previous generation of filmmakers, and reveal how the best-known Latin American auteurist directors (to whom we can add Walter Salles and Fernando Meirelles from Brazil) are no longer tied to national representations in terms of their output. The career pathways of 'the three amigos' demonstrate that paradigms of national cinema cannot explain or contain the work of such filmmakers, and a careful application of specific aspects of transnational film culture will frame the readings in this book.

There is another strand of global Latin American auteurs whose productions are more rooted in purer spaces of art cinema and for whom transnational funding and distribution arrangements are intimately linked to representations of the national. The best-known of these directors are the Argentine Lucrecia Martel, the Peruvian Claudia Llosa, and the Mexican Carlos Reygadas, although there are other examples. Though there is much to say about this, it does not fall within the remit of this book.

There has been something of a boom in work on the transnational in cinema in the last decade, in response to more globalised forms of filmmaking. This field of work is usefully mapped by Higbee and Lim (2010) in their article 'Concepts of Transnational Cinema: Towards a Critical Transnationalism in Film Studies'. The authors outline three theoretical approaches (Higbee and Lim, 2010: 8–10). The first centres on a 'national/transnational binary' (Crofts, 1998; Higson, 2000) that privileges the transnational as a means to understanding the complex production, exhibition, and distribution models of filmmaking. The second approach considers regional cinema, seen in examples they cite, such as work on Chinese cinemas (Lu, 1997) and 1930s European cinema (Bergfelder *et al.*, 2007). These are 'film cultures/national cinemas which invest in a shared cultural heritage and/or geo-political boundary' (Higbee and Lim, 2010: 9). The third approach can be found in work on diasporic, exilic, and post-colonial cinemas, most prominent in the writings of Naficy (2001) and Marks (2000), which challenges 'the western (neocolonial) construct of nation and national culture' (Higbee and Lim, 2010: 9).

It is clear, then, that there is no straightforward, single transnational film theory that can be applied to film texts or working practices or the economics of the industry. Indeed, as a number of critics have argued, a lack of clarity has surrounded 'transnational cinema', along with a tendency to conflate a number of meanings in a fashionable umbrella term (Berry, 2010; Hjort, 2009; Shaw, 2013). One of the reasons for this can be found in the many meanings that can be ascribed to it. Chris Berry has argued:

> It is clear that the potential meanings of 'transnational cinema' are many and various. It can be traced back to the beginnings of cinema itself. Or it can be dated from the impact of globalization in the cinema. It can refer to big budget blockbuster cinema associated with the operations of global corporate capital. Or it can refer to small budget diasporic and exilic cinema. It can refer to films that challenge national identity, or it can refer to the consumption of foreign films as part of the process of a discourse about what national identity is. (Berry, 2010: 114)

Elsewhere, in a chapter entitled 'Deconstructing and Reconstructing "Transnational Cinema"' I consider overgeneralised applications of the label that fail to separate out these different aspects of the transnational, and propose a way forward through the creation of a series of fifteen sub-categories, which I outline and explain (Shaw, 2013). These sub-categories are as follows: transnational modes of production, distribution, and exhibition; transnational modes of narration; cinema of globalisation; films with multiple locations; exilic and diasporic filmmaking; film and cultural exchange; transnational influences; transnational critical approaches; transnational viewing practices; transregional or transcommunity films; transnational stars; transnational directors; the ethics of transnationalism; transnational collaborative networks; and national films. Since formulating this list, one of the gaps that emerged in the writing of this book is another category, 'the politics of the transnational', needed to address the political discourses into which global texts and paratexts are inserted, and the relationship between these and the production and distribution companies that provide the finance.

For an analysis of the filmmaking of del Toro, Iñárritu, and Cuarón, the most apposite of these classifications are 'transnational directors', 'transnational modes of production, distribution, and exhibition', 'transnational modes of narration', and 'the politics of the transnational'. I go on to explain their application in more depth below, but a number of the other categories also inform the readings in this study. Throughout, I consider the influence of filmmakers from across the world on the three directors ('transnational influences'). The term 'cinema of globalisation' is applied in the analysis of two specific texts, Iñárritu's *Babel* and Cuarón's *Children of Men*. The term was developed by Tom Zaniello in his book *The Cinema of Globalization: A Guide to Films About the New Economic Order* (2007) to encompass films 'about transnational organisations' and 'multinational corporations', and their effects on people and the environment (Zaniello, 2007: 17).

In addition, I consider and evaluate the place of the national and, in particular, ask whether there is a loss of national specificity in the search for global success. This question is foregrounded in the readings of *El laberinto*, *Babel*, and *Y tu mamá también*. I also explore the relationship between the national and the transnational in each part of the book: I conceptualise the most successful film that each director has made in Mexico (*Cronos*, *Amores perros*, and *Y tu mamá*

Introduction

también) as national/transnational texts. This can be seen in the ways they combine national and global thematic concerns, a predominantly Mexican cast and crew, and Mexican funding with elements of international and US filmmaking languages and genres. These texts are also transnational in the way that they have circulated in global film markets.

These films are central in establishing the status of 'transnational directors', the overarching category of analysis in this study. The term can be applied to an exclusive set of directors who have often acquired an auteurist status, usually as a result of the success of a first film (or films) most often made in their home country, which opens up funding possibilities in other national production contexts. This definition can be applied to a number of respected filmmakers in addition to del Toro, Iñárritu, and Cuarón, including the Chilean/Spanish director Alejandro Amenábar, the Austrian Michael Haneke, the Taiwanese Ang Lee, the Australian Baz Luhrmann, the Brazilian directors Fernando Meirelles and Walter Salles, and the Danish director Lars von Trier, among others. It is helpful to distinguish between this group of 'transnational directors' and globally successful directors/auteurs who make films within a specific national/local context, but whose films circulate in the international market through transnational distribution and exhibition networks. We can cite Lucrecia Martel and Pedro Almodóvar as examples of Hispanic filmmakers who fall into this grouping.

It is important to note that the category 'transnational directors' is dependent on its relationship to the other categories highlighted for this study. Thus, all three of my case studies have benefited from a range of transnational production and distribution arrangements, the specifics of which will be seen in each chapter. This, in turn, is the result of the fact that the films made employ 'transnational modes of narration', that is, globally inflected film languages that can be understood in international markets, and make the product desirable to producers, distributors, and audiences. That does not mean that the three directors share approaches to film language, as will be seen; however, del Toro, Iñárritu, and Cuarón are all cine-literate, and understand the need to reach global audiences.

To give a few examples, discussed in more depth in each part, in del Toro's films, as he himself reveals, ideas are borrowed from directors such as Alfred Hitchcock and Victor Erice, and the creator of monsters Ray Harryhausen. Iñárritu has located himself, with his first three films, within the multi-stranded storytelling strategies of global art cinema and independent filmmaking. Cuarón has adopted a number of visual and narrative approaches with his cinematographer Emmanuel Lubezki. In their Hollywood films they have cultivated a rich and distinctive use of mise-en-scène to carve out an authorial signature for the director, while in *Y tu mamá también* and *Children of Men* they address important social themes and favour the long take and innovative use of the camera.

The effect of the film language each director cultivates is also related to the explorations of 'the politics of the transnational'. There are two central recurring questions throughout this book. Where do the directors position themselves politically through their texts? And, what is the relationship between declared statements of political intent and the commercial demands of the sector of the film industry in which each project can be located? I consider whether there is a possibility of radical social visions from directors who have global ambitions, a question that is foregrounded in the readings of *El laberinto*, *Babel*, *Y tu mamá también*, and *Children of Men*.

Structure and chapter outlines

There are three parts to the book, organised around each director, each with three chapters dedicated to readings of key films they have directed. In the case of Guillermo del Toro I begin with an analysis of his first Mexican film, with the chapter '*Cronos*: introducing Guillermo del Toro'. Here I examine a stripped down del Toro; that is, I explore the elements that make up his cinematic universe without the possibilities that bigger budgets afforded in his later work. I consider his transnational influences, and analyse a Mexican take on the vampire film, and identify thematic and visual signature markers that will be developed and expanded in later work.

Chapter 2, 'Generating an authorial presence with *Hellboy II: The Golden Army*', considers the complex issues at play when discussing auteurism in a studio-backed commercial film (Universal Pictures). I use this case study to present an analysis of the construction of an auteurist discourse through the use of paratexts: the director's commentary in the DVD extras, personal notes, observations, and drawings presented in the book *Hellboy II: Art of the Movie* (Sandoval and Velasco, 2008), and extensive interviews. I also consider what fans bring to this debate and how they have their own position on del

Introduction

Toro's adaptation and appropriation of Mignola's comic stories, which often clash with academic readings of adaptations and auteurism.

Chapter 3, '*El laberinto del fauno*: breaking through the barriers of filmmaking', makes the case that del Toro's third Spanish-language feature (after *El espinazo del diablo*) is an important text in the history of film, as it disrupts traditional boundaries between art cinema and fantasy filmmaking, and was the precursor to a series of European films that brought elements of genre filmmaking to the creation of popular non-English-language texts that circulated in global markets. I also consider the relationship between fantasy filmmaking and political historical storytelling, and discuss the ethical and social implications of this pairing.

I begin part II, on Alejandro González Iñárritu, with the chapter 'Crashing into the international film market with *Amores perros*', in which I examine the way the director and his team adopt stylistic features associated with a new international film language in vogue. I apply David Bordwell's notion of intensified continuity (2002a) and Eleftheria Thanouli's understanding of a post-classical style (2006, 2008) to develop the concept of the national/transnational film, which explains the film's success both in Mexico and around the world.

The title of the next chapter, '*21 Grams*: an American independent film made by Mexicans', indicates how I approach Iñárritu's first US film. This film can be seen as a continuation of the styles and themes essayed in *Amores perros*, but reframed in Memphis and distributed by Focus Features, the independent arm of Universal Pictures. I ask what constitutes an independent film and explore the ways in which *21 Grams* fits within the models presented. I also assess the relationship between independence and auteurism, both in general and in the specific case of Iñárritu.

In the final chapter in part II, '*Babel* and the global Hollywood gaze', I consider whether Iñárritu's *Babel* is a new form of world cinema text that de-exoticises 'other' cultures or whether it is a US-centric film conditioned by the fact that US companies were the primary sources of funding. I explore these questions by assessing the value of two types of gaze when reading the text: a tourist gaze, and a world cinema gaze. This is, of course, all connected to processes of othering, which Iñárritu claims he resists as a Mexican director, a claim I challenge.

As Cuarón is the director with the least consistency in terms of identifiable style, I have felt it necessary to take a slightly different approach in part III. It can be claimed that there are number of

'Cuaróns' in terms of his career: the national cinema director of the low-budget *Sólo con tu pareja*; the commercial director-for-hire who made *A Little Princess*, *Great Expectations*, and *Harry Potter and the Prisoner of Azkaban*; the Mexican auteur whose *Y tu mamá también*, along with Iñárritu's *Amores perros*, helped put contemporary Mexican film on the map; and the international filmmaker who made the acclaimed *Children of Men*. Part III is entitled 'Alfonso Cuarón: a study of auteurism in flux', and I conceptualise auteurism not as a fixed category, but as a subjective label, and something that directors have to work to claim. It is a status that emerges from a corpus of work, but also through individual film texts, and a single director can make auteurist films and non-auteurist films. Thus, Cuarón directs an auteurist low-budget Mexican film, *Y tu mamá también*, in which he had complete creative control, yet this was followed by *Harry Potter and the Prisoner of Azkaban*, with a huge crew, for which he was hired to do a job, with the rules of the franchise determining many of the creative choices.

For these reasons, in the first chapter of part III of the book I consider two films, *Sólo con tu pareja* and *Great Expectations*, as these are interesting, partially 'failed' texts that did not succeed in securing Cuarón a global auteurist status. They are also of interest as they helped determine future career choices, as the director moved away from the styles and approaches employed in these films. In the first part of chapter 7, '*Sólo con tu pareja*: bringing the middle classes back to Mexican cinemas', I analyse the factors that made Cuarón's first film a domestic hit, but prevented its international circulation. In the second part, 'Not such great expectations: working within the Hollywood system', I outline the director's frustrations on the project, and consider ways in which the director and cinematographer, Lubezki, compensated for weaknesses in the screenplay through the cultivation of a distinct visual style and elaborate mise-en-scène.

I dedicate more space to *Y tu mamá también* and *Children of Men* as they are where Cuarón finds his authorial voice, and they are significant in terms of subject matter and filmic approaches. They can also both be seen as transnational texts in different ways, as the chapters discuss. Chapter 8, 'Cuarón finds his own path: *Y tu mamá también*', explores the new personal style developed by the director and Lubezki, which they carry over to *Children of Men*. I examine Cuarón's choice to establish himself as a director of long takes, associated with a tradition of respected art-cinema auteurs, and the development of

Introduction 15

innovative and inventive camerawork. I also consider what makes *Y tu mamá también* a transnational text and examine the images of Mexico that have enabled the film to be exported to a global market, and the ways in which it plays with and provides a new take on familiar US genres. This is tied in with the political vision set out and the film's ambivalent takes on capitalism and feminism which work to sustain its commercial viability.

The final chapter on Cuarón, '*Children of Men*: the limits of radicalism', takes the film as a paradigmatic transnational text, as it fits a number of the categories associated with transnational cinema outlined above. I discuss the film's modes of production, distribution, and exhibition; the ways it can be seen as an example of the cinema of globalisation, and the modes of narration employed. There is a relationship between these factors which make it a global product and the limitations in radicalism espoused by the feature film. In the latter part of the chapter, I explore the conflict between commerce and radical politics and the relationship between *Children of Men* and the documentary *The Possibility of Hope*, also directed by Cuarón and available in the DVD and Blu-ray extras package. I ask how the feature film, co-produced by Universal Pictures and featuring such high-profile stars as Clive Owen and Julianne Moore, deals with issues such as migration, global warfare, state control and brutality, and terrorism. Other questions raised are: How do the fictional representations relate to the views, documented in *The Possibility of Hope*, of high-profile political and social theorists? And, to what extent does the position maintained by the film compare or contrast with that of two of these theorists, Naomi Klein and Slavoj Žižek?

Thus, the book aims to provide the first comprehensive academic analysis of some of the most significant films of Guillermo del Toro, Alejandro González Iñárritu, and Alfonso Cuarón, made over a period of seventeen years, from 1991 (*Sólo con tu pareja*) to 2008 (*Hellboy II: The Golden Army*). I have used approaches and asked questions that I have found most interesting and hope that others will do so too. I have attempted to link these questions and approaches to contemporary discussions within film scholarship and to offer some points of debate for future work in these areas.

Notes

1 *Babel* (Iñárritu, 2006) was partly shot in Mexico, but those scenes comprised a small part of a complex narrative.

2   *Amores perros* had a budget of $2 million, while even *Y tu mamá también*, made when Cuarón was well established, had a budget of $5 million, large by Mexican standards, but miniscule when compared with budgets for even small-scale Hollywood films.
3   The company was formed by the three directors along with Carlos Cuarón and Rodrigo García. The best-known films it has co-produced to date are *Rudo y cursi* (*Rough and Corny*), directed by Alfonso's brother Carlos Cuarón (2008), and *Mother and Child* (Rodrigo García, 2009). For more on the formation of Cha Cha Cha see Shaw (2013).
4   The director's re-edited cut of *Mimic* was released in October 2011 on Blu-ray. This features over ten additional minutes of footage and an editing out of some of the sequences filmed by the second unit (Lambie, 2011).
5   This study does not assume a director's auteurist status is weakened by recognising his/her collaborations with key members of a filmmaking team; rather, a strong team enhances this status by helping to give form to a director's creative vision.

PART I

Guillermo del Toro: the alchemist

1

Cronos: introducing Guillermo del Toro

Cronos is a film that has been given an afterlife with the subsequent global success of the director. The fact that a small Mexican film made in 1992 and released in 1993 is available in well known film outlets in modern urban centres and from online outlets throughout the world is entirely due to the auteurist status of the director. *Cronos* is an interesting film to explore, as it shows del Toro without big budgets. At the time, it was the most expensive Mexican film ever made, with a budget of $2 million, according to the Internet Movie Database (IMDB; uk.imdb.com); however, that is clearly miniscule in comparison with Hollywood and European art cinema productions. Del Toro has not made a film in Mexico since *Cronos*, and has escaped the limited funding possibilities that are encountered by most Mexican filmmakers. It is, then, fascinating to analyse his first feature, which was made without even the modest or medium-sized funds of his later films.

Most of the literature on *Cronos* has focused on the film's relationships to national cinema and to the vampire genre (Davies, 2008; Kantaris, 1998; Kraniauskas, 1998; Stock, 1999). Kraniauskas (1998), for instance, sees the vampire as a symbol of post-colonial/neo-colonial transnational economic relations in Latin America. Stock follows a similar line and, as well as highlighting the power relations that the film calls attention to between the USA and Mexico, argues against trying to perceive the film purely as a vehicle of Mexicanness; Stock (1999: 277–278) calls for a revalorisation of the hybrid film, and argues that, in its transnational nature, it subverts the traditions of the vampire film. Ann Davies questions Stock and argues effectively that vampire films are transnational by nature, and thus places the film firmly within the vampire tradition. In her words: 'most if not all vampire texts dissolve and cross boundaries and borders, that doing this in fact *is* one of the conventions of vampire texts' (Davies, 2008: 396).

I do not want to rehash ideas from this high-quality work, but I will consider the film's place within a national/transnational paradigm, with a clearer focus on the director himself and the production context as I argue that the approach to filmmaking taken in *Cronos* is central to understanding del Toro's subsequent positioning between global auteur and blockbuster director. No critics have focused on the way that del Toro's vision in his first film relates to his subsequent better-known texts. I read *Cronos* as a key film, in that it lays bare a personal vision which will be repeated and developed in subsequent films. While accepting financial realities and the importance of production contexts, I have found it more fruitful to seek out the authorial voice, which is large, ambitious, and always transnational, rather than categorising his films as straightforward examples of Mexican, Hollywood, or Spanish filmmaking.

In the analysis which follows I examine the way the film questions the fixity of borders while also making a political statement on US–Mexican relations. I consider the way in which the director alchemically utilises references from across cultural, mythical, and religious texts, from across continents and ages, to create a film which produces a personal and Mexican take on immortality, death, and morality. I explore the ways in which the writer-director applies his thesis on the importance of death to the horror genre, and examine how this subverts an understanding of death as the dark element to be feared. I go on to analyse how del Toro, through *Cronos*, establishes an auteurist identity, which will be developed with experience and access to larger budgets. I argue for the centrality of early horror filmmakers James Whale and Terence Fisher, and their interpretations of Dracula and Frankenstein. Finally, I consider traits which are common to del Toro's approach to filmmaking and outline how his defining characteristics – genre crossings, the marrying of the fantastical and the realist, and his political vision – are first essayed in his only film made in Mexico before being implemented in his later films.

Cronos: a national/transnational film

Cronos was made before the new possibilities for Mexican directors ushered in by the privatised financial approaches taken in the making and marketing of Iñárritu's *Amores perros* (2000) and Cuarón's *Y tu mamá también* (2001), and funding problems figure prominently in the narrative given by the director of the filmmaking process. Del Toro has spoken of the fact that, after much negotiation over three years, he eventually got funding from the Mexican Film Institute (Instituto Mexicano de Cinematografía, IMCINE), but that IMCINE refused to take the finished product to international festivals as it was a horror film, and it provided only a tiny budget to allow him to take the film to Cannes (Wood, 2006: 38). In the DVD commentary that accompanies the 2006 release from Optimum, he has also spoken of the producers' refusal to pay for the Cronos device, and the fact that he had to self-finance part of the project, resulting in crippling bank loans, with excessive interest rates and a debt that took four years to pay off. This was not helped by the very limited distribution given to the film when it was originally released – it was screened, for example, in only six theatres in Mexico City (Lázaro-Reboll, 2007: 44).

The roots of the source of contention between the director and IMCINE appear to lie in opposing visions of what cinema should be, with the national film institute endorsing social realist/art cinema forms rather than popular genre formats. Lázaro-Reboll summarises the attitude (at the time) of the official funding bodies well, with reference to Cuarón's *Y tu mamá también* and del Toro's *El espinazo del diablo* (*The Devil's Backbone*, 2001):

> These Mexican–Spanish co-productions and the generic forms chosen by the directors – horror and road-movie – are not embraced by official culture as illustrations of local cultural concerns or as representatives of national artistic pride, suggesting an institutional preference for indigenous cultural products, which are 'authentically Mexican'.
> (Lázaro-Reboll, 2007: 44)

Nevertheless, this is not the whole story, and many in Mexico welcomed this new direction in national filmmaking, signalled by the fact that it won nine Arieles, Mexico's prestigious national film awards. Subsequently, del Toro's international status has meant that within Mexico he has shifted from a being troublesome filmmaker who wanted money, but refused to fit into previously understood art cinema paradigms, to a star director who can influence national film policy, and who was the subject of a retrospective in the Mexican Cineteca nacional (Molina Ramírez, 2007). This is despite the fact that *Cronos* is the only film that del Toro has made in Mexico. It is thus ironic that the initial attitude from cinematic bodies and the lack of sustained financial support have led to his self-imposed exile from Mexico and success in the international market, and, following this, a canonised status in Mexico.

DVD and Blu-ray editions of the film were later released. For instance, Optimum Home Releasing brought out the film in the UK in 2006, and Criterion released the film on DVD and Blu-ray in 2010 with a number of special extra features. The transnational potential of the film was recognised by distribution companies due to: the reputation del Toro established with his subsequent films; the presence of internationally familiar performers such as Federico Luppi and Ron Perlman (who in large part owe their global status to their work with del Toro); and the nature of the film text itself. *Cronos* demonstrates that breaching borders separating horror and art cinema is a successful formula for global success, a formula del Toro would apply to later films such as *El espinazo del diablo* and *El laberinto del fauno*.

The plot of *Cronos* tells of Jesús Gris (Federico Luppi), an unassuming owner of an antiques shop. He and his wife, Mercedes, look after their granddaughter Aurora (Tamara Shanath) after her parents die in a car accident. By chance, Jesús discovers a Cronos device hidden inside a statue of an angel delivered to his shop. The Cronos device was invented by an alchemist in the sixteenth century and grants its users immortality after feeding from their blood. The user can, in turn, feed only from blood, as Jesús discovers after becoming addicted to the device. Unbeknownst to Jesús, the device is being sought by the business tycoon Dieter de la Guardia (Claudio Brook), who sends his nephew Angel (Ron Perlman) on a mission to track it down. A battle between Jesús and the de la Guardias forms the action for the rest of the film. From this basic storyline, del Toro creates a rich cinematic world. The transnational dimensions of the film can be seen in multiple ways beyond the fact that the film is available in the global market: they are apparent through the way in which nations are conceived; through the characterisation of the protagonists; through the numerous filmic and literary intertextual references; through generic hybridity; and through the establishment of an individual authorial style that has secured the director global success. In this section I explore both national and transnational elements, and the ways in which they interact.

Del Toro's transnational ambitions are apparent in *Cronos* from the planning to the conception of the project. The film was developed with US financing in mind. In the DVD commentary that accompanies the 2006 release, the director explains that he spent eight or nine years rewriting the script, originally written for his course thesis, following contact with an American film producer. He does not name the producer, but notes that the money never materialised. Nevertheless, this clearly affected the creative process, as he rewrites the script in English, then translates it back to Spanish, and it 'becomes more American, with a first, second and third act' (DVD commentary). This process reveals both a pragmatic and an auteurist approach to filmmaking: although del Toro rewrites the screenplay with an American producer in mind and, by implication, American/international audiences, at the same time he subverts a number of conventions of American mainstream cinema. This is seen from the very opening of the film, with its grand historical introduction, narrating and providing graphic images of the alchemist's arrival in Mexico and his eventual death, all voiced in English, like any other mainstream US feature. However, this is juxtaposed with a follow-up scene which appears to be from a different film; this is a dreary domestic shot, with a switch to Spanish dialogue that introduces Jesús and his family. This is quite deliberate and plays with expectations of Hollywood versus low-budget 'national' cinema. As del Toro tells Jason Wood:

> I was actually more interested in opening the movie like a Hollywood movie. Open it as if you are about to see a super-extensive production but then this production only lasts three minutes. Then you go to meet the most boring guy on earth. (Wood, 2006: 34)

Another example of 'Americanising' the screenplay while critiquing US culture can be seen in the fact that in the original script the 'Americans' were Nazis in hiding in Mexico. Their nationalities were altered as the investor wanted an American actor (DVD commentary); however, the younger American character, Angel de la Guardia, is a cartoon villain, a parody of a Hollywood villain, which appeals to a specifically Latin American desire to redress the representational balance. He is a sadistic brute who is only interested in his uncle's money; he is vain and obsessed with his nose, which suffers repeated blows. As has been noted by many critics (Berumen, 1995; Ramírez Berg, 1990, 2002; Richard, 1994; Shaw, 2007; Woll, 1980), Hollywood has long list of Mexican/Latin American stereotyped villains, which are constantly being reworked, and del Toro has stated that he liked the idea that he could gain some revenge with *Cronos* (DVD commentary).[1]

This idea of redressing a balance is also seen in the way that the plot makes clear connections between vampirism and both Spanish colonialism and, more explicitly, US neo-colonialism, as other critics have noted (Davies, 2008; Kantaris, 1998; Kraniauskas, 1998; Stock, 1999). Thus, the Cronos device finds its way into Mexico via the alchemist, Humberto Fulcanelli, in 1536, and resurfaces in a post-NAFTA Mexico in 1997, when the film was set. Del Toro has commented that as a result of the North American Free Trade Agreement (NAFTA), Mexican culture suffered, as 'we were raided and invaded by media companies and there was nothing to protect us' (Wood, 2006: 41). Although the NAFTA laws were passed in 1994, after the film was made, the effects are pre-figured through the relationship between Jesús Gris and the de la Guardias. As Ann Davies has noted, vampirism is the perfect medium to represent the crossing of borders, a central characteristic of vampire stories from the earliest tales to the present day (Davies, 2008: 396), and while *Cronos* is not interested in setting up the idea of a closed monocultural society, the film does give a sense of a multinational Mexico preyed on by its powerful North American neighbour. Geoffrey Kantaris (1998) observes that *Cronos*

> seems to encode, or at least play with, the anxiety produced in the pollution of frontiers. This, then, is an important example of the way in which post-national visual culture both reflects and partakes of disembedding processes.

However, the film problematises simplistic divisions between Mexico and the USA, and refutes unitary national identities, preferring to root the diegesis within sites of transnational complexities. The Mexico seen in *Cronos* is futuristically cosmopolitan (set in the then future of 1997), offering an interesting mix of past, present, and future, paralleled in the Cronos device. The antique shop's signage is in several languages, including Arabic, Russian, English, and Chinese. There are Russian newspapers covering Aurora's den, and a tin biscuit box in her room is decorated with Chinese characters.[2] Thus, the film speaks of a deterritorialised nation, reinforced by the wide range of intertextual references, as will be discussed.

The characterisation also speaks of the fluidity of national identities. The villains may be seen broadly as North American, yet Dieter de la Guardia has a Germanic/Hispanic name, is bi-lingual and within the diegesis speaks flawless, Mexican-inflected Spanish with a slight English accent, and English with a slight undetermined foreign accent. His North American identity is also undermined by the fact that Dieter is played by the Mexican actor Claudio Brook, best known internationally for his roles in a number of Buñuel films.[3]

Angel de la Guardia, despite his name, is more clearly figured as North American. He is played by Ron Perlman (who went on to become del Toro's Hellboy). He addresses Jesús in both flawed Spanish and English.[4] The 'American' characters, then, inhabit a bi-lingual linguistic borderland that characterises a Hispanic American space more clearly than an Anglophone one. Although Dieter and Angel address each other (abusively) in English, there is no clear sense whether they will speak English, Spanish or 'Spanglish' to Jesús. Dieter, for instance, tells Jesús referring to the missing pages of the book, 'me las comí, best meal I've had in years'. He follows this by 'peel it off' (referring to Jesús's skin), then, 'vea, ha vuelto a nacer'.[5] This is a pattern of speech also adopted by Angel. When he enters Jesús's shop and buys the angel, he says, 'no es mi dinero. Keep the change', followed by, 'can I ask your opinion on something [to Aurora] – a ti también – very importante'.[6] Ann Davies (2008: 398) notes correctly that Jesús 'replies in pure Spanish throughout' and suggests this is 'an attempt at purity'. However, this 'purity' is unclear. He is an Argentine (played by the famous Argentine actor Federico Luppi), living in Mexico with his wife Mercedes, played by the Mexican actress Margarita Isabel, who teaches tango in a make-shift dance school in their home.[7] A tango-dominated score is often used in the soundtrack to denote his Argentine identity, and the two are seen to be active members of the ex-pat Argentine community, celebrating New Year (until Jesús is abducted by Angel) amid a sea of blue and white balloons.

These complexities, along with the fact that the Cronos device was introduced by the Italian Humberto Fulcanelli, chief watchmaker to the Spanish Viceroy in New Spain (sixteenth-century Mexico), undermine a simplistic reading of the film in national terms. This is not to invalidate allegorical readings with conceptualisations of nations at their centre, as will be seen below; nevertheless, any notion of secure borders and fixed national identities are disrupted in the diegesis. The complexities reveal the fact that these borders have already been penetrated and this has been the case since the time of the Spanish conquest. The de la Guardias have an established (undetermined) business in Mexico, reflecting large-scale US business interests in the country; and the nationality of Jesús references other Latin Americans living within Mexico. Likewise, an obsession with artificial means of securing eternal youth, health, and beauty, and a desire for immortality, all secured via the Cronos device, are prevalent on a world stage, and are not exclusively North American concerns. Mercedes is obsessed with beauty, is terrified of ageing, and her favourite activity is reading obituaries, while Jesús is willingly 'contaminated' by the device, with its talon mimicking the drug user's needle, after the initial accidental 'injection'.

Alchemy and the Cronos device

In this section, I aim to explore the film's application of alchemy, with a focus on the Cronos device and its inventor. I argue that in his intertextual approach, Guillermo del Toro demonstrates that he is an alchemical filmmaker: from a range of transnational, transhistorical, and transgeneric sources, he creates something that he makes his own. A del Toro film is a curiously post-modern mix of multiple cultural borrowings and authorial appropriation. At same time, the message of the film is rooted in a specifically Mexican approach to death. Ideas of alchemy, immortality, and vampires provide the narrative mysteries and fantastic pleasures of the text, but ultimately the elixir of life is an unwelcome substance linked to insects, colonisers, addiction, and (demonic) possession.

The device itself is a hybrid creation, and takes both an insect and a mechanical form; it is animate and inanimate; alive and dead; ancient and modern. The mechanism is the result of the alchemical search for the elixir of life, the key to immortality. The cogs within the contraption are shown running backwards when drawing from Jesús's blood when he is alive to demonstrate its rejuvenating powers, but run forwards when he is dead to reverse the processes of death. The fatal flaw in the design (in moral terms) is that the user becomes vampirised, and needs human blood to sustain him, as the insect trapped within the device needs the blood of its user to power the contraption.[8] This aspect is where allegorical readings relating to nationhood can be found, despite the complexities outlined above. For instance, human sacrifice is linked with the Spanish colonisers,

Cronos

rather than the Aztecs, as would be expected (as the device was introduced by the watchmaker to the Viceroy in colonial times). It also suggests that the power structures of colonialism have persisted, as Fulcanelli continues his practices of human sacrifice until he is accidentally pierced through the heart when a building collapses in 1937, illustrated in a gruesome scene at the film's opening.

The need for human blood to sustain the immortal man also connects neo-colonial US transnational capitalism to vampiric practices, as the wealthy industrialist de la Guardia has dedicated what is left of his life to finding the device, after he secures the alchemist's manual relating to the invention and its use. This allegorical reading is signalled by del Toro when he notes, 'I wanted to show the vampiric relationship between the nephew and the uncle, and, of course, the vampiric relationship between Mexico and the U.S.' (Wood, 2006: 34).

The inspiration for the device comes from a number of origins, and also demonstrates the transnational and transhistorical range of creative sources the director borrows from, which is fitting for a contraption that is the source of vampirism. As Ann Davies points out, the vampire is not only a transnational symbol, but also a transhistorical symbol:

> As an embodied individual the vampire is localizable but contains infinite possibilities, to the extent of having the capacity to contain all spaces, places and times. (Davies, 2008: 396)

Del Toro has cited (in the DVD commentary) as a source for the inventor of the Cronos device the figure of Gerbert d'Aullirac, a French tenth-century monk who went on to become Pope Silvester II (see Díaz, n.d.). He is known for his creation of automatons, and he is believed to have invented the clock and a mechanised bronze head that indicated yes or no to important religious or political questions addressed to it (Childress, 2000: 92). The director also relates that he was influenced by a more contemporary and local phenomenon: a macabre form of jewellery that women in Mexico wore in 1970s which in some instances encased insects that were alive (DVD commentary).

The name Cronos (Chronos) indicates both time and destruction from Greek mythology: Chronos is the god of time, and Cronos/Kronos was the Greek Titan king who devoured his children (with the exception of Zeus) to prevent them from overthrowing him, although he was finally defeated by Zeus (Ancient Mythology, n.d.). The film creates parallels with this myth, as Jesús will devour his own granddaughter if he allows himself to become godlike, that is, immortal. By linking the two Greek figures of time and destruction, del Toro comments on the devastation that follows when humans try to manipulate the workings of time and interfere with its laws. All the characters involved with the device die: Dieter and Angel are killed in their battles with Jesús, and he is forced to kill himself (by destroying the device) in order not to become a killer.

There are a number of sources for the character of Humberto Fulcanelli. He seems to be based on a famous, yet mysterious, alchemist writing in the 1920s. Fulcanelli was the pseudonym of this French alchemist of unknown identity, author of *Le mystère des cathédrales* (1926, written in 1922) and *Les demeures philosophales* (*The Dwellings of the Philosophers*, 1929) (Riviere, 2006). According to the Amazon website's editorial review for his book *The Dwellings of the Philosophers*: 'His pseudonym, Fulcanelli, is derived from Vulcan, classical god of fire, smithing, the working of metals, and artifice' (Amazon, n.d.). Del Toro has said that he uses alchemical symbols in all his films, relating to the elements of air, water, fire, and earth (DVD commentary), and the element associated with Fulcanelli and his device is fire. The first symptom suffered by Jesús after being 'bitten' by it is a terrible thirst. He is shown desperately consuming vast amounts of water from the fridge, before spotting the tempting fiery red raw steak, which indicates that only blood can quench his thirst in his transformed state.

This biographical namesake is not the only source for the Fulcanelli of the film; another inspiration for the character and for the narrative as a whole is Melquíades, the wise gypsy and key character within the best-known Latin American novel *Cien años de soledad* (*One Hundred Years of Solitude*), by Gabriel García Márquez (1967). He too is an alchemist who has discovered the secret of immortality and defies the natural laws of mortality to return to life, as he cannot bear the solitude found in death (García Márquez, 1978: 47). However, he is the positive other side to del Toro's alchemist. Melquíades's search is for knowledge and understanding, and in this he is closer to Jesús, unlike the character José Arcadio Buendía, who illustrates one of the novel's central themes, the corruption of knowledge. There are clear thematic parallels with *Cronos*, with both works warning against the use of knowledge for personal gain. The alchemist's and de la Guardia's search for the elixir of life is an individual quest, with their survival dependent upon the blood of mortals.

There are other parallels between the two texts: *Cien años de soledad* contains within it a meta-narrative: the story of the Buendía family and the town of Macondo, written by Melquíades in a secret code that various generations of the family attempt to decipher. The final revelation of the last of the Buendías, who finally manages to decipher it, as the world of Macondo ends, reads as follows:

> It was the history of the family, written by Melquíades.... He had written it in Sanskrit..., and he had encoded the even lines in the private cipher of the Emperor Augustus and the odd ones in a Lacedemonian military code. (García Márquez, 1978: 446)

In a clear nod to García Márquez's novel, the manuscript of del Toro's alchemist is written backwards in Latin and also has to be decoded. However, the sharing of insights found within the manuscript is rejected by de la Guardia, who, as we have seen, eats the key pages to deny Jesús access to this knowledge. The science and wisdom involved in the invention of the device are reduced to one element, the need for human blood, which is all de la Guardia reveals to Jesús. Thus, the elixir for life has been distorted to a crude form of vampirism, a form of eternal life that Jesús rejects.

So, in *Cronos* we have: an Italian alchemist allied to the Spanish crown in New Spain (Mexico), who references a French alchemist and Melquíades from García Márquez's Colombian global bestseller; a Hispanic Germanic American industrialist (de la Guardia) and his American nephew; and an Argentine living in a multicultural Mexico. The device has crossed borders and ages, and is named after the Greek god of time and the Greek Titan king and god. The narrative is projected onto the most transnational of vehicles, the vampire story. This is without mentioning the numerous intertextual references to other films and literary texts, which I discuss below. Underpinning and extending these elements and the glue that gives the film its power and coherence is a celebration of death that is very Mexican – which is, of course, also transnational, as it rests on Aztec and Hispanic biblical influences.

Death in *Cronos*

As del Toro has stated, elements of vampirism can be found within Christianity, specifically in the ideas of the resurrection of the dead, and in the Catholic communion, in which worshippers symbolically eat the body of Christ in the wafer host, and drink His blood through the communion wine (DVD commentary). These ideas are played with and subverted in *Cronos*. The lead character is named Jesús, but Jesús Gris, with the surname meaning 'grey', acting as an earthly contrast to the divine. He is resurrected after being killed by Angel, on the third day, like his biblical namesake, with Angel thereby acting as a Borgesian guardian angel in the way that he allows Jesús to achieve his destiny. In Jorge Luis Borge's short story 'Tres versiones de Judas' ('Three Versions of Judas', 1944), the character of Judas is re-evaluated as the essential element in the divine plan, and the one who has sacrificed most, as it is his betrayal that allows Jesus to sacrifice himself for humankind within the biblical narrative, and will guarantee condemnation of the betrayer for subsequent generations (Borges, 1970a). Likewise, Angel reveals to Jesús the horrors of vampiric immortality, and allows him to choose eternal death over eternal life. In the DVD commentary, del Toro explains that this was a deliberate biblical reworking, and the paradoxical choice of name for his principal villain was deliberate. Like the biblical Jesus, Jesús Gris 'has to be heralded by an angel', and del Toro explains that Ron Perlman's character 'lets him fulfil his manifest destiny as without him there is no death or resurrection'.

Yet *Cronos* is 'a pagan reinterpretation of the biblical story' (DVD commentary), with this Jesús turning into a vampire, rather than a heavenly being. Redemption comes from his sacrifice: like his biblical counterpart, he martyrs himself so that others may live. The trigger for this is his beloved granddaughter Aurora, whose blood he would consume were he not to destroy the Cronos device, which keeps him alive and which he, in turn, keeps alive. However, in an inverse reworking of the messianic story, his sacrifice results in a rejection of immortality, and an embrace of death. He is the immortal being transformed into man. As he smashes the Cronos device with a rock, in a false religious ending, he declares 'soy Jesús' (I am Jesus), followed by a pause, then 'Gris'. He thus takes back his name and his human form. The happy ending comes from the regaining of humanity, and his subsequent release from a life without death.[9]

In an interview with Mark Kermode, del Toro explains his take on death and immortality in his first film:

> In that film the girl who does not mind dying is the truly immortal character. And the character played by Federico Luppi (Jesús) becomes

immortal at the moment he decides to die, the moment he says: 'Fuck it, I don't want to kill my granddaughter.' Immortality doesn't mean you live longer; it means you are immune to death. (Kermode, 2006)

An acceptance of death is, then, posited as an alternative and natural form of immortality. Unlike most US popular horror films, *Cronos* does not approach death (or ageing) as something to be feared or avoided. Indeed, the 'message' of the film is that death in its right time should be accepted and welcomed, as seen paradoxically in the Latin inscription on the Cronos device, 'suo tempore' ('everything at its right time').

The final scene highlights this need to accept the natural order of things and it stands in contrast to the previous scene, in which Jesús has taken on a monstrous form after his first feed (from Dieter de la Guardia's neck), with his skin decomposing, and a mixture of congealed and fresh blood staining his mouth. The colour palette is a cold, metallic dull blue, almost black and white, ensuring that life is drained from the screen, with just a few hints of red, from Aurora's coat and the blood on Jesús's face, highlighting the horror and her function as potential victim. The mood switches from horror to romance in the following death-bed scene. Classical harmonious music with a predominance of strings accompanies the dying Jesús: his decomposed skin has been removed to reveal new skin, suggesting death as rebirth; warm lights gradually return to the scene, where the family (Mercedes and Aurora) gather by his bed, replacing the discoloured grey blue tones. The light gradually increases and an overexposed brilliance indicates the moment when Jesús finally dies (a technique repeated in *El laberinto* when Ofelia dies), followed by a fade to white. The film's dedication follows, to the memory of Josefina Camberos (del Toro's grandmother), a dedication which reinforces the centrality of death in the narrative. The film, then, opens with the demise of the alchemist, and closes with that of Jesús and a reference to the deceased Camberos, with death positioned as resolution.[10]

Throughout the film there is a very Mexican familiarity with death. Mexico is a country with a specific relationship to death and it is well known for its graphic representations of images of the dead in the form of skeletons and the prominence given to the Day of the Dead festival. In his book *Death and the Idea of Mexico*, Claudio Lomnitz (2005) argues that intimacy with death is at the heart of Mexican national identity. The best-known theorist of death in Mexico is

Octavio Paz, whose ideas are developed in *El laberinto de soledad* (*The Labyrinth of Solitude*) (1959), and in particular in the chapter 'The Day of the Dead'. He writes:

> The word death is not pronounced in New York, in Paris, in London, because it burns the lips. The Mexican, in contrast, is familiar with death, jokes about it, caresses it, sleeps with it, celebrates it; it is one of his favourite toys and his most steadfast love. True there is perhaps as much fear in his attitude as in that of others, but at least death is not hidden away: he looks at it face to face, with impatience, disdain or irony. (Paz, 1967: 49)

Paz's ideas are incorporated into *Cronos*, and this love affair and familiarity with death explain Jesús's horror when he realises that his condition has made him immortal. For Paz, concepts of life, death, sacrifice, and rebirth in Mexico stem from Aztec beliefs in cosmic cycles, and Catholic more personalised ideas of sacrifice and resurrection embodied in a single man (Paz, 1967: 48–49). In both interpretations, death is a central part of life, as Paz explains: 'The cult of life, if it is truly profound and total, is also the cult of death, because the two are inseparable' (51). Paz's thesis lies behind del Toro's vision: life without death is a monstrous unnatural state, a living hell.[11] When Jesús is first resurrected, he bemoans, 'como me duele estar vivo – me siento ajeno a todo, la sed me quema' ('How it pains me to be alive – I feel apart from everything, thirst burns me'). His quest from this point becomes an inverse search to de la Guardia's: a search for death.

This is in stark contrast to the joyous mood in the morgue before he has come back to life. Del Toro has cited this scene as embodying a Mexican sensibility, and explains in the DVD commentary that when Universal Pictures asked him for the rights to the film, he declined, as what happens in the film (and he gives the example of the mortuary scene) can only happen in Mexico. Graphic scenes of the undertaker's work are shown when he stitches Jesús's gums, and this is accompanied by a cheerful, archetypal Mexican song, with lyrics by del Toro and his producer Alejandro Springall, and music by Javier Alvarez.[12] The lyrics refer to the 'muertito en la plancha' – 'the dead man on the slab' – with the Hispanic diminutive (muertito, literally 'little dead man') highlighting the affection for death in Mexican culture. The fast rhythm makes this a song to dance to and provides the soundtrack to this celebration of the rites of death. Tito (Daniel Giménez Cacho), the mortician, is compared to a makeup artist in films – his assistant notes that it is his best work and he describes himself as an artist as he marvels at the work he has done on Jesús's face. Fun and humour rather than horror, then, characterise this scene, highlighted when his assistant tells Tito that it is a shame he put so much work in, as Jesús is about to be cremated, which leads to a string of curses from Tito. He is dressed informally, in a vest, braces and loose-fitting trousers; he has rocker-styled hair, and constantly chews gum, apart from when he takes a break and sticks the gum onto his braces while he enjoys a banana. Everything about this scene is informal, relaxed, and lacking in any sense of the macabre, which begins only after Jesús has come back to life (escaping from the coffin before the cremation), demonstrating a very Mexican reworking of generic horror conventions.

It is worth making a small aside here to point out that a recent Mexican film, *Somos lo que hay* (*We Are What We Are*) (Grau, 2010) has an intertextual steal from this scene. In this film about modern-day cannibals in Mexico City, Daniel Giménez Cacho plays the same character as in *Cronos*; he is also called Tito, wears the same clothes as in del Toro's film, and his assistant even repeats the same humorous lines uttered in *Cronos* when he tells Giménez Cacho's character that he need not have gone to so much trouble preparing the body of the father of the cannibal family, as they are going to cremate the dead 'man'. *Somos lo que hay* can be seen as homage to *Cronos*, with the cannibal family becoming a version of what Jesús would have become had he not sacrificed himself.

Horror in *Cronos* has its roots in life and the denial of death, as seen in the decomposing, vampiric, resurrected Jesús. It is also best demonstrated in the character of Dieter de la Guardia. He is based on both the uncle of a friend of del Toro and Howard Hughes (DVD commentary).[13] Del Toro contrasts the 'American' de la Guardia with Jesús in his attitude to death. De la Guardia is suffering from cancer and has used his influence and wealth to prolong his life. He lives in a medically controlled environment in an acclimatised chamber at the top of the unproductive factory that could be anywhere in the world. The colour palette used for all scenes with de la Guardia (senior) is the metallic grey blue described above. This signifies the lifeless state that he is in, with his survival attained by artificial means. He explains to Jesús that half his organs are in jars, and his diet consists of different coloured pills (he notes ironically to Jesús that 'the red ones are especially good today').[14] Del Toro has argued that de la Guardia's desire to preserve everything in jars signifies 'the essence of capitalism'

(DVD commentary). Contraptions pump a substance that looks like dry ice, presumably to regulate the environment. All this highlights the unnatural state that the millionaire lives in and there are clear parallels to the lives of vampires. Like them, he feeds off others (as a wealthy capitalist), and he is unable to live in a natural environment, just as daylight will destroy the vampire. This is a character (and concept) that del Toro develops in his co-authored novel *The Strain* through the evil American billionaire Eldritch Palmer and his demonic pact with the super-vampire, the Master, also in the hope that he will overcome his diseased body and gain immortality (del Toro and Hogan, 2009).

Cronos in its attitude to death, then, rests largely on Paz's thesis in which life and death are inseparable and interdependent concepts. As Paz (1967: 46) has said summarising this connection, 'tell me how you die, and I will tell you who you are'. De la Guardia desires an eternal life in which he can feed from others, and this is reflected in his mortal life. It is worth noting that this form of vampirism, dependent as it is on the Cronos device, as well as on the blood of humans, does not grant eternal life to the victims as in traditional forms, but rather causes them to die. In this way, were de la Guardia to find the Cronos device, his new powers would benefit only him in this allegory of capitalism. Likewise, Jesús renounces immortality, as the existence it would force upon him would be in opposition to the way he has led his life, illuminated when Aurora speaks her only word of the film, 'abuelo' (grandfather), to plead with him as he looks hungrily at her bleeding finger. The world of life preserved beyond its natural time, then, is the site of horror and revulsion in the film, and this very transnational film paradoxically has a Mexican story of death as its beating heart.

Del Toro: the alchemist

In an alchemical process of filmmaking, del Toro achieves something with *Cronos* which he will go on to achieve with his other Spanish-language films. He takes elements of genres and the work of other directors and creates something new: a text that is at one time an auteurist art film, a genre piece, an example of new directions in national cinema, and a cult film in the global market. The last fact is illustrated in the award nominations it received and won in 1993/94 in both auteurist circles and in fantasy cinema circles. In the former category it won the Mercedes-Benz Award at Cannes, the above-cited Arieles in Mexico, and awards at festivals in Havana, Moscow, and Sitges (Spain). In fantasy categories it won awards at the Brussels International Festival of Fantasy Film, Fantafestival, the European Festival for Fantasy Film, the Portuguese Fantasy Film Festival (Fantasporto) and a Saturn award at the US Academy of Fantasy, Science Fiction and Horror Films (see IMDB). As Pam Cook has noted in an article on Baz Luhrmann, recent cinema has seen the rise of the popular art film, which, she argues, 'is characterized by a disregard for traditional boundaries between art and entertainment; it mixes classical forms with modernist strategies, and crosses over between popular and niche audiences' (Cook, 2010: 25). She continues, in what could be an analysis of *Cronos*:

> While it may have discernible national characteristics, it is transnational in approach and realization, and its national/transnational status is often contested via contextual discourses such as press and other critical responses. (Cook, 2010: 25)

One of the reasons for the generic fluidity of *Cronos* is the use made of a huge range of intertextual references from popular culture, horror films, and art cinema, among other generic forms. It is hard to know where to start when noting the borrowings of a director who has described himself as a film fan before a filmmaker (DVD commentary). A number of critics, as well as del Toro himself, have drawn attention to these. Stock (1999: 276) notes that *Cronos* is indebted to Mexican and Hollywood traditions, and argues that it borrows from genres as diverse as wrestling films, melodramas, horror movies, and B movies. Kantaris (1998) has also noted the vast array of cinematic texts that the film references, citing Murnau's *Nosferatu* (1922), Hitchcock's *Rear Window* (1954), and Cronenberg's *Videodrome* (1983) and *The Fly* (1986), among others. Del Toro himself mentions that Aurora was modelled on Ana (Ana Torrent), the young girl in the classic Spanish art film *El espíritu de la colmena* (*The Spirit of Beehive*) (Erice, 1973), and also cites James Whale's films as an influence (Wood, 2006: 38), with Whale's *Frankenstein* (1931) in turn so famously cited in Erice's film.[15] Del Toro also talks of his early love of horror films made by Universal Studios and Hammer Film Productions, and directly cites the influence of Terence Fisher's films made for Hammer. In addition, the director references Nicolas Roeg's *Don't Look Now* (1973), Charles Laughton's *The Night of the Hunter* (1955) (DVD commentary), and

William Peter Blatty's *The Ninth Configuration* (1980) (Kermode, 2006). Other influences the director cites are Sergio Leone, Mario Bava, Dario Argento (Wood, 2006: 36), Japanese horror, Italian and Spanish zombie movies, and the symbolist painters Julio Ruela, Gustave Moreau, and Carlos Schwabe (Díaz, n.d.).

Suffice it to say that there are so many transnational and transhistorical intertextual citations that critics or film buffs could spend many hours and days tracking them down and identifying them. This is not what I am interested in doing here; rather, I want to explore the ways in which the director uses influences and ingredients to create a del Toro film, with *Cronos* a low-budget prototype for what will become the auteurist brand. Del Toro is not simply a fan who pointlessly crams in as many references as possible; rather, these are used in *Cronos* and in many of his other films to deliberate effect, with a certain consistency, and with a moral and thematic coherence. My aim here is to outline and analyse his use of some of the key cultural texts that appear in *Cronos*, which will provide a grounding for the analysis in the subsequent chapters.

The primary influence for del Toro highlighted in *Cronos* are classical gothic horror films, principally those directed by James Whale and Terence Fisher, and centred around two monsters, Dracula and Frankenstein's creature. The production team were instructed by the director to watch Fisher's films for Hammer, in particular *The Curse of the Werewolf* (1961) and *The Curse of Frankenstein* (1957), in order to create the look of the film (Nafus, 1998). This is seen particularly in the colour palette, specifically in the use of greys and blues for death scenes and de la Guardia's warehouse/factory, which provide an updated allusion to the gothic castles and aristocratic homes of Hammer productions. The frequent use of red against this discoloured backdrop features in Fisher's Technicolor films, and is referenced in *Cronos* with Aurora's red coat and her red jumper, matched eerily with the brilliant red used to exaggerate the colour of the blood that so tempts Jesús. The images that stand out in this regard are: the raw steak in his fridge, the drops of blood from the man with the nose bleed at the New Year's party, and the blood that stains Jesús's lips and mouth after drinking from de la Guardia's neck/head. Del Toro's colour palette grew more sophisticated in later films, but he has continued to use this contrast, although with silvery blues and golden colours in place of the reds used in *Cronos*, as will be seen in chapters 2 and 3.

This love of early horror inspired his decision to begin his career working in special effects, after taking a course in New York run by the well known master of the craft Dick Smith, and it has been a clear influence in all his filmmaking (Wood, 2006: 29–30). Monsters, mythical creatures, and ghosts are central to the artistic and moral universe of del Toro, and the director has afforded them a key position in interviews. He tells Mark Kermode (2006):

> I really think that the most creative, most fragile part of the child that lives within me is a child that was literally transformed by monsters. Be they on the screen, or in myth, or in my own imagination.

The monsters/mythical creatures that emerge from del Toro's films all serve to illustrate the battle between good and evil in what, with some exceptions, is a fairly Manichaean view of the world. Dracula appears as the dark figure who stands behind del Toro's villains and is the source villain for the alchemist, who drinks the blood of others to survive, and for de la Guardia, who is weakened by his mortality, but who would be truly demonic with the powers afforded by the Cronos device. Del Toro makes his character a cross between Murnau's early Dracula prototype Nosferatu and Tod Browning's handsome yet sinister Dracula (1931), played by Bela Lugosi. He is sick and ailing like Nosferatu, but has the cloak and stick associated with the later figure, which came to define Dracula in many subsequent versions. This Dracula is most famously embodied by Christopher Lee in Fisher's *Dracula* (1958). It is worth noting that when Jesús first comes back to life, a wall behind has the word 'Dracula' written in graffiti form that can be faintly made out (and is easily missed), hinting at what he will become if he accepts this new identity. The father of vampires is not directly named in del Toro's films, but all his villains thrive and grow strong from the destruction of others, and in this they have their roots in the figure of Dracula. An obsession with vampires also led to del Toro agreeing to direct the very different commercial Hollywood film *Blade II* and to his novel co-authored with Chuck Hogan, *The Strain* (2009).

Frankenstein's creature, animated from the dead, in contrast, represents the monster as victim of the cruelty of humanity: an example of the refusal to grant respect to death, and the dangers of the misuse of science, all themes which figure prominently in *Cronos*. Del Toro has said of his fondness for the creature: 'To me, Frankenstein represents the essential human question: "Why did my creator throw me here, unprotected, unguided, unaided and lost?"' (Graser, 2008). As the monster's creator is human (Dr Frankenstein), del Toro's reading of the Frankenstein story is both a challenge to Catholicism (he is a lapsed Catholic) and existentialist.[16] This sympathy for Frankenstein's reanimated dead creation fits in with a thematic trope that runs through the director's work: the monstrous human, and the sympathetic otherworldly character, although it should be noted that in his other films the creatures are often more positive and empowered than is Frankenstein's creature. Del Toro has said of the conceit behind *El laberinto*, 'there was something incredibly attractive in creating a world full of creatures and monsters, but making the human characters much more monstrous than them' (Dalton, 2006). The monsters in *El laberinto* are the fascists as well as a selection of fantasy creatures, and in *Cronos* they are the capitalists. This is also a theme del Toro revisited in *Hellboy II*, as will be seen in chapter 2. Jesús in this context can be seen as a man-made monster, in the tradition of Frankenstein, while Dieter is a would-be vampiric monster in the tradition of Dracula.

Cronos: the key to del Toro's cinematic universe

In many ways, del Toro is a director of monsters; the figure of the monster (both human and otherworldly or supernatural) features in all of his films, and will be examined in the chapters which follow. In this area and in many others, there are elements of del Toro's cinematic universe that are first exemplified in *Cronos*, and which will be explored in the subsequent chapters. In these I consider how they are developed in other national contexts and are subject to different industrial and financial conditions, with a focus on *Hellboy II* and *El laberinto*. I argue that *Cronos* is the key film that unlocks the codes of the director's body of work in terms of his approach to film-making, the predominant themes, redefinition of genres, and visual style and artistry. Three characteristics that inter-relate in del Toro's filmmaking and which first appeared in *Cronos* are the crossing of genre boundaries, the coexistence of the magical/fantastical and the realist within a single text, and a concern to make a political statement (more explicit with his Spanish-language films). I have explained how del Toro incorporates an anti-capitalist political message in *Cronos*. He marries the fantastic and the realist by grounding the fantastic in a mundane reality: the hero is an ageing antiques dealer with nothing extraordinary about him, until he discovers the device. All the mythical elements relating to vampires, the magical device, and the elixir for life distinguish this from social realist national texts; however, as seen, the film still seeks to make a social comment on post-NAFTA Mexico and the USA.[17]

This combination of fantasy and realism is, of course, intimately bound up with the reworking of genres. Del Toro notes in relation to his first feature, 'I tried to take genre premises and explore them obliquely, where the fantastic is either tangential or illuminates reality in a different way' (Brown, 2009). Subverting and playing with generic codes has been seen as central to notions of auteurism by both the nouvelle vague theorists and the well known critic Andrew Sarris (see Langford, 2005: 8–9). As Barry Langford has noted, 'directors and films that strain against the limits of their given genre are ... evaluated as "superior" when compared to those who stick within rigid genre codes' (Langford, 2005: 9). He adds that 'it was the transcendence, not the comfortable inhabitation, of genre that marked the auteur' (10). Del Toro inhabits, reworks, and transcends generic borders in his films to greater or lesser degrees, depending on the production context in which they were made and on the source material, as will be explored in the chapters on *Hellboy II* and *El laberinto*, and this is the key to his popular auteurist status.

It has been seen here that *Cronos* is marked by its intertextual borrowings and generic reworkings and this sets the pattern for his subsequent films. In *El espinazo del diablo*, the Hellboy films and *El laberinto*, elements are taken, mixed together, and refashioned from children's stories and fantasy films, fairy tales, ghost stories, social realist drama, horror novels and films, comic books, and action adventure films. It is worth noting that none of these in themselves are 'pure' forms, and, as Janet Staiger (2003: 185) has argued with specific reference to Hollywood films, genres 'have never been pure', with both old (Fordian) Hollywood and new Hollywood films always 'a mixture of multiple genres' (191).[18] The director's auteurist persona, then, does not rest simply on the fact that he mixes generic elements, as this is intrinsic to all filmmaking. Rather, it has emerged as a result of the way del Toro has combined what are often seen as opposing genres and approaches (e.g. children's stories, horror, and social realism) to produce an identifiable style which straddles popular and art cinema niche markets, and contains recurrent visual patterns, and coherent visions of the world. What is most apparent from the range of elements and genres that make up del Toro's oeuvre is the way that they combine adult and children's sources, and a central characteristic of the filmmaker's work is the relationship between children and adults, and the child's connection with the supernatural. This is the key to the emotional heart of *El espinazo del diablo*, seen in the relationship between Dr Casares (also played by Luppi) and the civil war orphans, and in that between Mercedes and Ofelia in *El laberinto*, and even, to a degree, in the relationship between Liz and Hellboy in both Hellboy films, as he is presented as a teenager in his behaviour. This prototype relationship is first seen in *Cronos*, with Jesús redeemed through his love for Aurora, whose name significantly translates to English as 'dawn'.

Del Toro approaches the world of the child with great respect and shows children having a special affinity with magical/mythical worlds unattainable to many adults. They are able to befriend and make alliances with good otherworldly forces, in opposition to the villains of the films. These characteristics are repeated in the director's other Spanish-language films. In *El espinazo del diablo* Carlos finally accepts the ghost of Santi, which allows him to defeat the fascistic Jacinto, and in *El laberinto* Ofelia is guided by the faun, an alliance which allows her to escape from Captain Vidal. What is striking about Aurora (and replayed through the character of Ofelia in her reaction to the realm of the underworld) is her lack of shock and matter-of-fact response to the appearance of her grandfather as a vampire with decomposing skin, as she lovingly tends to him. Jesús returns home from the dead to be welcomed warmly by his granddaughter with a towel to dry him from the rain. Soft lighting and melodic classical tango-inflected music make this a tender love scene in another subversion of classical horror.

For del Toro, then, horror and children's fictional worlds are an organic match. He has commented:

> I think that children react very naturally to horror, perhaps in a more natural and pure way to adults, and are very much exposed to it. Horror comes from the unknown and you react with horror only to things that you don't know. (Wood, 2006: 27)

This focus on positive representations of children who are more in tune with the supernatural is, then, a key feature of del Toro's work. Thus, moral forces are played out often by pitting innocent yet insightful children against evil or corrupt adult belief systems (capitalism and neo-colonialism in *Cronos* and nationalist fascism in the case of the two Spanish Civil War films). This juxtaposition allows for the creation of a personal form of compassionate horror which characterises much of del Toro's filmmaking. These children have the ability to distinguish between good and evil and are guided by both intelligence and innocence. They are, like del Toro's adults, faced with serious moral choices, and the solution to these in the director's filmic universe is often self-sacrifice. This is another characteristic that first comes to light in *Cronos*, with Jesús the first in a line of good mythical beings and monsters to sacrifice themselves so that others may live. The director's heroes are also, in contrast to Hollywood's traditional heroes, old men, young girls, and mythical beings.

As well as a moral and thematic universe, del Toro creates a visual world with identifiable colours, symbols and designs throughout his films. *Cronos*, a film with a $2 million budget, provides the bones of what will be developed into a rich visual universe in subsequent, better-funded features. A full analysis of these and their meaning would constitute a chapter in its own right, so I will just outline some of the most significant here. There are number of objects and symbols introduced in his first film that make recurrent appearances in his later work. In *Cronos* we first see the objects in the jars (here containing de la Guardia's organs) that appear in a number of other texts, and feature so prominently in *El espinazo* in the 'medicinal' liquid containing unborn foetuses that Dr Casares sells to the villagers. Another repeated visual trope is the object wrapped in plastic/cellophane (angels in *Cronos* and animal carcasses in *Hellboy II*). The director's obsession with mechanical objects and contraptions that contain magical supernatural properties is also essayed in the first film, with the Cronos device, and reproduced in *Hellboy II*. This device contains cogs, which, as seen, run both forwards and backwards to symbolise the harmful effects of man-made mutations of the laws of time, caused by the alchemist's experiments. Circular cogs will also appear in other texts, most prominently in *Hellboy II* in the final fight scene between Hellboy and Prince Nuada, and in the design of the mill in *El laberinto*, clearly visible in Captain Vidal's room and in the fob watch which he obsessively fixes. Circular cogs often indicate the different conceptions of time within magical and realist human worlds, with the world of humans governed by laws which do not affect the world of mythical beings. As noted above, the device and the manuscript contain coded markings and language which has to be deciphered, and this idea of ancient mystical codes that unlock secrets and magical worlds is another favourite of the director, and is central to the visuals and narratives of the Hellboy films and *El laberinto*.

While del Toro borrows generously from popular canons, he has also staked his claim on art cinematic visual forms. Perhaps this and the way in which the director marks his authorial signature is most apparent in his attention to the colour palette in each film. I have already commented on the juxtaposition of muted metallic blues and reds to create the horror visuals, and these are, in turn, juxtaposed with warm colours, particularly in the intimate scenes in Jesús's home. As Ann Marie Stock observes, 'warm gold and orange tones characterize the familiar personal spaces, while blue and gray filters mediate the strange impersonal spaces' (Stock, 1999: 278). This colour coding of the world into cold and warm colours will be developed and enhanced as the director gains access to funds and more sophisticated means of painting his canvass, and provides the audience with the key to deciphering the moral codes of each scene, and, to put it crudely, of creating the distinction between good and evil. In terms of an identifiable visual style, *Cronos* predominantly relies on the colour coding and mise-en-scène, with warm or stark interiors, and rooms carefully arranged with such details as de la Guardia's futuristic medical anti-sceptic chamber, or elaborately crafted items within the antique shop such as angels and clocks. Del Toro subsequently develops other visual forms, and the following chapters will pay more attention to these. They will also explore the approach taken in the creation of special effects (practical effects versus computer-generated imagery), as del Toro develops his style with increased experience and the possibilities available with increased budgets.

Conclusion

In this chapter I have sought to demonstrate how a close study of the low-budget first film made by a director who would go on to become a global popular genre auteur can be illuminating. The transnational dimensions of this film set in Mexico, funded principally by IMCINE, and made by a Mexican director so well versed in international languages of cinema help explain how del Toro was able to make such a successful transition into Spanish and US filmmaking circles. A study of the some of the principal characteristics of his filmmaking when he has a budget of $2 million – compared with $19 million for

El laberinto and $72 million for *Hellboy II* – allows us to see del Toro metaphorically naked. This is an ideal starting point for exploring his subsequent work and identifying essential characteristics of his filmmaking and analysing how these evolve, depending on different contexts and increased funding.

Notes

1. The director cites Satipo in *Raiders of the Lost Ark* (Spielberg, 1981) as a particularly offensive example of this (DVD commentary).
2. I would like to thank Jude Gough for her help identifying the Russian Soviet-era newspapers in Aurora's room.
3. He has appeared in Buñuel's *El angel exterminador* (*The Exterminating Angel*, 1962) and *Simón del desierto* (*Simon of the Desert*, 1965), as well as a number of *lucha libre* (wrestling) films, and popular horror films such as *Los autómatas de la muerte* (Curiel, 1962) and *Neutrón contra el Dr Caronte* (Curiel, 1963), as well as art films such as *Frida* (Leduc, 1986).
4. In one exchange, he says to Gris, 'gracias para todos', featuring two basic grammatical mistakes.
5. 'Me las comí' translates as 'I ate them', and 'vea, ha vuelto a nacer' as 'look, you have been reborn'.
6. 'No es mi dinero' can be translated as 'it's not my money', and 'a ti también' as 'you too'. He proceeds to ask their advice about the best nose shape for his nose job – his main obsession.
7. Luppi also features in del Toro's *El espinazo del diablo* and makes a brief appearance as the king of the underworld in *El laberinto del fauno*.
8. The only two to have used the device and to have formed this symbiotic relationship with it are its inventor, Fulcanelli, and Jesús Gris.
9. Here there is another oblique reference to one of Borges's short stories, 'El inmortal' ('The Immortal', 1949), a fictional imagining of the devastating consequences of immortality (Borges, 1970b).
10. Del Toro has documented his relationship with his grandmother, who brought him up. He had conflicts with her over her strict Catholic values, although they were close (DVD commentary).
11. This is an idea developed by del Toro and his co-author, Chuck Hogan, in their vampire novel *The Strain* (2009), although the setting of the novel is New York.
12. The song is 'La pelancha' (1992) and credited to Springall's production company, Iguana Producciones, which co-produced the film.
13. In the DVD commentary, del Toro relates how his friend's uncle spent thirty years without leaving the house, and kept parts of his body in jars, such as toenail clippings, hair, and excrement.

14 Sadly, Claudio Brook, the actor who played de la Guardia senior, died in 1995 of stomach cancer. See http://pro.imdb.com/name/nm0111610.
15 Of *El espíritu de la colmena*, del Toro has said, 'that movie, along with the films of Buñuel and the films of Hitchcock is almost a part of my genetic DNA' (Wood 2006: 38).
16 In an interview, del Toro has spoken of his (still unfulfilled) desire to direct his version of Frankenstein: 'With that one, they will have to pry it from my cold dead hands to prevent me from directing it' (Graser, 2008).
17 This combination of myth, magic, and realism to demonstrate an anti-colonial or anti-capitalist political philosophy and to give voice to Latin American culture ties in with a long tradition of Latin American magical realism.
18 Staiger (2003: 197) prefers to talk of 'pattern mixing'.

2

Generating an authorial presence with *Hellboy II: The Golden Army*

In the previous chapter, I argued that *Cronos* can be seen to provide a key to Guillermo del Toro's artistic universe and world vision, and I identified a number of areas which can provide a framework for the readings of his subsequent films. *Hellboy II: The Golden Army* follows on from his first feature in a number of ways. In this film del Toro develops his role as a director of monsters; he continues to cross genre and cultural boundaries, bringing elements from high art and art cinema into this commercial venture; he intensifies the multiple and wide-ranging intertextual borrowings; and he blends all this together, adding recurrent visual motifs and thematic tropes to further a personal and identifiable style. Nevertheless, *Hellboy II* is a very different beast to *Cronos*: it is a Hollywood production funded, in the main, by Universal Pictures, with a much larger budget – $72 million in contrast with $2 million for the Mexican film, according to IMDB – to counter many of the financial obstacles del Toro reported in translating his ideas to the screen with *Cronos*.

As befits a commercial production, the DVD was released globally by Universal Pictures in 2008. In the director's commentary found among the DVD extras, del Toro has described *Hellboy II* as one of the films of which he is most proud, and he has claimed it as one of his most autobiographical works, thus ascribing an artistic stamp of quality and ownership over this studio-funded product. However, it would be too simple to argue that a larger budget allows us to witness an unproblematic rendition of the auteurist vision seen in *Cronos* writ large. There are two principal factors that problematise such an interpretation. First, the film is del Toro's take on the well established character devised, drawn, and written by Mike Mignola, who also co-created the story for this film.[1] Second, this is a studio film of an established hero, and there are certain conventions and expectations that any director would be required to follow, however many auteurist flourishes/deviations from the source texts he/she would be permitted.

These obstacles to the dominant artistic vision central to concepts of auteurism mean the director had to work hard to continue to cultivate the auteurist persona he consolidated with *El laberinto del fauno* (*Pan's Labyrinth*), and which was at risk of being diluted with such a mainstream choice of film as a follow-up. This effort to assert an authorial presence is seen in the volume of interviews given in a whole range of fora, including sci-fi fan sites, horror sites, respected film journals, and national newspapers. Del Toro also provided an extensive commentary on the DVD extras, and published his notes and copies of pages from his own notebooks in the *Hellboy II: Art of the Movie* book released to accompany the film (Sandoval and Velasco, 2008). There is also no shortage of pictures of the director with the actors at events such as New York's Comic Con 2008. When considering the auteur question with regard to del Toro, I am not overly concerned with 'is he or isn't he?' type questions, which are always constrained by subjective judgements; rather, I focus on the way del Toro seeks to generate an auteurist persona through the paratextual means outlined above.

Paratext is a term used by Catherine Grant, among other film scholars, which originates from the literary critic Gérard Genette, who aligns it with 'liminal devices ... that mediate the relations between the text and the reader' (Genette, cited in Grant, 2008: 103).[2] Jonathan Gray is another prominent critic who has written on paratexts (2010a), and in an interview he provides a useful definition, explaining that for him they are:

> all those things that surround a book that aren't quite the 'thing' (or 'the text') itself. Things like the cover, prefaces, typeface, and afterwords, but also reviews.... 'extra' means 'outside of,' whereas 'para' suggests a more complicated relationship to the film or show, outside of, alongside, and intrinsically part of all at the same time. Hence my fondness for that word in particular. (Gray, 2010b)

In this chapter, I engage in discourse analysis to see what these paratexts reveal about new ways in which auteurism can be cultivated through new media forms. Del Toro, like González Iñárritu and Alfonso Cuarón, represents a certain type of global auteur who can weave in and out of national contexts and challenge clear-cut distinctions made in the international market between Hollywood commercial film, independent cinema, and art house foreign-language film. However, unlike his compatriots, he is the one who has aligned auteurism with the most popular commercial forms of cinema, and this chapter explores the ways in which he seeks to do this.

In the next section I focus on the relationship between Mignola and del Toro through an analysis of interviews with both of them, and in the following section also through transnational fan response in a thread that I started on the fan forum at the official Hellboy website, Hellboy.com. I then go on to examine the ways that del Toro takes pains to insist on his creative power and authority through paratextual means. I will also provide an analysis of the text and consider its position within del Toro's filmic universe, and assess its relationship with *El laberinto*, a film which appears diametrically opposed in terms of genre and niche markets (Hollywood superhero film versus European art film), but with which it shares many visual and narrative traits. In this way, I further my argument relating to the way that the director blurs boundaries between traditionally demarcated ways in which films have traditionally been categorised.

Hellboy II – Guillermo del Toro and Mike Mignola

There is inevitably an auteurist premise behind a book, such as this one, that focuses on specific directors, and del Toro is the figure that looms largest of the three in this study in terms of popular and critical status, and the types of budgets that he has access to. An analysis of *Hellboy II* is, however, the most problematic of all my case studies when applying this frame of reference, as it is a Hollywood product from within the superhero stable of films, and is based, like *Hellboy* (2004), also directed by del Toro, on the character and the adult comics created by Mike Mignola. Funding came principally from Universal Pictures, but also from Dark Horse Entertainment, the company behind the Hellboy graphic novels. Publishers of comics are increasingly taking on the role of film producers, with film remakes providing a substantial proportion of their income (Furey, 2008). Del Toro, by successfully lobbying to become the director of the Hellboy films, agreed to play by a series of unwritten rules, with a certain logic relating to narrative and style contained within the genre (even with the subversions del Toro brings), as the director himself implicitly acknowledged:

> I just know that, if I want to paint these huge comic book panels, I need to go to a studio. I would never attempt to do 'Hellboy 2' with European funding, and I would never attempt to have 'Pan's Labyrinth' done with a studio. Imagine them testing that movie. (Roberts, 2008)[3]

Hellboy II is, then, a movie a studio can successfully test out on a mainstream audience. Thus, the director works not only within the constraints of the studio, but also within the self-imposed constraints of the genre.

Central to any questions of auteurism is the degree to which the vision is that of a single organising presence, usually the director, and the extent to which he/she has creative control. It is thus important here to outline the processes of creation, and to state that *Hellboy II* was not an adaptation of existing stories, but rather a new story formed in discussion between del Toro and Mignola, with the screenplay written by del Toro, using the characters created by Mignola. Thus, although the director did not adapt a pre-existing story, Mignola is still co-creator of this new film story. In his chapter 'The Adaptor as Auteur', from the book *Film Adaptation and Its Discontents*, Thomas Leitch (writing about Hitchcock) notes, 'to establish himself as an auteur ... Hitchcock has to wrest authority of his films away from another plausible candidate: the author of the original property', often refusing to allow the authors to work on 'his' films (Leitch, 2007: 239). While del Toro collaborates with Mignola and assigns him credit for the creation of the comics, in a series of ways which will be explored, he does establish his authority over the film text, with Mignola's acquiescence.

Del Toro stakes his claim on the second film and is afforded creative primacy by Mignola in all of the interviews given. In one example Mignola says:

> The first film was taking my world and adapting it into the Del Toro Hellboy universe, and the second film is very much a continuation of that Del Toro Hellboy universe.... It spoke to his interests and it became a vehicle for him to do things he wanted to do. (Albert, 2008)

A working partnership was formed where Mignola essentially became del Toro's employee, and attempted to translate the director's vision through his sketches, not usually to del Toro's satisfaction. He hands over the creative credit to the director and notes that 'all the

Hellboy II: The Golden Army

signature creature designs in the film are very much del Toro creature designs' (Furey, 2008), with the loaded term 'signature' conferring an auteurist status upon him. Mignola's language in a number of interviews makes it clear that del Toro is at the head of the creative hierarchy for the film, as the following examples demonstrate: 'as with my designs on the first film most of what I did on this film del Toro considered too simple' (Sandoval and Velasco, 2008: 39); of the drawing for Johan (Mignola's own creation in the comics), he notes in *The Art of the Movie* book, 'as soon as I started, I knew that no matter what I did, it was going to be way too simple for del Toro' (Sandoval and Velasco, 2008: 87). Mignola acknowledges that this shift in the hierarchy of power is intrinsic to the shift in medium:

> Once you've sold your property to Hollywood, you don't really control it. One of the questions I'm always asked is how much control do I have. Well, I don't really have any. Once I give up those rights, they can do what they want. Where I am very fortunate is I have a director who wants me there, a director who wants me involved. (Furey, 2008)[4]

Nevertheless, despite his above cited declarations and those of the director, which will be seen, Mignola's influence is felt beyond the designs he did for the films, and it is interesting that little is made in interviews by either him or del Toro of the influence of the comics on the film. Even though this was a new story, there are a number of plot parallels between this new fiction and the stories of the comic world, particularly with regard to the concept of the inanimate mechanical Golden Army, which requires the three interlocking pieces of the crown of Bethmoora to be activated. In one of Mignola's stories a minor demon tries to use Hellboy's crown and right hand to 'loose the dragon' and 'breathe life into the lifeless soldiers of hell and set that army to war against heaven' (Hall *et al.*, 2008: 63). In another parallel, the characters Herman von Klempt and Kroenen plan for the 'creation of a half-mechanical, half-human army of 666 soldiers who would bring plague and famine to the earth' (111).

Hellboy is Mignola's creation and he has had enormous success in the format of the comics through sales, as well as in the creation of dedicated fan sites (hellboy.com), and he has won 'every major award in the comics industry' (Hall *et al.*, 2008: 12). It is, therefore, worth noting that Mignola does remind del Toro of his position as the originator of Hellboy and has refused the director permission to use some of his characters on several occasions (Furey, 2008).[5] This would fit with the way in which Mignola sees his role within the world of Hellboy: as long as he remains master of the comic universe, he is happy to hand over authorship to others on their individual projects, up to a point.[6] This is illustrated in comments he has made:

> The Hellboy universe as I view the Hellboy universe, is not the movies.... There is a movie universe that I have little to do with. My Hellboy universe is the comics. (Alverson, 2010)

In the movie universe Mignola is working under del Toro; thus, there is an exchange of power which has interesting implications when considering questions of authorship.

Many of the 'failings' Mignola perceives in his work with del Toro are simply due to the difference in medium, and there are craftsmen on the team dedicated to drawing, sculpting, and the creation of three-dimensional images for specifically filmic creatures. In terms of method, as Francisco Velasco (one of the principal creature designers) explains, 'Guillermo asked Mike Mignola to sketch most of the main characters for the movie in order to define their main look. Next he brought all the sketches to me and asked me to render them in a more 3-D style' (Sandoval and Velasco, 2008: 43). Significant inputs came from other artists, including the creator of many of the creatures, Wayne Barlowe (see Sandoval and Velasco, 2008, for more details).[7] Mignola was, then, part of a team under the leadership of del Toro. While he had a significant input into the designs in the film, they were substantially changed, as a look at the creative process detailed in *The Art of the Movie* book for *Hellboy II* reveals.

The sense of Mignola as a diligent craftsman under the orders of the master filmmaker fits perfectly into the discourse of auteurism cultivated in the film's paratexts (interviews, *The Art of the Movie*, DVD commentary). Del Toro's tone, in keeping with this, and in contrast with Mignola, has the confidence of the auteurist director. While he acknowledges Mignola, he reinvents *Hellboy*, significantly using analogies of home in claiming ownership over the text:

> In the case of Hellboy, I've been blessed with a guy like Mike, who is the most generous landlord of the Hellboy real estate. He essentially says, 'Move in, decorate as you want, and make it yours'. (Roberts, 2008)

In terms of 'decorators', while seasoned Hollywood crew worked on the film, del Toro also managed to bring on board a significant

Hispanic contingent, most of whom he had already worked with. These included: his cinematographer, Guillermo Navarro; Bernat Vilaplana, editor for *El laberinto* and assistant editor for *El espinazo del diablo*; two Spanish storyboard artists whom he employed for *El laberinto*, Raúl Monge and Raul Villares (Sandoval and Velasco, 2008: 3); the Mexican Pablo Angeles, who came to him through his Mexican producer (and sister of his cinematographer), Bertha Navarro; and Francisco Ruiz Velasco, a Mexican comic book artist, who had moved to the USA and whose work, like Mignola's, is published by Dark Horse.

Fans and the auteur question

I will go on to examine other ways in which del Toro appropriates Mignola's character in his second *Hellboy* film and claims it as one of the signature films within his corpus. However, before this I want briefly to consider *Hellboy* fans' responses to the film, as they can also help in assessing the relationship between the two different *Hellboy* creators and their respective texts, and shed further light on the question of authorship. Fans who join chat rooms, threads and discussion boards are a transnational community linked by the internet and their access to source texts, rather than physical locations, and the national origin of fans cannot be determined through their postings. Fans are instrumental in determining the success of a film, and providing the value judgements on it, when it has its origins in a comic or graphic novel. They can be famously jealous in guarding a comic world and insisting on degrees of fidelity, and filmmakers, studios, and academics take them seriously. As Gordon *et al.* (2007: ix) argue, fans 'can be an asset to a film adapted from a comic, but also a liability particularly when taken for granted'. This is one of the reasons that studios and filmmakers court the fans at events such as the annual Comic Con, and often treat them to film previews (ix).[8] Henry Jenkins, in his well known book *Textual Poachers: Television Fans and Participatory Culture* (1992), validates fans as experts in fields of popular culture (Jenkins, 1992: 86), as well as their moral right to criticise, based as it is on informed debates among a community with shared interests and specialised knowledge (88).[9]

Fans bring an entirely different take to the question of auteurism. While film academics may expect directors to fundamentally alter literary texts in adaptations in order to make their own mark and gain auteurist credentials, fans, in contrast, may consider a work to be poor and a director sub-standard if the film deviates too much from the source text. *Hellboy* fans who posted comments on the thread that I started on the forum at hellboy.com fan forum, in the main, responded to the fact that this was del Toro's *Hellboy* and not Mignola's, despite the fact that he had collaborated in the production.[10] Here, del Toro's right to appropriate the text became the focus of a lively debate, with some feeling that del Toro did not have the right to 'distort' Mignola's creation by making fundamental changes to the *Hellboy* universe, while others accepted that this was a new text in a different medium, and thus changes were justified. The question I asked was deliberately open, as I wanted to ascertain the comic book fans' responses to the film and the way the director had adapted and altered some of the basic characteristics of Mignola's comic stories. The question was the following: 'I'm writing a book on Guillermo del Toro and currently writing on Hellboy II. Just wondering what the response to the film was from hellboy fans. I'd really appreciate any feedback.'[11] As of 24 August 2010, it had been viewed 1,000 times, and there were forty-five responses. I have selected the most apposite comments relating to this debate to analyse here.

The tone and varied content of the debate are neatly summarised by one of the posters, Gary Bolt (9 July 2010, 7.31 p.m.), who wrote:

> The most consistent criticism of the movies from Hellboy comics fans seem to center around the Hollywood need to make love triangles and romance tensions that don't exist in the comics canon. Adaptations of comics to film often bring out some fairly rabid criticism from die-hard comics fans, but my sense is that Hellboy comic nerds were quite a bit more accommodating and able to recognize that the comics are a separate universe from the films and that they don't need to match up in every detail.

I will focus here on the two positions (critical and accommodating), which in many cases rest on informed and considered views (I am reproducing their posts as they appeared). While a number of fans were indeed accommodating as Gary Bolt has indicated, there were some questions regarding del Toro's right to alter the content of the comic books. Linda Hutcheon's analysis of fans' responses to novel-to-film adaptations can be applied to some of the feelings expressed by those who participated in this thread; as Hutcheon (2006: 127) notes, 'the more popular and beloved the novel, the more likely the discontent'. As one of the posters in this thread writes, 'when you

Hellboy II: The Golden Army

love something, you can't help but be protective of it. It's part of the definition of "love"' (JR Wormwood, 9 July 2010, 12.03 p.m.). Some did express the view that the comics had been violated by del Toro, and in these posts it is interesting to note that value judgements focus on the question of changes, and these are what make *Hellboy II* a 'bad' film. Thus, while many critics have challenged the centrality of fidelity in ascribing value to an adaptation (Andrew, 2000; Leitch, 2003; Naremore, 2000), this is a still a central criterion for many fans. For instance, JR Wormwood (8 July 2010, 1.22 p.m.) writes:

> The second film, well ... I almost walked out of the theater. It just took many liberties with the source material for my taste. Now when I try to turn people onto the comic, they immediately think 'the movies'. It gets so tiring trying to explain how superior the book is, not to mention the glazed over look in the eyes of those I'm attempting to convince. My two cents.

Kidfromhell (10 July 2010, 3.03 a.m.) shares this view: while he liked the first film, he added 'Abe is HORRIBLE in the movies. HORRIBLE! The voice is horrible, the new powers are lame, his visual just sucks.... Why did Liz have black hair? Whats the point of that change?' Middenway also criticised the film over questions of fidelity, noting (among other things) that 'most of the main characters aren't portrayed even remotely faithful and the ones that are are more of a caricature than a fleshed-out person' (8 July 2010, 3.57 p.m.). The question of fidelity appears to rest on concepts of authorship, and the implicit opinion that one author (del Toro) does not have the right to reinvent the work of another (Mignola). Del Toro's auteurist appropriation of Hellboy is what makes this a bad film for these fans.

Jackson Brody (8 July 2010, 10.05 a.m.) can be seen to represent another one of the strands: critical, but measured and analytical. He argues that the film has qualities, but needs to be seen as del Toro's work and not Mignola's. He expresses a clearly felt sense of loss in the process of the translation from comic book to film, as is common with fans of any 'original' text (Hutcheon, 2006: 122–128; Leitch, 2007), and well documented among comic fans (Rae and Gray, 2007: 86–87). Jackson Brody writes, 'Hellboy II is a great but ultimately flawed film. I think the biggest criticisms tend to center around Liz's pregnancy, the mangling of Johann Kraus' character, and the juvenile humor'.[12] He then goes on to outline what he loves about the film (the characters of Prince Nuada and Princess Nuala, the scene with the forest elemental, the troll market scene, and the tooth fairies). His overall view of the quality of the film is considered, and he acknowledges del Toro as the principal author of the work, while critiquing him for occupying this position so fully:

> Hellboy I took great pains to be faithful to Mignola's work and not violate the tone of the comics. With Hellboy II, Mignola gave Del Toro more license, which is how you get jerk teenager Hellboy, obnoxious Johann, wacky pregnancies, and drunken singalongs. I do like the singalong, but it's definitely more Del Toro Hellboy than Mignola Hellboy.... There are elements that make me cringe in both movies, but I do love them, despite Del Toro's need to add his signature where he shouldn't. When he's serious and respectful of the material, it's some of my favorite filmmaking of the past ten years.

Kees_L (9 July 2010, 2.42 p.m.) also defends the adaptation by asserting that rules of fidelity should not be too strictly applied when dealing with different media, a position shared by BPRD (9 July 2010, 2.16 p.m.). These 'posters' are taking a theoretical stance adopted by many scholars in the area of adaptation studies, as noted. He directs the following response to Middenway:

> Are you appreciating how these movies came about: with Mike Mignola being alive and well and making Hellboy as it is already, namely a comic. Where apparently a guy like Del Toro, an acquaintance and likely a kindred pulp fan, was being allowed to TRANSLATE Hellboy onto a movie screen.... Because what would be the point of perfectly echoing what the comic will be about already? Can you see why Hellboy and a movie might not really be – and could not really be – the same thing?

While not all the fans gave the film their blessing, some accepted del Toro's right to make changes (although some grated more than others, as has been seen from the above). Interestingly, there were also a number of posts from people who became fans of the comics after seeing the *Hellboy* films. It is also true that many comics have come to depend on film adaptations to stay commercially viable, with a number of comic publishers venturing into film productions, as is the case with Black Horse.[13] In the words of Mignola:

> A few years ago we were all saying: 'Jeez, maybe comics are going to go away.' Sales had gotten really terrible. If for no other reason, comics will

stay around because publishers are going, 'Well, maybe we won't make any money on the comic, but, hey, maybe that will be a film'. (Furey, 2008)¹⁴

Thus, there is a symbiotic relationship between the author of the comic and the film auteur, with each depending on the other, as the case of Hellboy illustrates.

Hellboy II: generating auteurism

Nevertheless, as Leitch (2007) has argued, film auteurism rests on a hierarchy, with the director using a range of ways to establish their authority over collaborators and authors on whom their work is based.¹⁵ He explains that 'filmmakers like Hitchcock get a special dispensation from following these models [market-based concepts of fidelity to literary models] because they provide a brand name with even greater commercial and critical cachet' (Leitch, 2007: 6, my addition in brackets). While del Toro does not have the status of Hitchcock, he does bring an auteurist cachet to the *Hellboy* films, and he is certainly better known than Mignola, whom few outside the fan base of the *Hellboy* comics will have heard of. The fact that the film followed the internationally acclaimed *El laberinto* will also have altered the expectations of audiences, and helps to wrest authority away from the comic book author. As Mignola kept reminding the director, 'Don't forget! This is your follow-up to Pan's Labyrinth! Everybody's watchin'!' (Furey, 2008).

In this instance, one of the ways in which del Toro asserts that authority and cultivates an auteurist presence through paratextual and textual means is to insert a heightened sense of self into interviews and define the character of Hellboy in autobiographical terms. He says that *Hellboy II* is one of his favourite films, along with his critically acclaimed Spanish-language texts, *El laberinto* and *El espinazo del diablo*, calling it 'a truly personal film' (DVD commentary). He also aligns himself with Hellboy the character, commenting that the plotline of whether his protagonist is ready to be a father is 'as autobiographical as it gets' (DVD commentary). The new storyline relating to Hellboy and Liz's relationship, entirely absent from the comics, in which the two have a 'brother-and-sister connection' (Hall et al., 2008: 57), is also filled with personal details that del Toro relates to his relationship with his wife. In one interview he explains his personal connection to the moment in the film where Liz asks 'Do you need *everybody* to like you, or am I enough?':

> The two movies are semi-autographical. And I do put a lot [sic] – my wife recognizes a lot of the details, including the moment when you get asked, 'Do you need everyone to love you or am I enough?' which has never been verbalized, but you have those moments. (Roberts, 2008)

The new paratextual forms – interviews freely available and easy to access on the internet, and commentaries by directors (and other key members of the team) on DVD extras packages – create new forms of authorship, and enable what Nicholas Rombes (2005) terms 'the dictatorship of the author in the digital age'. As Catherine Grant argues, 'DVDs often ... function as "Auteur Machines" ... potentially engendering different, more comprehensive forms of auteurism than were previously possible' (Grant, 2008: 104).[16] Perhaps as a consequence of this, film academics are now often more concerned with 'the discursive construction of the auteur status' than with defining auteurism (Czyzydlo, 2011: 38). Although del Toro had acquired an auteurist aura through his three Spanish-language films, his involvement in a superhero movie produced by a major studio could work to downgrade this coveted status. His director's commentary and the media persona he cultivates around the film work to militate against this.

The DVD commentary establishes del Toro as the authoritative voice within the world of the film: he thus creates a self who is both the organising presence behind the text and the one with the legitimacy to give it meaning. In some respects, this paratext seeks to supplant critical works, by explaining the themes and the processes, outlining the director's cultural references, and guiding the viewers and telling them what to watch out for. In this way, he seeks to become the viewers' personal tutor. He acknowledges this role in an interview:

> I try to make my DVD's and BLU-RAY's an 'all-access' educational glimpse into our filmmaking process. We try to keep it very candid and educational. Not just 'everything worked out' and 'we are all great' but we allow you to glimpse our tribulations, the way decisions are affected by budget or an FX that doesn't work. (Del Toro, 2008a)

On several occasions he instructs his audience to rewind, pause, and watch certain scenes in *Hellboy II* more carefully. For instance, he instructs us to look carefully at symbols on the streets of New York (actually shot in Budapest) relating to Liz's pregnancy, and he alerts

Hellboy II: The Golden Army

us to the goddesses of fertility in the auction house that also reference her state. He draws attention to the artistry behind the creation of the creatures within the film and gives specific instructions to rewatch the troll market scene to appreciate them fully.

David Bordwell (2007) asks a question highly relevant to the analysis here: 'knowing that films are seen on DVD, don't filmmakers adjust their art and craft to this new medium?' He adds, 'the ease of DVD replay can encourage filmmakers to pack their films with more details that repay rewatching'. It can be argued that both points are true of del Toro, who was prepared to spend a large proportion of his budget on *Hellboy II* (which was rather small by Hollywood standards) on creatures that are barely glimpsed (Roberts, 2008). The DVD or Blu-ray format offers a solution to this, as viewers can rewind and admire these creations, something that, as we have seen, the director advises us to do at many points in his DVD commentary.

In that commentary, del Toro informs viewers that his principal cultural references for *Hellboy II* include Ray Harryhausen, the innovative creator of monsters and creatures for many films, including the Sinbad series, and Bernard Hermann, musical director for the Sinbad films (among many others), whom he instructs his composer Danny Elfman to mimic at key moments. What is interesting about his reference to Harryhausen here is that he has been seen as an auteurist presence in the films in which he was involved for his special effects, creature designs, and use of stop-motion animation (Wells, 2002). John Landis, whose *An American Werewolf in London* (1981) is another cultural reference cited by del Toro, writes in a tribute to Harryhausen:

> Ray is truly unique in the history of movies as a special effects technician who is really the auteur of his films. Working with many directors and screenwriters, the stop motion creatures and vehicles Ray created were not only the stars of those movies, but the main reason for those movies to exist at all. (Landis, n.d.)

In chapter 1, on *Cronos*, I described del Toro as a director of monsters, and he, like Harryhausen, whom he references so closely in parts, implicitly claims an auteur status for his creature designs. The DVD commentary presents the references to Harryhausen as tribute rather than plagiarism, and the format allows him to cite his sources. He even informs viewers where they can find the reference, and in one case a quick search on YouTube allows for a direct comparison between the scenes. The director explains that he wanted the stone giant in the scene set on the Giant's Causeway in Northern Ireland (actually shot in Hungary) to be 'a Harryhausen moment'. He explains that he asked Elfman to imitate Hermann's score for the awakening of Talos in *Jason and the Argonauts* (Chaffey, 1963), and expounds on the staging and the use of wide shots in homage to this scene, which, at the time of writing could be found on YouTube.[17]

Del Toro's interest lies in the artistry of the design of creatures, which is fitting for a director who initially trained in special effects and make-up, studying with the horror specialist Dick Smith in New York, and supervising special effects for a number of Mexican productions before he began directing his own films (Wood, 2006: 29–32). This is one of the principal areas in which, then, he seeks to make a case for his auteur status: 'If I could say anything about the movies I do, I would love for them to become my personal bestiaries of fanciful creatures' (del Toro, 2008b). The director in the DVD commentary and interviews places great emphasis on the creativity that went into the designs and effects, and on his own role in ensuring that 'artistic quality' was not supplanted by computer-generated imagery (CGI). In this way, he deliberately creates a hierarchy of value between the two approaches, and, in the tradition of Harryhausen, assigns auteurist value to practical effects. He makes much of the fact that he prefers practical effects to digital effects, although he accepts that you have to know when to 'go digital' (Roberts, 2008). He explains that:

> Of the 32 creatures we created for the movie, about 90 per cent were created physically. Only the creatures that were too big, like the Elemental character, or too small, like the tooth fairies, were created using CGI. (Del Toro, 2008b)

In interviews and the DVD commentary, the director provides 'behind the scenes' insights into the genesis of the monsters. For instance, he explains how he assigned an individual creature to each member of the design crew to create, 'from maquette all the way to final realization, wardrobe, sculpting, painting, like you give a lead animator on a character in an animated film' (Furey, 2008). In the commentary he informs viewers that Mr Wink is 'a completely self-contained animatronic puppet' that was over seven feet tall, although there were digital elements (his fist and mouth and tongue). He thus consolidates his position as overarching author of the work, by (co)-creating the text, overseeing the creation of its 'monsters',

Hellboy II: The Golden Army

then providing the commentary on the process in a way that a critic without access to the set could never do, and finally assigning value to it. He, for example, decrees Mr Wink to be 'one of the most beautiful practical puppets ever built'.

It is interesting to examine del Toro's language when he discusses the process of monster and creature creation, and the ways that he claims an artistic status for his version of a superhero movie:

> It's extremely unusual to make a movie like this nowadays, but I feel the film acquires an artistry and a textural value and a handmade feel – a human touch – that CGI by itself does not give. (Del Toro, 2008b)

In this way, through textual and paratextual means, del Toro sets his film apart from others, and attempts to raise it above them. In this regard is worth mentioning Ang Lee's *Hulk* (2003), another auteurist director's attempt to take on the comic book movie. This film relied much more on CGI and the Hulk was entirely computer generated. While the film was praised for its more thoughtful and artistic take within the genre, the digital effects are a source of criticism for a number of reviewers. Todd McCarthy (2003) writes that Hulk is 'an obvious special effect', while A. O. Scott (2003) describes him as 'a computer generated Gumby on steroids'. The sense of these types of review appears to be that computer-generated effects are (within popular film criticism) placed lower on the hierarchy of artistic credentials than practical effects.

In addition, del Toro attributes artistic value to his creature designs by referencing sources from the realms of both popular and high culture, in another example of a hybrid approach to genres. In one interview with the magazine *Icons of Fright*, he explains that he based the long-legged elephant creatures that make a brief appearance in the film on a drawing by Salvador Dalí (Roberts, 2008), while he ensured that the creature designs belonged to a high art tradition:

> I urged everyone to NOT look into other movie monsters or comics and to look into engravings, old illustrations and fine painters of the Fantastique (BOCKLIN, REDON, ROPS, SCHWABE, etc) for inspiration. (Del Toro, 2008a, upper case used in original)

Elsewhere, he reiterates these sources and adds others: 'Pieter Bruegel, Arnold Böcklin and Hieronymus Bosch, as well as the Belgian Symbolists, the Surrealists, the Dadaists' (del Toro, 2008b). He roots his design of the Angel of Death in 'medieval engravings and Mexican baroque carvings and paintings' (DVD commentary). In another context del Toro disrupts the boundaries between cultural realms by having his mythical princess, Princess Nuala, recite an extract of a poem by Tennyson, 'In Memorium'.[18] The director links this to his creative universe by explaining in the DVD commentary that this is also the poem that Dr Casares recites to Carmen in his esteemed 'Spanish' film *El espinazo del diablo*. In an example of the boundaries he attempts to dissolve between European art cinema and Hollywood fare, the director assigns the poem the same function in both films. For del Toro the poem speaks to unfulfilled love, as Carmen does not reciprocate Dr Casares's love and Nuala and Abe cannot be together as their fight against the prince stands in their way. The film is also full of popular references: in another scene Hellboy and Abe sing drunkenly to Barry Manilow's 'Can't Smile Without You', when they are both lovesick.

Del Toro's Hellboy in this film inhabits a rich world informed by great artists and popular cultural references. He creates his own artistic identity to add to the intertextual references by talking about the screen as a palette. He explains his choice of colour schemes, which follow on from his Spanish-language films (analysed in chapter 1), with cold blue and grey colours chosen for the human world, while golden and earth colours are selected for the underworld of the mythical creatures. In an interview in *The Observer* he explains:

> I colour-coded everything in the movie before talking to the art director and cinematographer, and one idea I liked was to have the elf world in earth, gold, crimson and black, echoing the colours of Hellboy's library at the BPRD [Bureau for Paranormal Research and Defense]. That would emphasise the fact that Hellboy has something in common with the magic world. (Del Toro, 2008b)

Like an artist, he presents his aesthetic decisions in portrait-like terms: in addition to the colour palette, he alerts audiences to the 'straight neo-classical lines of [the] human world', which contrast with the 'round and golden and very very earthy' shapes and images in the creature world (DVD commentary).

Hellboy II and *El laberinto del fauno*

This consistency in the use of colours is one of the ways in which the director ensures that the film becomes a continuation of del Toro's

Hellboy II: The Golden Army

visual and mythical universe, and consolidates his artistic status. It is significant that the royal family in *Hellboy II* are rulers of the kingdom of Bethmoora, the name of the underworld kingdom in *El laberinto*, and that he invents a royal family who visually reference that of his previous film (see figures 2.1 and 2.2). The director informs viewers in the DVD commentary for *Hellboy II* that 'this movie came from the same place that *Pan's Labyrinth* came from', and notes that he wrote it both while he was filming *El laberinto* and during post-production. It is interesting to look at del Toro's notebook included in the published shooting script for *El laberinto*, as single pages have written and pictorial ideas for both films (del Toro, 2006).

Many of the differences in storyline are dictated by the contexts in which the two films were made. *El laberinto*, a film which celebrates resistance to the Franco regime, is more political in nature than would be acceptable in a US summer superhero movie; nevertheless, the two films share fairies and animatronic mythical creatures. They also share the belief that the human world is corrupt and full of evil, and alternative and better realities can be found in a magical underworld. While the elf prince, Nuada, may be the ostensible villain of the piece in his desire to wipe out humankind, he is motivated by human flaws and the exile of the elves. The elvish world is seen as a better world than that of the humans, embodied in the characters of Princess Naula and the King, while the troll market is presented as a wondrous place where Hellboy and his friends are no longer seen as freaks. The evil in *El laberinto* resides within Franco's nationalists, embodied in the figure of Captain Vidal, while modern consumerism is the site of evil in *Hellboy II*. As Prince Nuada exclaims, 'parking lots, shopping malls – greed has burned a hole in their heart that will never be filled, they will never have enough'.

In both texts, an underworld offers a richer, more natural, beautiful alternative, signalled not only in the narrative, but also through the visual imagery, and the colour coding. There are many visual parallels between the underworld in *Hellboy II* and that in *El laberinto* (compare figures 2.1 and 2.2). The shared look of the films is also a result of the fact that the two productions shared some of the same key crew members (e.g. cinematographer Guillermo Navarro and editor Bernat Vilaplana). There is an emphasis on warm earthy colours (golden, reds, and browns) to connote a sense of magic, royalty, and oneness with nature. The floating pollen shown in the death scene of the Elemental is a common visual reference in *El laberinto*, and another

2.1 The King of Bethmoora in *Hellboy II*

2.2 The King of Bethmoora in *El laberinto del fauno*

Hellboy II: The Golden Army

image that connects the two films. In these two films and in *Cronos* there are recurring visual motifs: the objects wrapped in cellophane, the beautifully designed magical mechanical objects, the circular wheels and cogs, medieval figures sculpted in stone, and codes and symbols that resemble alchemical figures.

The framing of some of the key scenes in *Hellboy II* and *El laberinto* is also remarkably similar. Two examples are the scenes where Prince Nuada enters the royal court in exile, and when Ofelia (now transformed into Princess Moanna) enters the underground kingdom. In these, both are in the centre of the shot and are flanked by subjects, with the monarchs at the far end of the frame, opposite the Prince (*Hellboy II*) and the Princess (*El laberinto*) (see figures 2.3 and 2.4). The two kings also inhabit the same visual universe, despite some key differences. These correspond to their circumstances. King Balor (Roy Dotrice) is a king in exile, as seen by the pipes which surround him, and the fact that he is shot at ground level (in the DVD commentary del Toro informs viewers that this is to indicate that these are 'gods holding court in a disused steam engine repair area'). The King in *El laberinto* (Federico Luppi), in contrast, represents a utopian space, an escape from the worldly realities of Franco's Spain: he towers over his subjects, emphasised through a low-angle shot; he is dressed more opulently and is seated on a golden throne. In these scenes brighter colours contrast with the browner earth colours used for Balor, who wears armour in place of the other king's sash. But there are important similarities to indicate that they are from the same imaginary family, and products of the same creator. Indeed, Balor would take on an appearance much like that of the King in *El laberinto* were he to return to the kingdom of Bethmoora. They are both dressed in robes of gold and red, and circular golden shapes feature behind their heads, taking the form of sun halos, reminiscent of medieval paintings of the Christian Holy family. The King's throne in *El laberinto* resembles Balor's antlers, as they appear to be an extension of his head.

The subtext in *Hellboy II* that del Toro is generating through references to high art, his defence of practical effects, and the visual and mythical links to his Spanish-language films, in particular *El laberinto*, is that this is a superhero movie with a difference. In this way, he implicitly aligns himself with other auteurist filmmakers who have directed comic book films, including Tim Burton (*Batman*, 1989), Christopher Nolan (*Batman Begins*, 2005, and *The Dark Knight*, 2008), and Ang Lee (*Hulk*, 2003). This stance is more than a subtext

2.3 Prince Nuada enters the underworld of the elves in exile in *Hellboy II*

2.4 Ofelia enters the underworld in *El laberinto del fauno*

elsewhere, as the director spells out his intention at various points in the DVD commentary. He expresses his satisfaction with the fact that he has made an 'anti-summer summer movie', describes it as almost an 'anti-superhero movie', and says of the tragic and beautiful tone he generates after Hellboy has shot the forest god, the Elemental, that to deny an audience pleasure through the destruction of the monster is 'pretty insane in a summer movie'.

In *El laberinto* there is a clear-cut sense of good and evil, and a clear distinction between heroes and villains, with the exception of the morally ambivalent figure of the faun, while in the Hollywood production *Hellboy II* the characters are all morally ambiguous. The 'heroes', Liz and Abe, are prepared to make choices that threaten to bring about the earth's destruction in order to save their loved ones, while Hellboy carries out orders to destroy and kill even when the ethical implications of these actions are questionable. Likewise, the apparent villain of the film, Prince Nuada, is seeking to create a better natural world through the destruction of the human order. Del Toro has thus commercialised his third Spanish-language film, and brought certain art cinema values and aesthetics to his fourth Hollywood film. Repeated visual motifs, a shared colour palette, imaginative creature designs, and a dominant paratextual and media presence all work together to create a sense of Guillermo del Toro as a popular genre auteur.

Notes

1 Three of the Hellboy books were drawn by Duncan Fegredo, as Mignola has said he would not have time to write and draw the comics (Furey, 2008).
2 Grant's focus is on auteurist strategies cultivated by directors through DVD extras, and her case study is *Timecode* (Figgis, 2001).
3 On the fact that he lobbied to direct the films, del Toro has said, 'I was not approached to direct – I went after the project like a Fat Mexican Missile of Joy!! I begged, cried and threw myself at it–!!' (del Toro, 2008a).
4 *Sin City* (Miller and Rodriguez, 2005) stands in contrast to this very free translation of Mignola's world, in which the graphic novel artist Frank Miller co-directed the cinematic rendition of his book with Robert Rodriguez. Gordon *et al.* (2007: viii) note that it is a frame-by-frame reproduction.
5 These characters were Lobster Johnson, and the Baba Yaga, whom del Toro replaced with the Angel of Death (Furey, 2008).

6 There are a number of other spin-offs from the original comics in addition to del Toro's films, including the Abe Sapien stories, the animated films, and the BPRD stories; the BPRD comics are written by John Arcudi and drawn by Guy Davis.
7 Barlowe has many other films to his credit, including several Harry Potter films, *Avatar* (Cameron, 2009), *Blade II* (del Toro, 2002), and the first *Hellboy* film (del Toro, 2004).
8 Both del Toro and Mignola, as well as other key cast and crew, attended New York Comic Con event of 2008 to promote *Hellboy II*; see M&C News (2008).
9 Jenkins's book was written before the advent of online communities, but these have only served to strengthen his arguments.
10 The thread can be accessed on http://forums.comicbookresources.com/showthread.php?329642-Guillermo-del-Toro.
11 In a later post, I asked anyone to let me know if they did not want me to publish their comments, and no one has written to refuse permission.
12 He also wrote 'Feel free to quote my statement. And you can use my real name, Eamon R. McIvor'.
13 See Gordon et al. (2007: ix) on deals between studios and comic companies to maximise profits for comic publishers. They cite the collaboration between Marvel and Paramount in 2005.
14 He adds, 'a publisher looks at your material, and they might say, "Yeah, we'll sell 10,000 copies of this, but we might be able to develop it as a film property, so we will publish it." So at least things are getting published that might not otherwise get published' (Furey, 2008).
15 Leitch (2007: 236–237) references Lubitsch, Welles, Bresson, and Kubrick as auteurist directors who made films from novels or plays.
16 For further discussion of the different uses directors make of digital media, and the relationship this has to their construction of their auteurist personae, see Zoran Samardzija (2010).
17 The YouTube link is at www.youtube.com/watch?v=Q17dL_aUNf4. There are many references to the Sinbad films; del Toro claims that the film was inspired by *The Golden Voyage of Sinbad* (Hessler, 1973), which he had to hand as he was writing the screenplay (Sandoval and Velasco, 2008: 2). The narrative device of the three pieces of the golden crown required to animate the golden army is also remarkably similar to this film. Here, three pieces of a golden tablet are needed for the fountain of destiny to yield its treasures: youth, a shield of darkness, and riches.
18 The title of the poem is given in *The Art of the Movie* (Sandoval and Velasco, 2008: 152). The poem is reproduced at www.online-literature.com/donne/718.

3

El laberinto del fauno: breaking through the barriers of filmmaking

For many, *El laberinto del fauno* (*Pan's Labyrinth*, 2006) marks the pinnacle of Guillermo del Toro's filmmaking career (Ebert, 2006; Guzmán Urrero, 2006; Kermode, 2006). It is a film that has allowed del Toro to realise his creative potential, unencumbered by the budgetary limitations of *Cronos* or the rules governing Hollywood-funded genre products. My argument here is that, with *El laberinto*, the director takes the key ingredients that I outlined in chapter 1, on *Cronos*, and succeeds in creating something new within film culture. Thus, it extends and develops both the visual approach and the themes essayed in *Cronos*: it combines the magical and the realist, the fantastical and the political; its narrative centres on the child's connection with the magical underworld; and it develops the visual world with a rich and contrasting colour palette, with previously separate colour schemes beginning to merge within a single frame. As with *Cronos* and *Hellboy II*, there is an emphasis on circular cogs and gears, coded symbols, and medieval figures carved in stone, while the creature designs are even more imaginative, seen in the characters of the faun, the fairies, and the terrifying figure of the Pale Man. Themes established in the first film (and returned to in *Hellboy II*) are also reprised and developed: *El laberinto* builds on the concept of the monstrous human through the character of the fascist Captain Vidal, and the idea of sacrifice is once again central to the plot and to the idea of redemption; the importance of moral choices is at the heart of Ofelia's character, while the characters come to embody good and evil, with the exception of the morally ambiguous faun.

So, *El laberinto* helps to establish the authorial signature traits of del Toro, but what is new about this film, and why is it so significant within film history? The answers to these questions lie in the ways in which conceptual barriers are broken down. It travels freely between the borders of art cinema, commercial filmmaking, social realist drama, political cinema, horror, and fantasy film. It is a Spanish-language film with funding from Spanish production companies, and co-produced by del Toro and Alfonso Cuarón's Mexican companies.[1] It is rooted in the specific national context of post-Civil War Spanish society (it is set in 1944), and conflicts between the Maquis resistance and the Nationalist forces, yet the director and cinematographer, Guillermo Navarro, are Mexican. It is a 'foreign'-language film, yet, unusually, it was shown in multiplexes all over the world and broke records for a non-English-language movie. It was marketed by the US distributors Picturehouse to the niche sectors of art cinema, genre, and Latino audiences, who are usually targeted separately (Galloway, 2007). It features a young girl as the protagonist, borrows from Lewis Carroll's *Alice in Wonderland* and *The Wizard of Oz* (Fleming, 1939), and uses a fairy tale structure, yet in the UK it has an 18 certificate due to the levels of psychological and physical violence, and is not for children.[2] What this crowded paragraph demonstrates is that *El laberinto* breaks many of the rules governing how we have seen cinema in terms of production, text, and reception. What holds this all together is the name/brand of the director: *El laberinto* makes sense in the marketplace as it is a del Toro film.

In this chapter, I briefly return to the comparisons with *Hellboy II* initiated in the previous chapter, here to elucidate the differences occasioned by the shift in production and generic context, rather than the similarities, which I have already outlined. I go on to explore the ways in which a freedom to create a new form of cinema is manifested in *El laberinto* by examining how the film traverses borders and creates a new hybrid form. Few of the aspects of *El laberinto* in themselves are exceptional or represent new forms of filmmaking: what is unique is the way that elements from discrete modes are combined and brought together through the vision of del Toro. I return to the idea of the director as alchemist, blending together ingredients from different genres to create something original. One focus in this chapter is on the way *El laberinto* is part of a European trend in filmmaking to redefine texts' relationship to art cinema, and on resulting new forms of categorisation, with the term 'specialised film' coming to replace 'art cinema' in a number of cases.

Boundary breaking is also the prime consideration in my analysis of the lack of clarity which arises when assigning national identity to the film. This is linked to a question that is a recurring theme throughout the book: the tension between local specificity, global forms of filmmaking, and the political. I examine the ways in which del Toro presents the Spanish Civil War and its aftermath to international audiences, analyse the relationship between the fantastic and the realist, and consider the strengths and weaknesses of this pairing, which has become the main characteristic of the director's Spanish-language films. In addition, I consider whether *El laberinto* can be read as a feminist film.

El laberinto del fauno and *Hellboy II*

In the chapter on *Hellboy II* I argue that del Toro stamps his authorial seal on Hollywood productions through the text and paratexts, and the film reveals many instances of creative invention. Nevertheless, while generally critically well received, it was not seen as a groundbreaking film in the same way that the Spanish-language film was. It is interesting to consider briefly the reasons for this, when the popular critical response to *El laberinto* was so different. *Sight and Sound* critic Michael Atkinson (2008) summarises the high-end critical response to *Hellboy II* opinion well in his review of the film:

> [while] it's a breeze to watch, undemanding of empathy, constantly inventive in its monsters and always ironic ... the problem with *Hellboy II* is that too much of it is sub-literate, and too convinced that flashy physical combat tells stories, rather than stalls them to a halt. It's a universal presumption in modern Hollywood, and audiences have tacitly agreed to forgive pulp movies their bully reflexes. Here's to sending del Toro back to Spain.

There is a sense here that the 'real' auteur can be revealed only through Spanish-language films such as *El espinazo del diablo* and *El laberinto*. While this could be seen to lie in critical snobbery towards Hollywood, as del Toro would no doubt argue, there are some generic industry constraints that work against more traditional notions of quality. Despite the incorporation of artistic elements outlined in the previous chapter, which brings elements from high art to a commercial enterprise, it can be argued that the generic markers of the comic book necessitate action-filled set-pieces and resolution through violence. Del Toro makes the following telling statement when interviewed about *Hellboy II*:

In many ways, it will hit some of the beats. You know, you see an Indiana Jones movie, you expect certain beats. If you watch a Bond movie, you know you're going to have your opening sequence, he's going to get laid, there's going to be explosions, he's going to have a great car and gadgets. In that way, it will be a Hellboy movie, but to me, the best second parts are the ones that take what was done right on the first one and try to reinvent it. (Tallerico, 2008)

Despite the film's ambivalence towards violence as outlined in the previous chapter, the character of Hellboy is a creation who functions only through physical force and his ability to defeat enemies, even if the film casts doubt on who his enemies are. In commercial terms, the point is that *Hellboy II* does not have to do anything, indeed, should not do anything to disrupt *certain* narrative conventions, as its global audience is assured, provided that the film respects some fundamental rules. These rules, at their most basic level, require plenty of action sequences, and the use of violence to secure a resolution. This does allow space for authorial presence to be asserted, specifically in visual terms, as I have explained. However, a director accepts a contract, either written or unwritten, when she/he agrees to work within a specific production context: in this case commercial Hollywood. Thus, while *Hellboy II* is an artistic film, it can be clearly demarcated as a fantasy film.

Del Toro acknowledges the increased freedom to break generic codes in his Spanish-language films when asked how he feels about remakes of these in English:

> I don't mind anyone remaking any of my Hollywood efforts, because they are comfortably sat within one genre or another. For me, 'Cronos' is and it isn't a vampire movie; 'Devil's Backbone' is and it isn't a ghost story; and 'Pan's Labyrinth' is and it isn't a fantasy film. I don't want them to be homogenised into a genre. (Jenkins, 2006)

The production context of these two types of film is clearly central when discussing concepts of creative possibilities and constraints. Universal Pictures, which produced *Hellboy II*, is an entirely different organisation to the Tequila Gang and Esperanto Filmoj, the production companies with the most creative input behind *El laberinto*. They are principally controlled by the two director friends, del Toro himself and Cuarón, while the other main financial backer, the Spanish television company and film producer Telecinco, allowed del Toro complete creative control (see commentary with director

Guillermo del Toro in the extras package on the DVD release). No one at Universal needed to give up producers' salaries, as did del Toro, Cuarón, and Frida Torresblanco (Cuarón's partner at Esperanto Filmoj) for *El laberinto* in order to get the project completed (DVD commentary).[3] In other words, there is a freedom to break rules and reconfigure generic tropes in a film of this nature not seen in a Hollywood film, despite del Toro's protestations that *Hellboy II* is as personal a project as *El laberinto*. Working within constraints does not mean a project cannot be personal, but the fact that these constraints are common to the genre makes it more difficult to make a case for the film as an auteurist piece, hence the hard work the director had to put into reinforcing this status, as seen in the previous chapter.

Art cinema, genre cinema, and *El laberinto del fauno*

Of course, borders between film genres and forms are porous, and many are themselves an amalgam of styles and tropes, as I have noted. When looking at film's relationship with art cinema it is important to acknowledge that it is characterised by its 'mongrel identity', as Galt and Schoonover have argued (2010: 3). For these authors, art cinema is a hybrid form and contested term that has 'intersected with popular genres, national cinema, revolutionary filmmaking and the avant-garde, and has mixed corporate, state, and independent capital' (3). Nevertheless, there are certain aspects that have been seen to delineate 'art cinema'. David Bordwell, in his well known essay 'The Art Cinema as a Mode of Film Practice', sets the parameters for definitions for critics: he has noted that art cinema is characterised by 'realism, authorship, and ambiguity', as one of his subheadings indicates. He has a European focus and cites as examples Italian neo-realist films, films of Ingmar Bergman, and films of the French New Wave, among others; the only non-European director he includes in his account is Kurosawa. Art cinema is, for Bordwell (2002b: 97), 'lacking identifiable stars and familiar genres', and is a distinct mode which can be seen in opposition to classical Hollywood narrative norms through its rejection of the logic of a narrative cause and effect (95). There is, thus, frequently a 'drifting episodic quality' to the narrative, while the characters are both 'psychologically complex' and realistic (96).

Stephen Neale concurs with much of this, and also roots art cinema in a European context (his focus is on France, Germany, Italy, and Britain).[4] For Neale:

Art films tend to be marked by a stress on visual style (an engagement of the look in terms of a marked individual point of view rather than in terms of institutionalised spectacle), by a suppression of action in the Hollywood sense, by a consequent stress on character rather than plot and by an interiorisation of dramatic conflict. (Neale, 2002: 104)

He also highlights the privileged position of the director as author (104) and foregrounds the importance of realism (104); he notes the '*primacy* of art' in a classical and romantic sense (104), and, like Bordwell, stresses its differentiation from Hollywood products (105), although he focuses on art cinema as an institution, intimately linked to state film policies and constructions of national identities (118). For Neale, the 'art cinema' label is crucial as a marketing tool, allowing for the creation of 'a niche within the international film market' (118), sustained by the brand name of the author (119). It provides a 'mechanism of discrimination' (119), and is a 'means of producing and sustaining a division within the field of cinema overall; a division that functions economically, ideologically and aesthetically' (119). Art cinema films thus have 'rarely disturbed or altered' (119) the commercial film industry.

These definitions were extremely useful in establishing a film practice, industry category, and narrative mode that came to characterise European filmmaking for many. European films that were seen in other territories often conformed to these definitions. Thus, European film became art film for international audiences, despite many popular, more low-brow national films that were never exported.[5] It should, however, be noted that, as Galt and Schoonover (2010: 7) observe, a number of film texts become art cinema only once they have entered into transnational circulation, and may be placed in this category simply because they are not in English and are limited in release to art cinemas.

There has been a shift in the European films that are available to international audiences, and films that conform to strict art cinema definitions are only part of the story. Genre films are challenging traditional concepts of European art cinema. Many recent films from Europe are breaking down the division in the film market, noted by Neale, that previously worked to sustain 'foreign'-language films by restricting them to the art cinema category. Thus, a number of films are reaching global audiences by both relying on and reworking generic tropes found within sci-fi, thriller, horror, and gangster films. These include: *Abre los ojos* (*Open Your Eyes*) (Amenábar, 1997), *Caché*

(*Hidden*) (Haneke, 2005), *Låt den rätte komma in* (*Let the Right One In*) (Alfredson, 2008), *Män som hatar kvinnor* (*The Girl with the Dragon Tattoo*) (Oplev, 2009), *L'instinct de mort* (*Mesrine: Killer Instinct*) (Richet, 2008a) and *L'ennemi public no. 1* (*Mesrine: Part 2 – Public Enemy No. 1*) (Richet, 2008b), *Un prophète* (*A Prophet*) (Audiard, 2009), *El orfanato* (*The Orphanage*) (Bayona, 2007), *Los ojos de Julia* (*Julia's Eyes*) (Morales, 2010 – the last two both produced by del Toro – and *[Rec]* (Balagueró and Plaza, 2007) and *[Rec]2* (Balagueró and Plaza, 2009). These films are all working within, and at times against, specific genres, and many of them also refuse easy categorisation. Thus, *Caché* sets itself up as a thriller only to refuse the obvious final reveal and focus on what initially appear to be tangential issues; *Abre los ojos* is based on a sci-fi premise but is set in contemporary Madrid and is free of all the hi-tech tricks associated with the genre, unlike its Hollywood remake, *Vanilla Sky* (Crowe, 2001).

Del Toro is a prime exponent of the commercial turn seen in the evolution of auteurist European art cinema, partly, paradoxically, because he is not European and the national identity of the film is uncertain. The director and screen writer has the experience of making films in Mexico, Hollywood, and Spain, and was thus able to bring something new to this Spanish–Mexican co-production, which has arguably influenced European film production. *El laberinto* can, for instance, be seen to have set a trend of merging the fantastic with the realist: in *Un prophète* the ghost angel of Reyeb regularly visits Malik, after he has murdered him, while the use of a social realist aesthetic to tell the story of the vampire girl next door and her young, lonely human boyfriend gave the Swedish film *Låt den rätte komma in* its power.[6] My point here is that *El laberinto* is paradigmatic of a trend within European filmmaking in its shift away from rigid boundaries of art cinema, while retaining some of its characteristics, to create a form of cinema which has resulted in increased global consumption.

Thus, aspects of *El laberinto* can be neatly fitted into Bordwell's formulation of 'realism, authorship, and ambiguity', and Neale's notion of the 'primacy of art'. Art cinema audiences have their expectations met by cultural references from the realms of 'high art', the use of the colour palette, and the engagement with serious social issues. Nonetheless, other elements of del Toro's film have no place within prior definitions of art cinema. The worlds of the faun, the Pale Man, the fairies, and the royal underworld to which Ofelia/Princess Moanna returns belong within the genre of fantasy. The stress on plot and action, rather than an 'interiorisation of dramatic conflict' (Neale, 2002: 104), also place it closer to Hollywood storytelling practices, as does the resolution seen in the 'happy ending'. There is, effectively, a fusion between two normally opposing forms of filmmaking – social realist art cinema and US fantasy filmmaking – and these factors provide the film's strengths and, as I go on to argue, its main weakness when applying a political reading of the film. The crossover success of the film can perhaps be attributed to the fact that both traditional art cinema and genre audiences are provided with some of the blatant pleasures of the mainstream text, often deliberately withheld from art cinema audiences, or presented more subtly, while serious and worthy issues are addressed.

A useful focus to explore the combination of fantasy and realist elements in *El laberinto* is the colour palette. Del Toro applies his signature colour design of metallic blues and greys that contrast with warm earthy tones. What is different in this film is the way that the colour palettes begin to contaminate each separate sphere for specific purposes, an aspect the director as guide alerts viewers to in the commentary on the DVD and Blu-ray. In broad terms, the bluish grey tones colour exterior scenes that feature the cruelty of Vidal's nationalist soldiers and the activities of the Maquis. Nevertheless, they also accompany the faun's appearances to Ofelia, even when these take place in interiors, perhaps signalling his affinity with the natural outdoor world. Earthy brown tones are used for most of the interior shots in the home, the granary, where the food is stored, the cave inhabited by the resistance fighters, and the false paradise of the Pale Man's underground banquet room. Golden colours signal the world of magic and fantasy, and are reserved for the magical world of the royal family of the underworld. They are, for instance, used in the sequence where Ofelia tells her baby brother the magical story she has made up for him, thus directly linking storytelling and fantasy.[7] It is also worth noting that as Ofelia first opens the magical book that the faun has given her and the images take shape, a bright white light streams in through the round windows (resembling portals) in her bathroom. Shapes are used as deliberately as the colour scheme in the film: circular shapes are used for the feminine magical places of the film, while straight lines and angular shapes are used for the masculine militaristic worlds (DVD commentary).

In *El laberinto* the blues and earth tones of the inside and outside world come together in, for example, the realist scene where el

El laberinto del fauno

3.1 The post-torture scene in *El laberinto del fauno*

Tartamudo (the Stutterer) has been tortured by the Captain and is receiving the comfort of a lethal painkiller from the doctor. Vidal is always seen in his blue uniform, and here we see he is aligned with the outdoor battle scenes, rather than the earthy domestic spaces (figure 3.1). The film also uses the coming together of different worlds of colour to show the gradual encroachment of the magical over the realist. As Ofelia succeeds in her tasks (despite failing the task of the Pale Man), and comes closer to returning to her royal immortal identity, golden colours begins to infiltrate in the blue realist world. Viewers are shown the burning mill, with the golden light transforming the naturalistic forest into a fantasy setting. This is the setting for the mythic film ending of the killing of the Captain by the rebels and Ofelia's death and entry into her magical kingdom (figure 3.2). It is signalled by the exaggerated intense yellow colouring given to the frame, with the notion of fantasy compounded by the fact that her clothing is magically transformed and she is seen wearing a red silk cloak and (Dorothy-like) red shoes. In an inverse reference to the *Wizard of Oz*, Ofelia (now Princess Moanna) is finally home when she enters the magical world, not, in contrast to Dorothy, when she returns from it. This inversion links to the fact that del Toro is more at home in a magical world than in a realist one.[8]

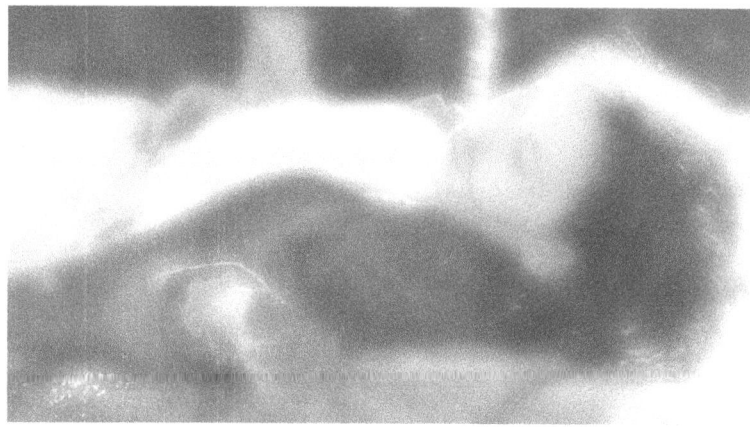

3.2 Ofelia is reborn as Princess Moanna in *El laberinto del fauno*

Thus, the colour coding signals the primacy of film as art, with the director cast as the modern-day version of the classical artist. Yet, even in his use of colour palettes, del Toro is signalling his dual identity as both serious realist and imaginative fantasy director, a feature apparent in the artistic sources for realist and fantasy scenes. Paul Julian Smith notes that in many of the kitchen scenes there is 'an aesthetic reminiscent of Velasquez' (Smith, 2007: 8), with particular reference to the painting *Old Woman Cooking Eggs* (in the National Gallery of Scotland). While Velásquez provides the realist look for the homely kitchen shots, the director turns to Goya, the other best-known classical Spanish artist, for the film's most famous fantasy/horror scene, where Ofelia has her encounter with the Pale Man, the monster double of Captain Vidal. Del Toro alerts viewers in the DVD commentary to the influence of Goya's 'black' paintings, particularly in this monstrous scene, and notes what he calls an 'almost verbatim quote' from Goya's painting *Saturn Devouring His Son* when the fairy's head is bitten off.[9] References for the fantasy visuals are rooted in more popular sources and he acknowledges a number of influences in the DVD commentary, including the golden age fairy tale illustrator Arthur Rackham, who illustrated the Grimms' fairy tales in 1909, and symbolist painters such as Arnold Böcklin and

Carlos Schwabe. Thus, in the intertextual popular artistic sources and the creature designs, the film inhabits the realms of fantasy film and more commercial cinematic forms.

Shifts in the nature of European and global films breaking into international film circuits have resulted in changes in forms of classifying film, with programmers, trade papers such as *Variety*, and film councils, such as the (now defunct) UK Film Council preferring to use the term 'specialised', rather than 'art cinema'.[10] This provides another example of how transnational textual and distribution practices are changing how films have been understood and categorised. It is interesting to note that in a section on distribution and exhibition, the Council uses an image of *Pan's Labyrinth*: this was one of the four films, along with *Volver* (Almodóvar, 2006), *Caché*, and the South African film *Tsotsi* (Hood, 2005), which received Council grants to pay for 'additional prints and advertising, providing a greater opportunity for people to see the films' (UK Film Council, 2007: 63). Del Toro's film was awarded £158,000 from the Prints and Advertising Fund, which is supported by the National Lottery.[11] The high profile awarded to *El laberinto* by the UK Film Council signals its status as a key example of a specialised film, a Spanish-language film which is neither art cinema, nor mainstream Hollywood fare, but which takes components from both, and which can thus have broader appeal than 'foreign'-language films, which fall more neatly into the definitions of art cinema seen above.

It can be argued, then, that the success of *El laberinto* lies in its redefinition of the borders of art cinema, and in its use of generic tropes. In this way, the film works to undermine Neale's notion of market differentiation, a differentiation which has traditionally guaranteed art cinema films a small but stable audience. This is reflected in the ways that the film was marketed by its US distributors, Picturehouse, specifically to three audience sectors: Latino audiences, genre audiences, and art cinema goers, with the auteurist presence of the director harnessed to bring these three usually diverse sectors into the cinemas (Galloway, 2007). Bob Berney, then President of Picturehouse, explains the process:

> The challenges of marketing a Spanish-language film were daunting. And the period of the film and the harsh violence were definitely major challenges. I was concerned that the traditional art audience, the older audience, might be put off by the extreme violence and that the younger

audience might not understand the period and the politics of the film. We decided to promote Guillermo as the star. He has younger fans, of (2004's) 'Hellboy' and (2002's) 'Blade II,' and he has critics who are fans because of … 'Cronos' and (2001's) 'The Devil's Backbone,' and we wanted to merge both those audiences. Also, we really believed that the Latino audience in the US was under-served and ready for a bigger film. These are very different audiences, and we had to pull all these elements together. (Galloway, 2007)

This approach is illustrated by the fact that the film competed in diverse sectors of the festival and awards circuit. It was promoted at the traditional art festival Cannes in 2006 through collaboration with French distributors Wild Bunch, and a huge promotion was organised at the San Diego Comic Con fantasy and science fiction convention of 2006. At Comic Con del Toro signed autographs for thousands of fans by a replica tree of that which appears in the film (Galloway, 2007). This way of targeting the fantasy market bore fruit, as seen in audience figures; according to the database Box Office Mojo (www.boxofficemojo.com), the film (made with a budget of €13,500,000) grossed $37,634,615 in the USA alone and was shown in 1,143 theatres, an unusually high number for a foreign-language release. It is also worth noting that the film was nominated for the Saturn Awards of the US Academy of Science Fiction, Fantasy and Horror Films, for which it won in the categories of Best International Film and Best Performance by a Younger Actor, for Ivana Baquero (see IMDB).

El laberinto and national identities

Just as market categories and generic markers for the film are blurred, assigning it national or regional identity is not straightforward and whether *El laberinto* is a Spanish or a Mexican film is mired in some confusion. For many, it is a Spanish film, due to the setting, themes, and location, as well as the Spanish nationalities of the actors. Smith (2007: 9) notes the 'expert art design with its reference to a famously devastated village' of Belchite (in the province of Zaragoza), where it was set and partially shot.[12] This is reinforced by the fact that it was entered in and won a number of categories for the high-profile Spanish annual film awards, the Goyas, including Best Cinematography for Guillermo Navarro, Best Editing for Bernat Vilaplana, Best New Actress for Ivana Baquero, as well as Best Screenplay for del Toro.

El laberinto del fauno

Nevertheless, this is problematised by the nationality of key crew and the complexity of the funding arrangements; this was hinted at by del Toro himself when he declared '¡Viva México y viva España!' on accepting his Goya award (Smith, 2007). A number of the key crew members were Mexican, including del Toro, Navarro, the production designer Eugenio Caballero, and a number of the producers. As seen, the film was a Spanish–Mexican co-production: the financial muscle was provided by the Spanish companies, while the hands-on production work was done by the Mexicans (DVD commentary). The global ambitions of the film were realised through the fact that the film was taken up by the major US distributor Picturehouse, while it was distributed elsewhere by other large companies, including Warner Bros in Spain, Culture Publishers in Japan, and Optimum Home Entertainment in the UK.[13]

It appears that while the Spanish film world chose to claim the film as its own, the same was true for the Mexican film world: *El laberinto* was nominated for twelve of the fifteen categories for the Arieles, the Mexican national film awards, and won nine (Tovar, 2007). The Mexican film academy (La Academia Mexicana de Artes y Ciencias Cinematográficas) selected the film to represent the country in the Oscars of 2007, a rather controversial act which rested principally on the nationality of the director and demonstrated the Academia's desire to align itself with the highest-profile Spanish-language film of the year (alongside Almodóvar's *Volver*), rather than a desire to promote cinema that engages with national issues.[14] Uncharacteristically, *Pan's Labyrinth* was entered in other non-foreign-language categories, dominated by US productions, including Best Original Screenplay, Best Original Score, Best Art Direction, Best Cinematography, and Best Make-Up, winning awards for the last three nominations.[15]

So, is *El laberinto* Spanish or Mexican? Or is this the wrong question? I would argue that to select one or the other is to fall into a false dichotomy: it is a Spanish–Mexican co-production set in Spain and focusing on Spanish topics with Spanish actors; it is made by a predominantly Mexican creative team, with collaboration from a Spanish film crew, using globalised patterns of storytelling, individualised through an auteurist vision (of which more later). Del Toro speaks to this lack of clear definition in both generic and national terms in an interview given to *Time Out* magazine. He gives the following answer when asked whether he considers himself to be an art-house or a mainstream director:

> I see myself as a perennial expatriate, because frankly, I don't think I fit comfortably in any conventional form of filmmaking and I feel at the same time, depending on the project, I fit into many different ones. If you ask me, I alternate between truly bizarre, what you would call 'Hollywood' movies and truly bizarre, what you would call 'arthouse' movies. But, then again, I don't feel the movies fit perfectly in either one of them. The same question would be, am I a Spanish filmmaker, a Mexican filmmaker, a Hollywood filmmaker? I feel I'm just a filmmaker who is hopefully equally at odds with all of the above definitions. (Jenkins, 2006)

Thus, del Toro sees strength in his refusal to conform to strict parameters of filmmaking and clear national demarcations.

In terms of the national identity of the film, I partially share the position of Ann Davies (2012), who argues that in *El laberinto* (as well as *El espinazo del diablo*) 'del Toro converts local specificities to a globalised form', and 'the isolation and lack of specificity' in the landscapes, as well as the archetypal nature of the forest, serve 'to de-nationalise and internationalise them'.[16] Despite this, for Davies, the history in the film 'is nonetheless specific and local as well as global, and as such it resonates with meaning'. Thus, she argues, del Toro can have his cake and eat it by making a film rooted in the specifics of post-Civil War Spanish society, while its use of an international film language and elements from fantasy and horror makes this vision easily accessible to international audiences. She summarises her position thus:

> We can have it both ways: the setting can be landscape, the site of spectacle, generic in the sense of genre, allowing history to be rewritten as fantasy for the pleasure of audiences within Spain and without. But it is also territory, the land that was literally fought over, and we see the landscape in both films in that sense as well – and thus the landscape acquires a local specificity. (Davies, 2012)

Although Davies acknowledges potential problems with the re-creation of history as an alternative fiction, this can be justified through the pleasures of the text.

While del Toro, to a degree, achieves the feat of universalising a version of the local, I do challenge the notion that history can be 'rewritten as fantasy' and maintain its specificity. The universalist concept of the happy ending inherent in the fantasy genre necessitates a resolution which is false in historical terms, and this can be seen as problematic, particularly when considering audiences who are not familiar with Spanish history. These audiences are given the impression of the victory of the Maquis forces through the defeat of the Francoist Captain Vidal, while the new Spain, symbolised through Ofelia's baby brother, is seen safe in the arms of the progressive Republicans. This is disturbing in a way that the obviously fantasy ending of Ofelia's transformation into the mythical Princess Moanna is not, as it is couched in realist aesthetics and belies the extra-textual truth of nearly thirty years of Francoism that Spain endured following the period in which the film is set.[17] Francisco Franco's rule continued until his death in 1975, and neither he nor his generals were subject to any judicial proceedings for human rights abuses, following an amnesty granted to those who collaborated in such abuses committed during or after the war (Preston, 1990), although contemporary Spain is challenging the official amnesia (Sciolino and Daly, 2002).[18] The engraving in Latin at the entrance to the labyrinth translates as 'in your hands is your destiny' (DVD commentary); this concept – central to the rules of fantasy storytelling – would not be a truth recognised by the defeated Republicans in the Spain of 1944.

Paul Julian Smith also shares this sense of *El laberinto* as a successful 'world cinema' text rooted in national specifics. Spanish and Mexican film cultures are, he suggests, united by the film, which has a rightful subject for a Mexican director, as Mexico gave refuge to many Republican victims of the Spanish Civil War (Smith, 2007: 4).[19] For Smith, the film 'is a feat of cinematic Esperanto that transcends both the supposed exile of Mexican cinema and the alleged non-communication of national cultures' (9). Rather than consider the ways that the film de-nationalises its landscapes (as suggested by Davies, quoted above), Smith highlights the very Spanish references, seen in the Don Quixote-like mill (5), the above cited references to Belchite (9), the intertextual reference that Ofelia makes to the young girl Ana (Ana Torrent) in Erice's *El espíritu de la colmena* (*The Spirit of the Beehive*) (1973) (6), and the artistic references to Diego Velásquez (5), noted above. Smith also makes the point that the film resonates 'with current trends in Spain, where a "Law of Memory" on the legacy of the Civil War has been bitterly debated and where mass war graves are only now being disinterred' (6).[20]

Nonetheless, there is, despite these national elements, a selection of transnational intertextual references which root the text more firmly within globalised structures of storytelling than a specific period of

3.3 Professor Pomona Sprout (Miriam Margolyes) holds up the mandrake in *Harry Potter and the Chamber of Secrets*

3.4 Ofelia looks at the mandrake in *El laberinto del fauno*

Spanish history, identifiable only to Hispanophiles. These include some rather less Spanish references to popular fantasy sources. The mandrake appears to be a direct lift from the mandrakes in *Harry Potter and the Chamber of Secrets* (Columbus, 2002), with the function of these anthropomorphic plants being to heal in both texts (figures 3.3 and 3.4).

This Harry Potter film also features a magical book with pages that are blank until they are activated by the ink in Harry's pen. Likewise, the blank pages of Ofelia's book, given to her by the faun, show words and pictures only when it is opened in the sanctuary of the bathroom. Del Toro also informs us that he cites a number of global classical sources when approaching the fairy tale structure of the storyline and the use of archetype:

> Hans Christian Anderson, Lewis Carroll, The Wizard of Oz, C. S. Lewis, everyone, but the main book in the creation of the film was called The Science of Fairy Tales. It's a nineteenth century volume [by Edwin Sidney Hartland] that essentially tracks what it calls 'the marchen,' a German word, which is the fantastic tale. It tracks it through the ages and through the cultures of the world. I found myself intoxicated by reading it. A lot of the things the book does is tell you what are the primordial mythologies. (Tallerico, 2008)

What is most apposite here is the fact that the main feature of the *Märchen*, the type of fairy tale which forms the basis of Hartland's analysis, is the happy ending (Hartland, 1890: 23). This clearly relates to the structure of classical Hollywood cinema, with the problems that this entails discussed above.[21] This fairy tale structure behind many forms of 'globalised' storytelling is what takes the film away from its historical specificity. The magical dimensions ultimately take over the realist elements, so that these fantasy elements, while responsible for the film's global success, are also at the root of the historical distortion, as seen.

The fairy tale and *El laberinto del fauno*

Del Toro has always had global ambitions for his filmmaking, and has thus studied and applied archetypal universalist laws of storytelling, all the while transforming them to give them an auteurist spin. As he has noted, one of the chief sources for the writing of the screenplay was Edwin Sidney Hartland's *The Science of Fairy Tales: An Inquiry Into Fairy Mythology*, originally published in 1890 (Tallerico, 2008), and now freely available via the Gutenberg Project.[22] One of the key ideas expressed by Hartland, underpinned by an essentialist understanding of human imagination, is that within fairy tales there are universal laws. These are ideas which were developed by structuralist readings of folktales based on the idea that there are common underlying structures to popular stories. The best-known of these is Vladimir Propp's *Morphology of the Folktale* (1928), which sought to demonstrate that thirty-one narrative functions could be identified from 150 Russian folk/fairy tales. Hartland argues that 'Man's imagination, like every other known power, works by fixed laws, the existence and operation of which it is possible to trace' (3). He sets out to trace this in his erudite book by looking for patterns within fairy tales, and highlighting the repetition of plots and incidents. In his words: 'The name of Fairy Tales is legion; but they are made up of incidents whose number is comparatively limited' (3). It is interesting that the lesser-known Hartland pre-dates Propp's formulation that 'the number of functions known to the fairy tale is limited' (Propp, 1968 edition: 10) by thirty-eight years.

These generalised storytelling principles are also behind Joseph Campbell's idea of a shared transhistorical and transnational structure, which he develops in the notion of a monomyth in his influential book *The Hero with a Thousand Faces* (1968). The hero's adventure is divided into stages, which fall under the subheadings 'Departure, Initiation and Return', and 'the nuclear unit of the monomyth' (23), which feature key concepts such as the call to adventure, a road of trials, the goal or 'boon', the return to the ordinary world, the application of the boon. Campbell explains:

> A hero ventures forth from the world of common day into a region of supernatural wonder (x): fabulous forces are there encountered and a decisive victory is won (y): the hero comes back from this mysterious adventure with the power to bestow boons on his fellow man (z). (Campbell, 1968: 23)

These ideas were applied by Christopher Vogler in his influential screenwriting guide *The Writer's Journey: Mythic Structure for Writers* (1998), in which he develops this formulaic structure and includes key journey stages for his hero, which are made up of 'the ordinary world', 'the call to adventure', 'refusal of the call', 'meeting with the mentor', 'crossing the threshold', 'tests, allies and enemies', 'approach', 'the ordeal', 'the reward', 'the road back', 'the resurrection', and 'return with the elixir'.

The ways in which structuralist accounts of fairy tales and folktales transmuted into Hollywood screenwriting guides illustrate that, whether due to the notion of a Jungian collective unconscious, ingrained learnt patterns of storytelling, or a deliberate commercial engagement, there are popular formulae for fantasy hero-based storytelling which have their roots in fairy tales. In the DVD commentary to the film, del Toro has said that (to paraphrase) it is possible to preserve the structure of the fairy tale and deconstruct characters, or to deconstruct the fairy tale and preserve the simplicity of characters, but that it is not possible to do both, as the fairy tale would be unrecognisable. He thus claims that he retains the fairy tale archetypes (he cites Red Riding Hood and the Big Bad Wolf for the characters of Ofelia and the Captain), while reconfiguring essential structural elements of the fairy tale. I will consider the degree to which this is indeed the approach taken in the film, and will examine the extent to which del Toro remains within these popular generic rules or deviates from them within *El laberinto*. A consistent theme throughout this book is the question of deviation from and subversion of generic norms, and here I consider the tensions between a subversive desire to carve out a singular voice that goes against the grain and the application of a conventional form of storytelling with the widest possible appeal.

A good starting point for this analysis is the text the director cites as his primary source: *The Science of Fairy Tales*, whose very title reveals a desire to quantify and measure tropes within global storytelling. The main difference between Hartland and del Toro's vision is that the former sees the beliefs expressed within fairy tales as symptomatic of the superstitions of 'primitive' minds and a society at a low stage of development. In his words: 'the root whence all these phenomena spring is the predominance of imagination over reason in the uncivilized' (Hartland, 1890: 34). For del Toro, in contrast, magic offers a better, 'more civilised' reality than that embraced by rationalists such as Captain Vidal, who are unable to see the other world Ofelia inhabits. Despite this difference in vision, many of the central ideas within *El laberinto* are identified in Hartland's *Science of Fairy Tales*. The author tells of numerous instances of the 'doctrine of Transformation' (335), where spirits can 'quit the body and roam at will in different shapes about the world, returning to the body as to its natural home' (334). This is an idea manifested in the spirit of the Princess Moanna, which has taken temporary residence in the body of Ofelia. Hartland also gives many instances throughout the world of stories which feature the prohibition of a mortal eating food from a magical world lest she/he be confined to that world. He notes:

> We have found the supposition that to eat of fairy food is to return no more, equally applicable to the world of the dead as to Fairyland.... Hence to partake of food in the land of spirits, whether they are human dead, or fairies, is to proclaim one's union with them and to renounce the fellowship of mortals. (Hartland, 1890: 51)[23]

This is an idea that del Toro also puts to excellent use in the scene with Ofelia and the Pale Man; she is almost murdered by the Pale Man after eating the sumptuous grapes he has left to tempt children at his banquet. Nevertheless, the overriding prerequisite of the happy ending of the fantasy film ensures that she is allowed to escape just as the hourglass is about to be empty, signalling that her time to escape would be over.

Another trope common to fairy tales and utilised by del Toro is the concept of a magical world which only a few are able to see. Hartland recounts stories of magical ointments acquired by humans through their meddling, that allows them to see fairies (often punishable by loss of sight) (60). In *El laberinto* Ofelia is the only one who is able to see the faun (along with the privileged audience); however, she does not need magical ointment, as she is the embodiment of the Princess Moanna. The other key magical element adopted by the director is the importance of special times for supernatural happenings to occur and for fairies to appear. Hartland chronicles the centrality of full moons, and notes key dates such as Midsummer Day or Midsummer Eve and holy days which have evolved from pagan celebrations (250). The moon provides del Toro with the idea of the propitious moment for the fulfilment of the magical premise within the film and affords it its mythical structure. Ofelia has to complete her three tasks before the full moon; she is, the faun tells her, born of the moon, and to indicate her royal lineage she has the mark of the moon on her shoulder. She can, most importantly, enter the portal her father made for her only on the night of the full moon, when her blood enters the portal after she has sacrificed herself for her brother.

This links to another concept which is central within del Toro's filmic universe and also to the fairy tale tradition chronicled by Hartland: that of sacrifice. The author notes:

> it is a very widespread custom to sacrifice to a divinity his living representative or incarnation, whether in animal or human form. It is believed in such cases that the victim's spirit, released by sacrifice, forthwith finds a home in another body. (Hartland, 1890: 253)

He adds that 'what looks like murder [is] ... enjoined in a number of stories for the purpose of disenchanting a bewitched person' (253), and these were a common element in the 'enchanted princess' stories (253). Ofelia can be seen as the living representative of the divine Princess Moanna, and, in line with the numerous fairy tales Hartland chronicles, it is her sacrifice which allows for the disenchantment and her return to her original, supernatural identity

Thus, del Toro can be seen to follow of a number of key concepts that are common to fairy tales across ages and nations. This can be seen as a bid to appeal to the widest possible audience by applying tried and tested ingredients of a 'good story'. He can also be seen to have maintained many of the journey stages of the hero narratives outlined above. The main difference between del Toro's story and the stages of Campbell's monomyth and Vogler's headings is that in *El laberinto del fauno* there is no 'return to the ordinary world'. Nonetheless, Ofelia's return to her true home as Princess Moanna does fit within the structure of the happy resolved ending. Any subversion of the fantasy tale is found in del Toro's use of a realist aesthetic and the rooting of the story in the social historical context of post-Civil War Spain, although this ultimately falls victim to the prerequisites of fantasy storytelling, as I have argued. The ending is almost a perfect fit within the final stages of the structure that is identified in the Russian fairy tales he mapped. There is a transfiguration, with 'the hero ... given a new appearance' (Propp, 1968: 42). This is seen where Ofelia transforms into the Princess and this fits with Propp's formulation of the girl who 'puts on a (magical) dress and suddenly is endowed with radiant beauty' (43), although the transformation is here more magical, as the new clothes are part of the transformation. In the next stage, 'the villain is punished' (63), which fits with Captain Vidal's shooting at the hands of the rebels. Finally, 'the hero is married and ascends the throne' (43).

This final point leads us to the key area where there is subversion of traditional folktales and fairy tales. Ofelia does not need to be rescued by a male hero, whose prize is often to marry the princess. Neither does she become a princess through marriage to a handsome prince; rather she tackles the tasks herself, and assumes her royal status thanks to her own efforts. Indeed, she saves her brother and her sacrifice results in the Captain being exposed and alone, which, in turn, leads to his ambush by the rebels. Despite del Toro's statement that structures are subverted while archetypes are retained, the main generic subversion comes through the overturning of traditions associated with the female characters in fairy tales and fantasy films.[24]

El Laberinto del fauno: a feminist film?

Traditional fairy tales are known to often have a conservative social function, as have many more recent reworkings. As Jack Zipes notes in his well known study *When Dreams Came True: Classical Fairy Tales and Their Tradition* (1999), it is crude but broadly true to say that early fairy tales 'served the hegemonic interests of males within the upper classes of particular communities and societies' (7). There have, of course, been feminist revisions of these, mainly in literature (but also through the Shrek films), through writers such as Angela Carter, Margaret Atwood, Donna Jo Napoli, and Marina Warner. Yet Zipes, writing on more contemporary adaptations of fairy tales (from Disney onwards), asserts that, 'in all forms and shapes, the classical fairytales continue to be moneymakers and thrive on basic sexist messages and conservative notions of social behaviour' (26). In Ofelia, del Toro creates a feisty, courageous, disobedient, rebellious, imaginative, good-hearted heroine to counter the passive feminine archetype in the traditional fairy tale.

In spite of this, there has been some debate over whether *El laberinto* can be seen as a feminist film: Janell Hobson (2008: 242) argues that the film 'maintains a feminist stance', while Laura Hubner (2010: 52), despite reservations over some of the gender essentialism within the film, provides a mainly positive take on the feminist potential within the film. She argues that it 'goes some way in subverting some of the fears of the female body in fairy tales' (58). In contrast, Kim Edwards bemoans what she sees as the patriarchal ending of the film, where Princess Moanna is under the rule of the King; she writes, 'in a text so concerned with unearthing and empowering the repressed, it is unsettling that such an active, rebellious and subversive heroine is finally reduced to a traditionally passive female role' (Edwards, 2008: 145).

I would argue that *El laberinto* is a broadly feminist text, and this is where the subversion of the fairy tale lies. The narrator's words towards the end of the story appear to go against Edwards' reading: 'descendió el reino de su padre … Y que ahí reinó con justicia y bondad por muchos siglos. Que fue amada por sus súbditos.' This translates as 'she descended to the Kingdom of her father … and there she reigned with justice and a kind heart for many centuries' (my translation). The Princess may be in her father's kingdom, but she has power, and is given the freedom to rule, which she does in an idealised way, with no sense of the control that would reduce her to a passive role.

While gender distinctions are rigid in the text, with violence reserved for the masculine Nationalist and Republican forces (with the exception of Mercedes' attack on the Captain), *El laberinto* can nonetheless be categorised as a feminist film. Ofelia refuses the passive position embodied in her mother, disabled by her pregnancy and entirely controlled by her husband, Captain Vidal, who sees her as no more than a vessel for his son. Ofelia's power lies in the peaceful means she uses to achieve her aims. Indeed, her ultimate success in the final task comes about via a refusal of violence wherein she sacrifices herself. In a reworking of the Abrahamic myth, she disobeys the faun's instructions to stab her brother with the phallic dagger and through this act of disobedience regains her immortal royal identity.

Conclusion

So, to bring these ideas together, what marks del Toro out as a singular filmmaker is not the structural reconfiguration of the storytelling formula of fairy tales and hero narratives, but the way he rewrites the female role to allow for the development of a feminist (young) heroine. He is also noted for the fact that he uses this fantasy format in a Spanish-language film ostensibly about Francoists and Republicans. In this way, the director has spearheaded a generic trend in 'European' filmmaking away from realist art cinema. *El laberinto del fauno* was a global commercial and critical success and did achieve something new in the ways that it combines elements from what have been placed within the fantastic or the political, and the magical or the realist, usually discrete forms of filmmaking. I have argued here that a commercial imperative to generate the pleasures of the text has led to the fantasy structure imposing itself on the realist forms, with the resulting falsification of history. It appears fair to conclude that *El laberinto* is an enormously accomplished film and is central to the enhancement of the auteurist status of del Toro. Nonetheless, it also appears to demonstrate the difficulties of incorporating an accurate, progressive political vision in a commercial text driven by the requirement of the happy ending wherein the heroes triumph and the villain is punished. Audiences are delighted to see the defeat of the Nationalist Captain Vidal, while many will remain unaware of the many years of Franco's dictatorship which Spaniards in the real world had to endure.

Notes

1. It was initially produced by the Spanish company Estudios Picasso, then taken on by Telecinco when funding from Estudios Picasso fell through. It was co-produced by the Tequila Gang, the Mexican production company co-founded by del Toro, Bertha Navarro and Alfonso Cuarón, and Frida Torresblanco's Mexican company Esperanto Filmoj.
2. In this it has parallels with *The City of Lost Children* (Caro and Jeunet, 1995), starring del Toro favourite Ron Perlman, and Ofelia can be compared to Miette (Judith Vittet), the feisty orphan in a red dress.
3. Although they are certain to have recouped this following the massive profits the film generated.
4. Galt and Schoonover rightly challenge such a Euro-American focus, and prefer a more global focus that is not limited to serious cinema (Galt and Schoonover, 2010: 4).
5. Núria Triana-Toribio in her book *Spanish National Cinema* provides the examples of popular Spanish sex comedies that were not distributed abroad, while films falling into the art cinema category were (Triana-Toribio, 2003: 152–154).
6. The film was remade in the USA as *Let Me In* (Reeves, 2010).
7. Ofelia tells the tale of a magical rose which grants immortality, but is protected by poisonous thorns. The rose dies daily as it cannot grant its gift to men who are too fearful of pain to seek immortality.
8. It is worth considering the evolution of the characters played by Federico Luppi. In *Cronos,* as Jesús Gris, he is the failed vampire who sacrifices his immortality to protect his granddaughter; in *El espinazo* he is shot dead by Nationalists while protecting the boys in his care; he finally ascends to a state of royal immortality in his cameo in *El laberinto.*
9. It is worth noting that Saturn is the Roman version of Kronos, who, as seen (chapter 1), is also referenced in *Cronos.*
10. The UK Film Council's definition of 'specialised film' can be found at www.ukfilmcouncil.org.uk/media/pdf/r/2/Defining_Specialsied_Film_Update_20_04_08_.pdf. In July 2010, the UK Conservative–Liberal coalition government announced plans to close down the Council (Shoard, 2010). It was decided that the funding role would be taken over by the British Film Institute.
11. This clearly helped in making it one of the highest-grossing foreign-language films in the UK in 2006. The others were *Volver, Kabhi Alvida*

El laberinto del fauno 91

   Naa Kehna, and *Caché* (UK Film Council, 2007). Further information on the Prints and Advertising Fund can be found at http://industry.bfi.org.uk/printsandadvertising.
12 The Battle of Belchite took place in 1937 and was the site of bitter confrontation between Republicans and Nationalists. The town was devastated and Franco ordered that the site of destruction be preserved as a monument to the war and the ultimate victory of the Nationalists (Thomas, 1988: 725–726). IMDB lists the other filming locations (in Spain) as Segovia and the Sierra de Guadarrama mountain range.
13 For the full list of distributors, see www.imdb.com/title/tt0457430/companycredits.
14 Some felt the documentary *En el hoyo* (*In the Pit*) (Rulfo, 2006) would have represented Mexican film better (see Huerta, 2006). The film which ultimately won in the category of Best Foreign Language Film of the Year was *Das Leben der Anderen* (*The Lives of Others*) (Von Donnersmark, 2006).
15 A full listing of the 2007 Oscar nominations and awards is given on *The Guardian*'s website, at www.guardian.co.uk/culture/2007/feb/26/awardsandprizes.oscars2007.
16 I am grateful to Ann for allowing me to see an early draft of her work on del Toro for her book *Spanish Spaces: Landscape, Space and Place in Contemporary Spanish Culture*, now published by Liverpool University Press (2012).
17 For a contrasting reading of the ending, see Hubner (2010). Hubner argues that 'the final ending offers a cyclical return to the fairytale realm of the father, but Franco's regime as historical actuality remains. This is the true horror' (58).
18 Mercedes Camino (2009: 48) provides some useful context to post-Franco films which represent the Maquis in Spanish cinema (and she includes *El laberinto* in this category). These include *Los días del pasado* (*The Days of the Past*) (Camus, 1978) and *El corazón del bosque* (*The Heart of the Forest*) (Aragón, 1978), as well as *Silencio roto* (*Broken Silence*) (Armendáriz, 2001).
19 Del Toro has spoken of the personal impact of meeting Spanish exiles. He has said in an interview, 'these expatriates heavily shaped Mexican culture and cinema. Some of them became key mentors of mine growing up. They had tales of leaving Spain behind as children. These tales affected me a lot' (Levy, 2006).
20 This is also a point made by Mercedes Camino (2009: 62), who notes, 'Much information about the protracted aftermath of the Spanish war has only started to be made public since the mid-1990s, culminating in the creation of the *Asociación para la Recuperación de la Memoria Histórica* (Association for the Recovery of Historical Memory) in 2001 and the passing of the *Ley de Memoria Histórica* (Law of Historical Memory) in 2007'.

21 *Märchen*, according to Hartland, are tales 'told simply for amusement, like Jack and the Beanstalk, Cinderella, Beauty and the Beast, and Puss in Boots' (Hartland, 1890: 23). The other category of fairy tales is 'sagas': 'these are looked upon as narratives of actual occurrences' and include 'the legends of Lady Godiva and Whittington and his Cat, which, however improbable, contain nothing of the supernatural' (23).
22 The book can be accessed from www.gutenberg.org/ebooks/24614. The Gutenberg Project offers free access to ebooks where copyright has expired.
23 He notes the following examples of this myth: 'to eat the food of the dead in New Zealand prevents a living man from returning to the land of the living, just as Persephone was retained in Hades by partaking of the pomegranate, and just as to eat the food of fairies hinders the Manx or the Hebrew adventurer from rejoining his friends on the surface of the earth' (Hartland, 1890: 351).
24 Hartland (1890: 242) notes many instances where male protagonists of fairy tales are assigned tasks to save a princess.

PART II

Alejandro González Iñárritu: independent filmmaker

4

Crashing into the international film market with *Amores perros*

From *Amores perros* (2000), to *21 Grams* (2003), to *Babel* (2006), to *Biutiful* (2010), Iñárritu and his team have travelled from Mexico, to the USA, to multinational landscapes, and to the immigrant world of Barcelona. Despite the fact that this book is a directorial study, it is not possible to downplay the significance of Iñárritu's co-creators, and *Amores perros* set up an international career for all of the core filmmaking team. For the first three films this team has consisted of Iñárritu, screenwriter Guillermo Arriaga, cinematographer Rodrigo Prieto, German-born production designer Brigitte Broch, and the Argentine composer Gustavo Santoalalla. All, with the exception of Arriaga, following a well documented spilt with the director after *Babel*, continued working with Iñárritu on *Biutiful*.[1] Significantly, all four members of Iñárritu's team have broken into international filmmaking circles. This chapter argues that one of the central reasons for the global success of *Amores perros* was its use of an international film language, and in their application of this language all the key crew demonstrate their potential to work in other national contexts.[2] Despite their significant input, in line with this book's focus on directors, Iñárritu's auteurist aspirations and the focus on the director in terms of reception, I concentrate on Iñárritu. As Deleyto and Azcona (2010: xii) note, 'Iñárritu, the director, is a very real presence behind the movies and the central force under whose leadership the input of Arriaga and the rest has come to fruition'. Nonetheless, part II of the book also pays particular attention to the work of cinematographer Rodrigo Prieto and screenwriter Guillermo Arriaga, who have been central to the creation of the director's style and filmic world.

Through the trajectory outlined above, and with the help of his collaborators, Iñárritu, then, demonstrates his aspirations to become a 'world' cinema auteur, unrestricted by national borders.[3] Indeed, Iñárritu has seen the first three films as a trilogy, and has spoken of how each film has taken him to a new level, using geographical language to reveal these ambitions:

> I thought it was a good possibility to close that trilogy, which started with *Amores perros* in a local way, in a foreign way as *21 Grams* and then on a global scale. I thought it was a good way to find a triptych. (IGN Movies, 2006)

Nevertheless, it can be argued that this distinction between local (national), foreign (US), and global is rather simplistic, as I seek to demonstrate throughout the three chapters on Iñárritu. In this chapter I demonstrate that, from his first Mexican film, Iñárritu and his collaborators strategically employ techniques from a strand of international cinema to ensure that this 'national' film enters into transnational circulation.

A good deal has been written on *Amores perros* (Amaya, 2007; Deleyto and Azcona, 2010; D'Lugo, 2003b; Kantaris, 2006; Podalsky, 2003; Shaw, 2003, 2004; Smith, 2003a), and I certainly do not want to repeat myself or re-tread critical debates on this film. Rather, I focus on the cinematic languages employed within the text in an attempt to locate it within a contemporary international sphere, and ask to what extent does *Amores perros* borrow from US models and emerging global patterns of filmmaking? I consider *Amores perros* within the context of Iñárritu's trajectory as a filmmaker, and demonstrate the ways in which it establishes signature traits that will be developed in the subsequent films that he directs, despite the shifts in national contexts and production modes.

Amores perros: a national/transnational film

Recent writings on contemporary Mexican cinema rightly highlight the importance of *Amores perros* in the revitalisation of Mexican cinema, and as signalling a new order in national film financing, with the shift from public to private funding arrangements (Deleyto and Azcona, 2010; Menne, 2007; Miller *et al.*, 2012; Shaw, 2003; Smith, 2003a). As Paul Julian Smith has noted, within Mexico the film's enormous success was largely due to more professional marketing strategies, achieved through the vertical integration of the producer, Altavista, and its parent company, Estudio México, part of CIE, the giant live entertainment company (Smith, 2003b: 396).[4] Nevertheless, if the film's success was limited to domestic audiences, Iñárritu would not be such an internationally known director, and, in fact, it was the first Mexican film since *Como agua para chocolate* (*Like Water for Chocolate*) (Arau, 1992) to gain a widespread international release, followed a year later by Cuarón's *Y tu mamá también* (the subject of chapter 8). Once national success was achieved, the film attracted big international distribution companies, including Lion's Gate in the USA, Optimum Releasing in the UK, and Warner Home Video in Germany and Switzerland.

I have written of the national and international awards and box office success of the film elsewhere (Shaw, 2003: 51–52), but it is worth reiterating that it had unprecedented success for a Mexican film in the international market, and competed with English-language independent films at the US box office.[5] The production team knew that they had a 'hot' product on their hands and sought to promote the film at Cannes, where it was entered in competition and won the Critics' Week grand prize, and subsequently attracted international buyers (Smith, 2003a: 13). The film's producer, Martha Sosa, has described the ways in which they used Cannes to launch the film:

> We created something extraordinary, spinning an aura around the film to make it seem much bigger than it actually was. From a Mexican perspective we made it look as if we'd won the world cup.... We needed to create a lot of noise and you cannot do that with advertising alone.
> (Wood, 2006: 85)

Iñárritu himself is from a marketing background and had been making advertisements before his first feature film, so also knew the importance of promotion. He is described by Sosa as 'the best salesman you will ever meet' (Wood, 2006: 86), and he seduced the media through multiple interviews given to promote the film. Likewise, he worked on the trailers and was heavily involved in marketing the film (86–87). The team also cannily employed a Los Angeles publicist in their bid to secure an Oscar nomination for the best foreign film, which paid off, thus dramatically raising the film's profile, despite losing out to *Crouching Tiger, Hidden Dragon* (Lee, 2000) (Smith, 2003a: 13). The global circulation of the film continued with the DVD release of the film by recognised distribution companies, including Optimum Releasing in the UK, Lions Gate Home Entertainment in the USA, Nu Vision in Mexico, Pyramide Distribution in France, and

Warner Home Video in Germany and Switzerland. Thus, a nationally produced film, filmed and set in Mexico City, with a predominantly Mexican cast and crew, entered the international market, making *Amores perros* a national transnational film, and setting the scene for Iñárritu and team's future career path.

A new international style and *Amores perros*

While marketing strategies are thus central to the creation of a national hit and a 'world cinema' text, we cannot, of course, forget the film itself. A close examination of the narrative modes and cinematic techniques used for *Amores perros* reveals what made it so attractive to international distributors, and highlights the fact that Iñárritu and his team had transnational aspirations from the start of their filmmaking careers. It can be argued that, in a number of areas, the film fits within current trends in international filmmaking. In two illuminating articles, Eleftheria Thanouli looks at some recent developments in narrative modes used in internationally successful films from around the world, and argues for a new 'post-classical' style that exists contemporaneously with a classical Hollywood style favoured by most mainstream US films (Thanouli, 2006, 2008). She identifies key features of this style from her analyses of a number of popular films made in a range of countries, including: *Arizona Dream* (Kusturica, 1993), *Europa* (Von Trier, 1991), *Chungking Express* (Wong, 1994), *Trainspotting* (Boyle, 1996), *Lola rennt (Run Lola Run)* (Tykwer, 1998), *Magnolia* (Anderson, 1999), *Fight Club* (Fincher, 1999), *The Million Dollar Hotel* (Wenders, 2000), *Natural Born Killers* (Stone, 1994), *Requiem for a Dream* (Aronofsky, 2000), *Amélie* (Jeunet, 2001), and *Cidade de deus (City of God)* (Meirelles, 2002). The features of this post-classical style can be summarised as: an increased number of plotlines and protagonists, with no single traditional hero; and a complex use of time, with a rejection of a linear narrative, and the use of chronological tricks such as flashbacks, flashforwards, and loops,[6] as well as repeating forms in which the same instance is shot from different perspectives (Thanouli, 2006, 2008). As will be seen, a number of these features can be seen in *Amores perros* and the team's subsequent films.

David Bordwell disagrees with the term 'post-classical cinema', as he argues that in the last forty years Hollywood storytelling has not fundamentally changed in its representation of space, time, and narrative relations (Bordwell, 2002a: 16). Nevertheless, he does identify important shifts in contemporary filmmaking, which he sees as characterised by 'intensified continuity', and, indeed, Thanouli (2006: 188) co-opts this notion to characterise her use of the term 'post-classical' style to which Bordwell so objects. Thanouli notes that she favours the term post-classical 'partly because it appeared after the demise of the classical studio system and partly because it bears a complicated relation with the classical model' (Thanouli, 2008: 8).

Notwithstanding the disagreement over the label 'post-classical', the two critics are both keen to map this new style, and share a fundamental understanding of its key elements. It is worth summarising Bordwell's ideas on intensified continuity, as they form the basis of Thanouli's ideas, and are central to any discussion of a new cinematic style. It will then be possible to examine the extent to which Iñárritu and team adopt these contemporary international filmmaking trends in their first international hit. Although the focus of his study is US film, Bordwell also notes that an increasing number of non-American directors use intensified continuity techniques, including Werner Herzog, Rainer Werner Fassbinder, the Cinema du Look directors, Tom Tykwer, Neil Jordan, John Woo, Tsui Hark, and Guy Ritchie. In his words: 'It is now the baseline style for both international mass-market cinema and a sizeable fraction of exportable art-cinema' (Bordwell, 2002a: 21–22). Bordwell compares the average shot length of films made between 1930 and 1960 (8–11 seconds) with those used in contemporary films (1999–2000) (3–6 seconds), and demonstrates that rapid editing is one of the main characteristics of the new approach to filmmaking (Bordwell, 2002a: 16–17). He also explores the ways that filmmakers increasingly exploit the extremes of lens length (18), another central feature of the style. Linked to this is the use of closer framings in dialogue scenes, with more close-ups and extreme close-ups (18–19). Finally, camera work is less rigid, with films utilising a free-ranging camera (20).

In *The Way Hollywood Tells It: Story and Style in Modern Movies* (2006), Bordwell also documents the increasing use of subjective stories and network narratives. His description of this has clear parallels with his analysis of intensified continuity, and with the characteristics described by Thanouli as 'post-classical', as can be seen from the following account:

> Another era of experimental storytelling was launched in the 1990s, when a fresh batch of films seemed to shatter the classical norms.

> Movies boasted paradoxical time schemes, hypothetical futures, digressive and dawdling action lines, stories told backward and in loops, and plots stuffed with protagonists. It seemed filmmakers were competing to outdo one another in flashy nonconformity. (Bordwell, 2006: 73)

Here again, his focus is on both mainstream and independent Hollywood filmmaking, but he accepts the international dimension of this approach and highlights the influence of imported art cinema and the films of directors such as Tarkovsky, Wenders, Kieslowski, and Wong Kar-Wai (Bordwell, 2006: 75–76).

Not every aspect mentioned by Bordwell and Thanouli in their account of a new international style can be seen in *Amores perros*. Thanouli (2006), for instance, identifies parody (186) and self-conscious filmmaking that exposes 'the means of its own making' (192) as characteristics of a post-classical style, and neither of these features in *Amores perros*, or indeed in any of the films directed by Iñárritu. Deleyto and Azcona also point out slight differences from other network narratives in the way that each story comprising the film is presented:

> The three self-contained episodes of *Amores perros* ... allow us to engage with each set of characters almost as if a single story were being told, emphasizing the particular predicaments and the emotional intensity of each of the individual stories. (Deleyto and Azcona, 2010: 29)

In this way the filmmakers employ narrative elements associated with a contemporary filmmaking mode and provide their own take on these, and establish the director's auteurist credentials (helped by the input of Arriaga in creating the narrative structure and the expertise of Prieto's camerawork). Despite a personalised approach to intensified continuity, most of the temporal and narrative conventions utilised in the film fit within this trend of contemporary filmmaking, and this can account for the entry of all three into international film territories. As Deleyto and Azcona also argue, Iñárritu and team's films appropriate conventions associated with network narratives, which they see as a genre:

> The human mosaics assembled by these three movies need to be placed in the context of the experimentation with multiple characters and narrative lines that took place at the end of the 20th century and turned what had until then been just an alternative storytelling pattern into a proper genre with its own thematic concerns and narrative and visual conventions. (Deleyto and Azcona, 2010: 20)

4.1 A close-up of Octavio (Gael García Bernal) at the dog-fight in *Amores perros*

Specific features of their adoption of these generic tropes can be seen most specifically in the reliance on a network narrative, the film's rejection of a single hero, and the disruption of chronological time, all elements that have gone on to become the signature of Iñárritu and team. *Amores perros* is characterised by rapid editing in story 1 (Octavio and Susana), and a range of lens lengths applied, from extreme close-ups in story 1 (figure 4.1) to the use of longer lenses in story 3 (El Chivo and Maru) (figure 4.2).[7] In addition, stories 1 and 3 make full use of Prieto's handheld free-ranging camerawork, which has come to characterise his cinematography with Iñárritu.

While the film is largely a Mexican affair in terms of funding, cast, and crew, from the outset the filmmakers looked to their North American neighbours and other internationally acclaimed filmmakers for influence and in this way created a text that is easily consumed on the global stage. Marvin D'Lugo argues that:

> Precisely because of its clever balance between the cultural specificity of its Mexican subject-matter and what might be termed as its transnational texture, *Amores perros* needs to be read not simply as a product of a revived Mexican cinema, but as a pointed interrogation of the position of Latin America's increasingly urbanized culture. (D'Lugo, 2003b: 222)

4.2 A long shot from the point of view of El Chivo (Emilio Echevarría) as he stalks his next victim in *Amores perros*

This 'transnational texture' is seen in its narrative and cinematographic approach. Iñárritu has stated that the links created by writers/directors Paul Auster and Wayne Wang in the early network narratives *Smoke* (Wang, 1995) and *Blue in the Face* (Auster and Wang, 1995) were a key influence for his film's narrative. He comments: 'in *Amores perros* we had a similar starting point to the latter [Auster and Wang]: characters from different walks of life whom chance brings together' (Lawrenson and Pérez Soler, 2001).[8] Another source, unacknowledged by the team but often claimed by critics and popular reviewers, is Tarantino's *Pulp Fiction*.[9] In terms of narrative structure, Arriaga prefers to acknowledge the novels of William Faulkner (Wood, 2006: 68),[10] while cinematographer, director, and production designer credited the influence of the US photographer Nan Goldin in creating the look of the film (Wood, 2006: 78; Oppenheimer, 2001: 21).[11]

What is particularly significant is the lack of Mexican sources that any of the team claim, and Iñárritu has gone as far as to say 'I was born without Mexican cinema' (cited in Patterson, 2001), rather dismissing the previous generation of art cinema auteurs such as Arturo Ripstein, Paul Leduc, Jaime Humberto Hermosillo, and Felipe Cazals. There were, however, multi-stranded narratives in Mexican cinema prior to *Amores perros*. Dolores Tierney (2009: 108) cites the examples of *La mujer del puerto* (*The Woman of the Port*) (Ripstein, 1991), and *Callejón de los milagros* (*Midaq Alley*) (Fons, 1995). Likewise, Deleyto and Azcona (2010: 21–22) mention a number of Mexican multi-protagonist films, including María Novaro's *El jardín del Edén* (*The Garden of Eden*, 1994), Rafael Montero's *Cilantro y perejil* (*Recipes to Stay Together*, 1998), and Benjamin Cann's *Crónicas de un desayuno* (*A Breakfast Chronicle*, 2000). In their words: 'both before and after the impact of *Amores perros* the multi-protagonist format seems to be very much at home in contemporary Mexican cinema', as well as in telenovelas (21).

By not referring to these the director appears to wish to insert himself into a global film culture while not, perhaps, fully acknowledging his Mexican predecessors. Nonetheless, *Amores perros* is one of an increasing number of internationally successful films that cannily employs contemporary fashions in structure and cinematography to score an international hit. It is the first of three network narratives produced by Iñárritu and Arriaga, and is the style associated with their partnership. It is significant that *Biutiful*, the first film Iñárritu made following his separation from Arriaga, follows a more traditional, linear chronology, with a single protagonist, Uxbal, interpreted brilliantly by Javier Bardem.

'Network narrative' is a term coined by David Bordwell (2006, 2008) for multi-stranded and multi-protagonist films which tell interconnecting stories of several characters. Some of the best-known examples of films which fall into this category and which are referenced by Bordwell (2008: 197) are from a range of national contexts. These include Robert Altman's *Short Cuts* (1993), Michael Haneke's *71 Fragments of a Chronology of Chance* (1994), Atom Egoyan's *Exotica* (1994), Wong Kar-Wai's *Chunking Express* (1994), and Quentin Tarantino's *Pulp Fiction* (1994). There are many other examples from cinema throughout the world, as Paul Kerr (2010) outlines in his article on *Babel*, and as Bordwell lists in his chapter 'Mutual Friends and Chronologies of Chance' (2008).

Amores perros is divided into three stories or chapters – Octavio and Susana; Valeria and Daniel; and el Chivo and Maru – with each focusing on a key character. The film tells of the purely accidental and momentary intersections of three central characters from distinct sectors of society who do not know each other, and who are brought together by a physical and metaphorical car crash. The first tells the story of the working-class Octavio (Gael García Bernal), his affair with his brother's wife, Susana (Vanessa Bauche), and his attempts to make enough money for them to run away together through dog-fighting. The second story focuses on the relationship between an upper-middle-class couple, Daniel (Alvaro Guererro), the editor of a fashion magazine, and Valeria (Goya Toledo), who was a top model until she badly injures her leg in the crash, and has eventually to have it amputated. The final story is of el Chivo (the goat) (Emilio Echevarría), formerly a middle-class college lecturer who left his job and family to become a revolutionary, and after years in prison is living as a tramp, working as a hired assassin for a corrupt policeman, and spying on his daughter, whom he longs to contact.

As with a number of network or multi-stranded narratives, there is one central focal event that unites the characters, or, at least, brings them into a shared physical space, and this device allows thematic connections to be made between them. The chance central event in Arriaga and Iñárritu's film is the car crash caused by Octavio when escaping from rival dog-fighters. This device is increasingly common in contemporary US network narratives, and has prompted Bordwell (2006: 97) to write:

> If there's no overarching event frame, unacquainted characters might be granted more autonomy, pursuing their own lives but intersecting occasionally by sheer accident (most often a traffic accident: it's dangerous to take to the roads in today's movies). This version of the ensemble plot has come to be known as the 'converging fates' device.[12]

As seen, both Thanouli and Bordwell have written of the disruptions of chronological time in the new style of contemporary filmmaking and the use of the loop, and the crash in *Amores perros* perfectly illustrates this tendency, with the central event returned to and shot four times, each from a different character's point of view. Each instance supposedly takes the characters towards different chronological moments; however, this conceit is not fully successful. Arriaga argues in the extra feature on the DVD ('Behind the Scenes') that the first chapter (Octavio and Susana) of the film is set in a narrative past, the second (Valeria and Daniel) in the present, and the third (el Chivo and Maru) in the future. This time sequence is supposed to work by viewers orientating themselves around the car crash. In the case of Octavio and Susana, this works: the scene is shot at a frenetic pace to open the film and hook the viewers in, and, as we later discover in the second viewing of the chase and crash, it brings the first story to an initial close (the story of Octavio and Susana is brought to a final conclusion in an intercut in story 3). The crash, according to Arriaga, brings audiences to a narrative present in the story of Valeria and Daniel, as their relationship deals with the consequences of Valeria's disability following the accident. However, it is unclear how this differs chronologically from the story of el Chivo, as the story also picks up following the crash, and deals with the changes in his life once he acquires Octavio's killer dog. Thus, both stories can be seen to be set in a future if the crash is constructed as a narrative present.

Despite this flaw in the writer and director's vision of narrative time, the film sets out Arriaga and Iñárritu's trademark disruption of chronology, which they take to a more complex level in *21 Grams*, as will be seen in chapter 5. The frequent crosscuts to other characters' stories add to the sense of narrative fragmentation and give the film an aura of international sophistication. *Amores perros* also fits in with the trend of contemporary American independent narratives to focus on flawed characters, with all four protagonists deliberately complex in moral and ethical terms. This inevitably brings with it the loss of the central, individual, traditional hero. The production demonstrates both an alternative approach to mainstream hero-centred texts and a philosophical shift from an individualist notion of societal structures to a communal one. In many ways, the experimental stylistic conventions discussed above and adopted in Iñárritu's first feature are the mainstay of a number of US independent features (*Short Cuts, Magnolia, Crash*). As Dolores Tierney (2009: 108) has argued: 'Given its multiple similarities with American Independent cinema, *Amores perros* could almost be read as a proto "indie" film'. The way in which Iñárritu and team adopt aesthetics and approaches associated with American independent cinema forms the basis of the following chapter on *21 Grams*, so I will do no more than raise the point here.

Both Arriaga and Iñárritu have spoken of their intentions to create multifaceted characters. Arriaga has stated, 'I don't like characters who are good or bad. I do not like closed endings' (Chumo, 2000: 11), while Iñárritu affirms that the 'characters are multidimensional, which makes it difficult for the viewer to make a definitive judgement of them or their actions' (Pérez Soler, 2001: 19). Thus, in the film, Octavio wins money through the brutal 'sport' of dog-fighting, and tries to steal his brother's wife, but he also appears to love her and defends her against Ramiro's violence. Valeria and Daniel struggle to reconfigure their relationship when the accident causes them to look beyond fame, beauty, and sexual attraction. El Chivo secures the money he needs by stealing from two fratricidal brothers and then provides them with a gun in a final game of death; but he does this in order to leave behind his life of crime and seek a new life to be worthy of his daughter's affections. In this too, then, the film fits with the morality of many contemporary network narratives, independent, and even mainstream features that eschew easy moral judgements on the characters.

As with other network narratives, there are short intercuts in each storyline to the characters of the others, to highlight the thematic links between them, with the score composed by Gustavo Santoalalla, another central member of Iñárritu's team, helping to create a sense of a cohesive whole. The theme that connects the stories is the crisis in patriarchy illustrated through the absent father, a concept which is seen to cut across both generation and class.[13] While there are flaws in this rather forced narrative attempt to make connections, which I have pointed out elsewhere (Shaw, 2003: 57–61), my concern here is to show that the film belongs within a contemporary strand of international filmmaking.

Each section has its own look, and creatively employs cinematic devices to achieve this, with each story making use of different lenses, camera movements, and style to achieve a different visual look. 'Octavio and Susana' is in many ways a textbook example of intensified continuity. The scenes are given a dramatic, modern, experimental look through the use of the bleach-bypass process, whereby the colour black is intensified and whites are made brighter, while blues and reds are enhanced, the grain is enhanced, and skin tones are slightly bleached (Oppenheimer, 2001: 22; Wood, 2006: 79). The first section employs a shaky, fast-moving handheld camera in the dog-fight scenes; indeed, a handheld camera is used throughout, which facilitates the free-ranging camera movements that characterise this section. In addition, the 'Octavio and Susana' section is shot using a number of extreme close-ups, with Prieto keeping the camera very close to the actors. This gives the opening story of the film a deliberately imperfect and edgy look. A sophisticated film-literate viewer is interpolated through the structure established in the first story, with abrupt, short, unexplained cuts to other locations and storylines which initially seem unrelated, and which make sense only as the film's narrative structure unfolds with the telling of the stories in sections 2 and 3.

Story 1 also speaks to a young and hip viewer. This is perhaps most apparent in the use of a music video aesthetic, a key example of intensified continuity, followed in two key scenes. This appeal to a youth market is capitalised on in the DVD package, which includes pop videos with the title *Amores perros*. One of these is co-directed by Iñárritu (with Oliver Castro); this is a video featuring fashionable acts Control Machete and Ely Guerra.[14] A second video, sung by the Mexican Julieta Venegas, directed by Jorge Aguilera, includes lengthy clips from the film.[15] Thus the videos form paratexts which help to promote the film to a young audience. Indeed, the soundtrack was released along with the film, and heavily promoted, tying the film in with a youth-oriented pop market (Smith, 2003a). There are also two music videos in the film itself: in the first, the images of the key ingredients of story 1 are shot to Control Machete's 'Sí señor', a rap song with a catchy guitar riff. The focus is on dog-fights, sex, money, crime, and conflict. Rapidly edited images include Octavio counting his money from fight wins and buying a car, Ramiro having hurried sex with his shop-assistant lover, Ramiro and his partner in crime holding up a pharmacy, and Jarocho (Gustavo Sánchez Parra) – Octavio's rival – plotting his revenge with Mauricio (Gerardo Campbell) – the owner of the dog-fight circuit. The images are cut to fit the rhythm of the music, and the ambience is infused with a youthful, cool energy, principally generated by the rap's rhythm and lyrics, that suggest the force of the city ('tell me that you can feel the sweat on your brow' is the repeated refrain). Thus, while the film purports to speak against violence, crime, fratricidal relationships, and the lack of solidarity in society, it relies on these factors for pace and excitement – an example of the medium (the fast-paced music video) generating its own meaning. It is worth noting that the music video of this song in the DVD extras package has a harsher, more negative take on love, with images of lovers that crosscut to images of dog's fucking. This provides a graphic illustration of the film's title and themes associated with 'amores perros', literally dog love, but translated cleverly as *Love's a Bitch* (with the term associated with the traumas, cruelty, and even animalistic nature of love).[16]

The second 'music video' sequence is more thoughtful, and set to the indie ballad 'Lucha de gigantes' ('Battle of the Giants') by the Spanish rock band Nacha Pop. While it also relies on sex and violence for its power, the tone is very different, and the serious implications of the affair between Octavio and Susana, and the brutality of the violence, are used to take away any glamour seen in the previous musical composition. Octavio's mistaken course of action is suggested in the lyrics, which speak of deception, nightmares, foolish dreams, and personal fragility in an enormous world. Shots of Susana and Octavio making love are interrupted with cuts to the severe beating that Octavio has organised for his brother, so that he is safe to run off with Ramiro's wife. The implication is that Octavio's love for Susana is fuelled and tainted by fraternal hatred and rivalry.

Nevertheless, despite the images, pace, and lyrics of the music, which, taken together, critique violence and fraternal hatred, this sequence still fits within the definitions of intensified continuity, with abrupt crosscuts from Octavio and Susana to Ramiro, a roaming handheld camera, and extreme close-ups as the defining stylistic techniques. All in all, it can be argued that the pop videos follow established international conventions, and through their incorporation into the film text, the film invites a global youth audience to participate in its consumption, despite the use of Spanish lyrics and Hispanic artists.

Story 2 (Valeria and Daniel) follows a more classical form of storytelling, with longer average shot lengths, a less mobile camera (although still handheld), and fewer examples of crosscutting to other sections: there are just two short cuts of el Chivo – spying on his next target, and entering his daughter's apartment – which act as previews to story 3. The section also concentrates on only two characters, and is less interested in the peripheral characters than the other two. The lives of all three principal protagonists intersect for a filmic moment at the third showing of the crash; however, el Chivo is glimpsed only briefly, and only the car is seen, not the occupants. The feel of the section is more theatrical and is really a close study of a relationship in decline, with a thematic focus on the ephemeral nature of fame, glamour, celebrity, and passion. This is a bourgeois love story, and feels very much like a French art film, with obvious linguistic shifts. It does not, then, fit within the paradigms of the models provided by Bordwell and Thanouli of the new styles of filmmaking of so many contemporary international hits. It is not surprising that the director, looking to make an impact in the international market, was persuaded, after initial resistance, to cut a large amount of this section by Guillermo del Toro, who worked with the director on the editing process (Wood, 2006: 83). In the original cut this section ran for 1 hour 58 minutes, and would have radically changed the dominant style of the film. In the words of Iñárritu, it worked 'as a stand alone piece', but jarred in the composite movie (Wood, 2006: 80).[17]

The fact that story 1, with so many of the characteristics of intensified continuity, dominates the narrative is, then, a deliberate strategy to have the film fit within an international style that is in vogue. 'Octavio and Susana' is approximately 54 minutes long, story 2 is approximately 35 minutes long, while story 3 (el Chivo and Maru) is 53 minutes long, and includes three substantial crosscuts to reveal the denouement of story 1, reinforcing the dominance of this section.[18] Story 3 does return to intensified continuity techniques, and, though slower-paced than story 1, certainly exploits extremes of lens length, and employs a free-ranging camera, with the camera frequently following el Chivo's point of view, and using longer zoom lenses. Experimental camera techniques are put to good use as here they capture the fact that el Chivo sees the world at a distance. He is an outsider, who spends much of his time spying on others, either his daughter or the targets he has been paid to kill.[19]

A transnational Mexico

Amores perros' very reliance on global paradigms also resulted in its success in Mexico, and especially with Mexican young, urban, middle-class audiences familiar with the sophistication of the independent end of Hollywood productions, European art cinema productions, and a music video aesthetic. Nevertheless, the success of the film in Mexico and the national foci of area studies film scholars have resulted in some Hispanic cultural critics (including myself) over-emphasising Hispanic influences, and seeking to produce national allegorical readings of the film, while underemphasising the film as a transnational text.

Several critics have focused on the Hispanic and specifically Mexican elements of the film. I consider the allegorical implications of the parallels made between absent fathers and the failing state under the ruling Institutional Revolutionary Party (Partido Revolucionario Institucional, PRI) (Shaw, 2003: 59–60; Shaw, 2004: 94–99). D'Lugo argues that in addition to its 'international cinematic sources', the film has intertextual references to Luis Buñuel's *Los olvidados* (*The Young and the Damned*, 1950) and *Tristana* (1970), and Arturo Ripstein's films, in the use of morally ambiguous characters, the focus on a violent city, and the critique of superficial elements of modernity

(D'Lugo, 2003b: 227–228).[20] Paul Julian Smith has pointed out the film's debt to traditions of Mexican cinema and, citing Charles Ramírez Berg's notions of *mexicanidad* in national cinema, explores the film's thematic reliance on capitalism, machismo in crisis, and the use of the common types of virgin/whore and sacrificial mother (Smith, 2003a: 36–37). Smith does, however, also note the thematic absences when holding the film up against Ramírez Berg's *mexicanidad*. While I am not denying Mexican cultural reference, these absence are, I would argue, as important, if not more important, than the boxes ticked in making a case for the film's lack of national specificity. He points out that there are no Indians represented; history is treated superficially, with a brief undeveloped reference to the political tensions of the 1970s; while the theme of migration is downplayed (37).

There is very little in the film's representation of the nation that would be unreadable to foreign audiences, with almost no undecipherable nationally specific references. At one point Gustavo (Rodrigo Murray) does note that El Chivo is like Comandante Marcos, when Leonardo (the corrupt police officer played by José Sefami) explains that he was a former revolutionary. But this is not developed and would not substantially affect the reading of the film if not picked up. There is just a broad critique of El Chivo's militant past life, as it caused him to abandon his daughter and to become another absent father (along with Ramiro, Ramiro's unnamed father, Octavio, Daniel, and Valeria's father). In this, *Amores perros* can be contrasted with *El violín* (*The Violin*) (Vargas, 2005), a film rooted in rural Mexico, and in the guerrilla conflicts of the 1970s. *El violín* has clear pro-Revolutionary sympathies, and implicit parallels are made to the present-day conflict in Chiapas, with the neo-Zapatista movement led by Subcomandante Marcos.[21]

The image of the nation given to domestic audiences in *Amores perros* is global and modern, with political issues couched in universal messages of anti-violence (story 1), a critique of the emptiness of fame, beauty, and consumerism (story 2), and a further critique of violence in the parallels made between revolutionary activities and contract assassinations (story 3). In interviews, writer and director speak of the broad themes that the film addresses, none of which is exclusive to Mexican society. Arriaga, for example, comments that the film focuses on 'a world where we are losing our social values, our sense of fraternity' and claims that it laments the excessive emphasis on individual values (Chumo, 2000: 11). Iñárritu, in turn, speaks of the film's focus on 'human pain, love and death – which make no distinction of social class' (Pérez Soler, 2001), thus emphasising the universal message of *Amores perros*.[22]

The film also presents a foreigner-friendly vision of Mexico in its representation of the city, which is largely an unmarked space. *Amores perros* tells stories that could be located in any urban cityscape. Geoffrey Kantaris (2006: 524), in his analysis of the virtual flows in *Amores perros*, notes the lack of national roots of the geographical sites in the film:

> virtually all of the locations in the film are non-places, spaces of transit, from precariously rented accommodation to transitory and illegal dog-fighting venues, from garages to bus terminals, and, most spectacularly, from the high-speed car chase in the city streets to the global television studio.

These 'spaces of transit' could be found in any urban centre, with the exception of the dog-fighting venues, which confirm foreign viewers' expectations of a rough, violent Mexico City. In addition to this, the interiors are archetypal, suitable locations for the archetypal protagonists: Octavio's family home is a suitably non-specific location for the working-class, tough, street-wise teenager; Daniel and Valeria's bourgeois, modern home could be found in any developed city; while El Chivo's make-shift hovel could belong to any tramp/*clochard* figure.

The focus on the universal aspects of urban life, together with the adoption of an international visual style, demonstrates the transnational aspirations of the filmmakers, who would prove to be so adept at working in other geographical locations for global US production companies with their subsequent films. I would argue that the film works in both the international and the domestic market not because of what it reveals about Mexico, but because of the use of a cinematic style that fits in with internationally successful models, a structure that sees it take its place within the US-dominated genre of network narratives, its modern urban setting, which never appears specifically Mexican, a reliance on urban youth culture that sustains the first and dominant section of the narrative, and a focus on universal themes cultivated in all of Arriaga and Iñárritu's collaborations.

Notes

1 The sound designer Martín Hernández has also worked on all of Iñárritu's films, while the American editor Stephen Mirrione has edited *21 Grams*, *Babel*, and *Biutiful*.
2 Arriaga has gone on to write *The Three Burials of Melquiades Estrada* (Jones, 2005), and write and direct *The Burning Plain* (2008). Prieto has been even more successful and was the cinematographer on a number of high-profile US-funded features, including *Brokeback Mountain* (Lee, 2005), *8 Mile* (Hanson, 2002), and *Frida* (Taymor, 2002), as well as working again with Ang Lee as the cinematographer for *Lust, Caution* (2007) and for Pedro Almodóvar for *Los abrazos rotos* (*Broken Embraces*, 2009). His work with Terrence Malik has also won him wide acclaim, in particular, his cinematography on *The Tree of Life* (2011). He has also continued to act as cinematographer for all of Iñárritu's films, including his 2010 work, *Biutiful*. Santoalalla has composed music for a number of other important films besides those of Iñárritu, including *Brokeback Mountain* and *Diarios de motocicleta* (*Motorcycle Diaries*) (Salles, 2004). For full list of films on which he has worked see IMDB, www.imdb.com/name/nm0763395.
3 It is worth noting in relation to this that Dolores Tierney (2009) has given her paper on the director the following title, 'Alejandro González Iñárritu: Director Without Borders'.
4 For a description of the unprecedented scale of the marketing campaign, see Smith (2003a).
5 I noted that 'it was the fifth most successful independent film at the US box-office from January to July 2001, and the most successful foreign language film of that period. The success was repeated elsewhere and the film was seen in 30 countries' (Shaw, 2003: 51–52).
6 Thanouli (2008: 12) writes, 'a popular choice seems to be the structure of the loop, as in *Pulp Fiction* and *City of God*, which open at a certain point in time, then make a long leap into the past and eventually return to the opening scene to pick it up from there'.
7 There is more use of medium-length shots in story 2 (Valeria and Daniel), the most conventional of the three stories.
8 He also cites Lars von Trier and Wong Kar-Wai as influences (Lawrenson and Pérez Soler, 2001).
9 See Marvin D'Lugo (2003b) for a convincing case made for this film as an intertextual reference. See also the *Sight and Sound* article and interview by Edward Lawrenson and Pérez Soler (2001). Although Lawrenson says the comparisons between the films are only superficial, the fact that the article is given the title 'Pup Fiction' rather weakens his point.
10 He also credits his attention deficit disorder as a source for the multi-stranded structure of his writing (Wood, 2006: 68).

Amores perros

11 For similarities and differences in visual style and approach of *Amores perros* and Goldin's photos see Smith (2003a: 76–77).
12 One of the most obvious examples of this approach used after the release of *Amores perros* is *Crash* (Haggis, 2004). For further analysis of the techniques used in the filming of the car crash and the narrative functions of the event, see Smith (2003b).
13 I have written about this in some depth in my article 'The Figure of the Absent Father in Recent Latin American Films' (Shaw, 2004).
14 Control Machete is a highly successful Mexican rap group, while Ely Guerra is a well known Mexican singer who composes her own songs.
15 Julieta Venegas is a Mexican singer who has collaborated and been produced by Iñárritu's composer Gustavo Santoalalla. She is very popular throughout Latin America and among Latino audiences in the USA.
16 *Love Is a Bitch* is the official translation of the film's title, although the Spanish-language title was used in cinema and for the DVD releases. For instance, Optimum Releasing's DVD cover has 'amores perros' featuring prominently, with 'love's a bitch' in brackets underneath the Spanish title in a much smaller type size.
17 The deleted scenes can be found in the DVD extras.
18 Audiences are shown scenes of Ramiro being shot during a bank raid, Octavio and Susana at his funeral, and Octavio at the bus station in a futile wait for Susana.
19 Prieto and Iñárritu talk at some length of the techniques used to achieve the different visual styles in interviews with Jean Oppenheimer (2001).
20 D' Lugo (2003b: 227) says that Iñárritu 'borrows conspicuously from a variety of international cinematic sources which far from detracting from the film's power, lend force to its theme of the contradictions of Latin American modernity'. He references as such sources Tykwer's *Lola rennt* and Tarantino's *Pulp Fiction*.
21 In 1994, the Zapatista Army of National Liberation (Ejército Zapatista de Liberación Nacional, EZLN), led by Subcomandante Marcos, declared a revolutionary war against the Mexican government. The Zapatistas are a non-violent Mayan indigenous movement, and they were calling for land reform and indigenous rights, and attacking the inequalities associated with globalisation and neo-liberal economic policies. They were one of the first revolutionary groups to utilise the internet to promote their campaign. As a result, they became a movement with global reach and support; for more on the Zapatistas, see Harvey (1998).
22 I critique this focus on universals at the expense of class specifics in Shaw (2003: 54–57).

5

21 Grams: an American independent film made by Mexicans

Despite the fact that *Amores perros* uses techniques associated with a new international style of filmmaking, it is still regarded by most in the international community as a Mexican film. The film can be found in the world cinema sections of DVD outlets online and in stores, and academics' writings on the film have appeared in Hispanic film journals and books, while popular reviewers focus on the Mexican identity of film, cast, and crew. The next film, *21 Grams*, made by the same core team of Iñárritu, Arriaga, Prieto, and Broch, with the score again provided by Santoalalla, is taken by the critical community, both popular and academic, as an American independent film, with the Mexican identities of the central filmmakers glossed over.[1] Due to the lack of obvious identifiable Mexican or Latin American references in the film, Hispanic scholars have largely ignored *21 Grams* in their critical writings and conference papers. There are two important exceptions to this. One is found in the work of Deleyto and Azcona (2010), who note the Mexican influences in *21 Grams*, seen in the reliance on emotional excess, and the focus on death. They note, 'the familiarity and proximity of death, the shocking violence, and the sustained reluctance to refrain from the representation of intense experience are not features that mark Iñárritu's originality but rather signal his cultural origins' (16). The other is Dolores Tierney (2009: 110), who argues that first and third world paradigms are deconstructed in the way that Memphis, the location of the film, is seen through a third world lens. Tierney notes perceptively that:

> *21 Grams* subverts the First World/Third World binary by presenting a part of the United States in the same way it presents the Third World. We view violent, chaotic, shabby Mexico City, mediated through the same representational strategies through which we see Memphis.

While some of these aspects could be explained by the Iñárritu team's Mexican formation, I prefer to read *21 Grams* as an example of American independent filmmaking, and argue in this chapter that rather than illustrating the filmmakers' national backgrounds, it is a text which demonstrates that they have mastered and personalised the languages associated with this form.

The complexities involved in ascribing national identity to a film such as *21 Grams* point to the inability of simplistic categories of national cinema to adequately explain shifting cinematic landscapes. What becomes clear from this film is that a largely 'foreign' crew can make an American independent film. The notion of independence will be explored below; however, I take 'American' in this case to rest on the use of US production and distribution companies, the North American location, with most of the film shot and set in Memphis, and the use of (American) English. In addition, although the film relies on a multinational cast, with the American Sean Penn, the Australian Naomi Watts, the Puerto Rican-born Benicio del Toro, the British Eddie Marsan, and the Anglo-French actress Charlotte Gainsbourg, they are all actors who have largely formed their careers in the USA (with the exception of Gainsbourg, whose casting helps place the film within the art cinema end of independent filmmaking). The film's themes – evangelical Christianity, substance abuse, recovery, and relapse, life after loss, guilt and redemption – also speak (although are not exclusive) to a contemporary North American cultural landscape.

The fact that a creative team from Mexico can make an American film says much about the nature of Hollywood/Indiewood.[2] While US filmmaking is widely criticised for its hegemonic practices and international dominance of screens, it is a system that is relatively open to talented outsiders who have a hit behind them, and learn to speak its (film) languages, as the recent successes of Mexican directors and other crew, and the presence of numerous non-American-born filmmakers in Hollywood throughout its history have demonstrated.[3] Iñárritu and team have taken advantage of this and have shrewdly created a film product in *21 Grams* that positions itself firmly within the codes of American independent filmmaking. While Iñárritu directed a 'multilingual' film with *Amores perrros*, in that it used the languages of international filmmaking but with Spanish dialogue, in *21 Grams* the director adopts the languages of independent cinema.

Defining independence

Independent cinema is not easy to define, and there has been some debate as to what constitutes independence.[4] Greg Merritt (1999: xii) has argued that a film cannot qualify as such if it has received funding from a studio. In opposition to this, Geoff King advocates a broader, less rigid definition, which has, in fact, been adopted in most critical discourses. As he argues:

> A literal use of the term might suggest restriction to the domain of industry and economics, but this is not the manner in which 'independent cinema' has been established in its dominant usages in recent decades. (King, 2004: 83)

King prefers to focus on formal qualities in establishing whether a film is independent, and highlights the shift from classical Hollywood narrative paradigms to more experimental patterns of storytelling, often marked by a disruption of chronology and multiple narrative strands (84).

Clearly, if Merritt's approach were adopted over King's, most of the films that we take to be independent would have to be re-categorised, as they have received funding from powerful studios. As Yannis Tzioumakis (2006: 3) points out, 'independent' companies Miramax and Sony Picture Classics are subsidiaries of ABC Disney and Sony Columbia, and are therefore ultimately answerable to them, despite their apparent autonomy. Nevertheless, notwithstanding their affiliation with the majors, many of the films distributed by the subsidiaries are accepted as independent in critical and popular circles. Films released between 2005 and 2008 with commercial but independent credentials distributed by Miramax include *Blindness* (Meirelles, 2008), *There Will Be Blood* (Anderson, 2007), *No Country For Old Men* (Coen and Coen, 2007), and *Breaking and Entering* (Minghella, 2006). Those distributed by Sony Picture Classics include *Persepolis* (Paronnaud and Satrapi, 2007), *Quinceañera* (Glatzer and Westmoreland, 2006), *Breakfast on Pluto* (Jordan, 2005), and *The Three Burials of Melquiades Estrada* (Jones, 2005). 'Independence' in the texts cited here is ascribed through the status of the directors and the films' distinction from blockbusters and more mainstream commercial fare, with a focus on innovatory narrative devices, storytelling over action-adventure sequences, a politically progressive slant, and protagonists from ethnic or sexual minorities. In addition to this,

Chris Holmlund's definition of independent filmmaking can also be applied to the above examples:

> For numerous critics and many audience members too, the label suggests social engagement and/or aesthetic experimentation – a distinctive visual look, an unusual narrative pattern, a self-reflexive style. (Holmlund, 2005: 2)[5]

From these definitions we can clearly situate US films that use the new international languages of cinema discussed in the previous chapter as independent films, and indeed apply the term to *Amores perros* – and in fact to all the films of Iñárritu and team.

Thus, while there is no single definition and the term is 'ill-defined and hotly debated' (Holmlund, 2005: 2), there is some consensus among many critics as to what constitutes independent cinema. Notwithstanding such agreement, it is a broad category and many traditions of filmmaking can fit within the above descriptions. As a number of critics have observed, independent film has been seen to include 'avant-garde', low-budget exploitation films, as well as cult films (King, 2005: 2; Holmlund, 2005: 11–12), while there has also always been a close relationship between independent and art cinema (King, 2004: 83; Insdorf, 2005: 26–33; Tzioumakis, 2006: 267–268). J. J. Murphy argues that:

> American Independent film does not constitute a unique and separate category, but instead represents a hybrid form that bridges the divide between classical Hollywood and Art cinema by freely incorporating elements from both of them. (Murphy, 2007: 16)

Some 'indie' films are more mainstream, and in this regard Tzioumakis' concept of a 'top-rank independent production' is useful. He argues that an emphasis on profit was a result of the low box office returns of some of the later New Hollywood films: 'this type of independent production became representative of mainstream cinema and has remained so to date' (Tzioumakis, 2006: 181). Clearly, there are degrees and variations of independence, with some more commercially orientated in nature, some closer to classical Hollywood in style and approach, and some closer to art cinema, while many low-budget exploitation films would eschew art cinema narrative and aesthetic modes. To complicate matters, the term 'art cinema' is itself a hybrid term, and the concept is also evolving, as I have argued in chapter 3. The national context is also central in the creation of labels, as 'art cinema' is more likely to be applied to European films, while 'independent cinema' is more likely to be used in a North American context, even if European films rely on independent industrial and aesthetic practices, and North American films adopt art cinema aesthetics. To attempt to summarise this section and all the complexities inherent in applying definitions to such a broad category, the concept of independence and the meaning of the label for critics, spectators, and marketing purposes rest predominantly on three areas: the relationship between the filmmakers, the film text, and the studios; the status of the director/auteur; and the cinematic languages used. In what follows, I explore all three of these areas with specific reference to *21 Grams*.

21 Grams, independence, and the studios

It is clear that we cannot ignore the industrial context, and the filmmakers' relationship with the studio is instrumental in any attempts to define a film as independent. Like most directors with auteurist aspirations, Iñárritu links independence with creative control, and the desire for financial backing without studio interference. As he has said in an interview with Jonathan Romney in *Sight and Sound*, 'I didn't want to go through the development process with a studio; I wanted to be completely independent' (Romney, 2004: 15). He elaborates on this in an interview with Jason Wood, affirming again his autonomy: 'I said to them, "this is the script, these are the actors, these are the cities and this is the budget. I want complete creative control and final cut"' (Wood, 2006: 145). He was lucky enough to work with the ideal distribution and production companies Focus Features (distribution) and This Is That Productions to achieve this desired working relationship.

Geoff King provides an excellent background to the formation of Focus, and tells of the company's development as an 'indie/speciality' outlet run by the experienced and respected David Linde and James Schamus, with good independent credentials (King, 2004: 81). Focus was set up as an independent arm of Universal, precisely to work with auteurist directors. The stated aim of the operation is to generate cinema 'somewhere between Hollywood and the farther reaches of independence' (81). This balance is struck by *21 Grams*, with its reliance on experimental narrative forms and melodramatic modes, and it can be seen as an example of a 'top-rank independent production'. It is no surprise, then, that Focus chose to enter a bidding war against DreamWorks, Miramax, and Regency Enterprises for 21 Grams, with the reputations of Linde and Schamus central to Iñárritu's choice to go with Focus (Wood, 2006: 145). This Is That formed a partnership with Focus in a 'three-year, first-look deal', with the company sharing a similar background and filmmaking ethos.[6] 21 Grams was the first film resulting from this partnership (King, 2004: 82), and seemed to be the model film text for companies wanting integrity and independent credentials along with commercial success. According to IMDB Pro, the film grossed an estimated $58.3 million globally, from a budget of $20 million.

Iñárritu sees the role of the studio as central to his own understanding of independence, which he conceptualises as a combination of institutional support with creative freedom. I would, however, argue that the concept of independence in the relationship between studio and filmmaker is not as straightforward as appears from all of this. On one level, Iñárritu seems to have transformed traditional power structures associated with Mexicans working across the border, in that not only has he come to the USA to make a film, but he is given creative control, a much larger budget than would be possible in his home country, and he has top American actors and crew working for him. Nevertheless, while there may have been minimal studio interference, there was a contract (both written and implied) between the director and the studios.

What is unsaid is that Iñárritu and his creative team applied key rules and codes implicit in such a contract and delivered a North American product to Focus and This Is That, following an American independent 'rulebook'. Despite the Mexican identities of the core team of filmmakers, there are no Hispanic characters, and there is no reference to Mexico, while any potential Hispanic identity associated with the casting of Benicio del Toro (of Puerto Rican origin) goes unfulfilled, as he plays the Anglo-American Jack Jordan.[7] The film, rather, focuses on 'universal' or at least 'Western' existential questions, and has them play out in a North American cultural context.[8]

Independence, the auteur question, and Iñárritu

If this line of argument is followed through, then we have to acknowledge that there will always be a relationship of co-dependence between director and studio, as studios will allow even auteurist directors freedom only if they deliver to them the products that they want, within budget. Profit and artistry are always interrelated, and freedom and creative control are always accompanied by financial constraints and some implicit rules. Rather than being anathema to art, commerce thus drives it in the case of studio-backed independent filmmaking, with the figure of the auteur serving as a bridge between art and commerce. In an article in *Screen*, Nuria Triana-Toribio reaffirms Tim Corrigan's view that 'the effect of auteurism was and is to serve commerce' (Triana-Toribio, 2008: 260), and she rightly argues that debates on auteurism need to be more rooted in an industrial and commercial context (260–261).

Despite theoretical challenges to auteurism, then, it still remains the foundation on which both independent film and art cinema stands. While mainstream films use the power and name of the producers (e.g. 'A Jerry Bruckheimer film'), and intertextual references to other films ('from the makers of…') to position their films in the market, the independent film relies largely on the status of the director and the cast he/she manages to attract to define it. Iñárritu, for instance, already had his cast on board before securing finance, including heavyweights Benicio del Toro, Naomi Watts, and Sean Penn, all actors associated with independent films.

Histories and critical analyses of independent film place auteurist directors as central to the construction of the category, with most mentioning George Lucas, Martin Scorcese, Robert Altman, Jim Jarmusch, and more recently Spike Lee, David Lynch, John Sayles, Steven Soderbergh, Kevin Smith, Gus Van Sant, and Todd Haynes, among others (see Berra, 2008; Holmlund and Wyatt, 2005; King, 2005; Levy, 1999; Murphy, 2007). When looked at in this context of American directors, it is quite an achievement that Iñárritu had managed to transform himself from Mexican director to independent auteur by only his second film.

Iñárritu carefully constructs an auteur identity through his media persona. In the above-mentioned article, Triana-Toribio (2008: 260) has written of the phenomenon of *autores mediáticos*, that is, 'media-minded/media friendly directors who first and foremost understand the need to treat marketing as an integral part of production'.[9] Iñárritu clearly qualifies for this label, as does del Toro, as seen in chapter 4. Iñárritu is a director with a very keen sense of the power of the media and knowledge of how to use it to his advantage. He claims ownership over his films and implicitly declares his auteur status through many interviews (in print, radio, and television), and takes the promotion of his films as seriously as do his stars. In such interviews, as seen in those cited above with *Sight and Sound* and Jason Wood, he places emphasis on his control over the filmmaking process, with freedom from interference again clearly linked to the construction of an auteur status.

In chapter 2, on *Hellboy II*, I have written of del Toro's use of the paratext of the DVD package to position himself as an auteur, and this is also true of Iñárritu. Indeed, Iñárritu is very much constructed as the star of the 'Behind the Scenes' short feature on the *21 Grams* DVD. The feature, entitled *21 Grams: In Fragments* (2004), was directed by Alfonso Gómez Reja, the research assistant on *21 Grams* and later assistant director on *Babel*. He is, thus, very much part of the team, and in an ideal position to create a promotional companion piece. *21 Grams: In Fragments* shows footage of Iñárritu's ritualistic opening and closing of his films. At the start, we see the director's wife and children, cast, and crew standing in a circle, listening to him speak of his fears and explaining the symbolism of the red roses (blood, passion etc.) that he asks all to throw in the air, while they shout 'Abba Eli' ('God the Father' in Hebrew) as a form of collective prayer. The fact that he shares and indeed controls physical space with the actors places him above them, and casts him as the biggest star in the movie firmament. Iñárritu delivers a speech to his cast and crew in which he explains to them what the film is about thematically, symbolically taking ownership of the film away from Arriaga, the screenwriter. He says to all that he wants them to feel the film as 'more than a work; it is a blessing, and it is a work of love', thus establishing his art cinema/independent credentials, shifting the discourse away from a commercial terrain, and establishing implicitly that he is more than the *metteur-en-scène*.[10]

The director's voice dominates *21 Grams: In Fragments*, with his voice-over accompanying selected images from the film, which again reinforces his ownership of them. Iñárritu, then, introduces 'his' team, whom, he tells us, he always works with: Prieto, Broch, José García (sound mixer), Martín Hernández (sound designer), Prieto, and Santoalalla. This emphasis on his core team who work for him again establishes his auteur status, with them helping to create his recurring style. Arriaga, the writer, is relegated to the same status as all the other crew members, praised briefly by Iñárritu, but glimpsed only for a moment, and not given a speaking part. Along with his team, or 'family', as he describes them, he introduces the US crew, including Stephen Mirrione (editor) and Robert Salerno (producer), whom he describes as among the 'best in the world', with the inclusion of the respected American crew another way of affirming his status as an auteur. The fact that he presents them as working under his control also emphasises his 'specialness', as, unlike most of his less privileged compatriots, he is in a position of power over North Americans, and, thus, on an individual basis appears to invert neo-colonial hierarchies.

In this short promotional 'extra', the director is seen in front of a monitor, giving instructions to the actors, and to his cinematographer, Prieto, in Spanish, and is generally seen to be in complete control of the filmmaking process. This is endorsed by his stars within *21 Grams: In Fragments*, where they sanction his auteur status through their comments: 'I think he's one of the best directors in the world; he's definitely a force' (del Toro); 'I think he's somebody who so owns his craft, and is so relentlessly after the story he wants to tell' (Penn); 'I'd seen *Amores perros*, and to me that was a perfect film' (Watts), which is why, she states, she immediately signed up for his subsequent film. Iñárritu, in turn, is generous in his praise of his three stars, and his crew, and presents himself as modest and magnanimous.

From this analysis, auterism can be seen as a product of the text, the marketing process, the stars attached to the film, and the paratexts (interviews, DVD extras, websites). It is a label that Iñárritu wears proudly, crafted from industrial, commercial, and artistic materials. Through *21 Grams*, the backing of high-profile studios, and the endorsement of respected actors, he emerges as an independent auteur.

21 Grams: an independent art film

21 Grams can be seen as a paradigmatic American independent film text if many of the definitions referred to above are applied: it certainly meets the criteria in terms of director-led filmmaking, the use of innovatory narrative devices, a preference for storytelling over action, aesthetic experimentation, and a distinctive visual look. It also 'bridges the divide between classical Hollywood and Art cinema' (Murphy, 2007: 16) in the way it marries formal experimentation with melodramatic devices. This status is illustrated in the fact that two critics, Geoff King (2004) and Michael Z. Newman (2006), have

21 Grams

chosen *21 Grams* as a case study to highlight some of the key features of independent filmmaking. In fact, King uses the film in an article to attempt an 'enquiry into the current identity of American independent cinema' (2004: 80).

Central to their situating of the film is its ambivalent relationship towards mainstream filmmaking that depends on more archetypal, classical Hollywood forms of storytelling. Newman, for instance, locates *21 Grams* within independent models predominantly due to its formal complexity, its disruption of 'causal or temporal relations' between events or characters, and its complexity in characterisation (Newman, 2006: 92), yet his article also considers its reliance on melodramatic structures (100). King focuses on the film's position 'in the industrial landscape' (80) and on its formal qualities (80), with a balance between alternative narrative structures, and more conventional plot devices (80).

My focus in this section is on the ways that a Mexican team of writer, director, and cinematographer creates a film that satisfies auteurist demands and fits within the codes of independent filmmaking that have incorporated elements of the new international style that I discussed in chapter 4, on *Amores perros*. After explaining ways in which *21 Grams* adopts approaches commensurate with this language, I explore the specific ways in which the film positions itself as an example of independent art cinema by focusing on the colour design, and the way that textual meaning is generated through the use of tones and lighting.

In the previous chapter, I argued that *Amores perros* belongs to a new international style of filmmaking, and, in terms of approach and aesthetics, many elements associated with intensified continuity and post-classical filmmaking are also central to the 'independent' label. *21 Grams* shares many stylistic and narrative features with *Amores perros:* it also relies on a number of plotlines (three, as in the first film) and protagonists (also three); there is a rejection of the traditional hero; and it makes use of free-ranging camera movements, experimental framing devices, and variations in lens length. It, too, plays with concepts of time, but takes this to a new level, with the film cultivating greater confusion regarding the chronological placing of elements of the plot.

This experimentation with time and the adoption of elements of many of the above-mentioned techniques have led to another author, James Harkin, to take the film as a paradigmatic text to illustrate a label he has coined for new forms of storytelling in film and television. Harkin sees *21 Grams* as an example of a 'cyber-realist' narration in an exposition remarkably similar to Bordwell's concept of 'intensified continuity' and Thanouli's notion of post-classical filmmaking. The ingredients of cyber-realism, so named for its connections with a culture of computer games and internet use (Harkin, 2009: 40), are a fragmented jigsaw structure that viewers have to piece together, multiple plot lines, the loop or circular structure of the narrative, and random or unlikely ties or connections (42).

Whatever terms we choose when referring to contemporary modes of storytelling that have been incorporated into America independent filmmaking, it is interesting that Iñárritu has won authorial recognition by adopting key components of this style/approach in the first three films he has directed (they are also applied in *Babel*). Auteurism is, thus, firmly inscribed within this new form of narration, even with the director so dependent on his cinematographer, screenwriter, production designer, and editor for its realisation. Indeed, having a strong team of collaborators working under his guidance reinforces rather than weakens this status, as seen in *21 Grams: In Fragments*.

In *21 Grams*, the filmmakers put their own stamp on these elements, creating an original artistic piece from within the prescribed language of independence. The film has three basic plotlines, as stated. These are character focused (another marker of independence), and none of the three is in any way a traditional hero; rather they are ordinary people struggling with difficult circumstances. After a deliberately confusing opening twenty-five minutes, the narrative begins to make sense to viewers, and the characters' stories ultimately converge. Jack Jordan (Benicio del Toro) is a reformed ex-con and evangelical Christian who accidentally runs over and kills Cristina Peck's (Naomi Watts) children and husband. This causes Jack to sink into depression, hand himself in and be sent to prison, before going into self-exile from his life and family. Cristina is a suburban housewife and mother, and ex-drug addict, who, once bereaved, returns to drug taking to bear the enormity of the tragedy. She enters into a relationship with Paul Rivers (Sean Penn), who has received the heart of her dead husband and has tracked her down, and then fallen in love with her. The film follows these three characters in what appear initially to be random short shots of their stories that make little sense. Gradually (from the twenty-fifth minute) the links become apparent, and the thematic and narrative connections are established.

As David Bordwell notes, the 'converging fates' device is common in independent Hollywood narratives (Bordwell, 2006: 74), and, as he explains, 'convergence is revealed not just through the selection of events but also through narrational strategies of ordering and emphasis' (98). Thus, while the fabula, the components of the story, is fairly conventional in *21 Grams*, the syuzhet, that is, the arrangement of these components, allows the form to fit the conceit of converging fates.[11] Through the use of editing, structure, and Santoalalla's unifying score, the filmmakers create a coherent text from a series of fragments and apparently separate worlds inhabited by the characters. In addition to these formal features, the principal way in which coherence is achieved is through the film's visual design, in particular its colour palette, realised through the collaborative work of Iñárritu, Prieto, and Broch. Broch explains the process in the production notes:

> Alejandro, Rodrigo, and I work closely together. I prepare a presentation, and the three of us go through the material. We talk about the colors. We talk about the moods and textures. Ours is the teamwork of three people who will ultimately agree on what the final product should look like by taking an overall view. (Hollywood Jesus, 2003)

This is a film that is read as an independent art film predominantly due to the symbolic value of the colour design, with the screen acting as a canvass on which the characters appear bathed in a range of tones. They emerge as products of the filmmakers' artistic vision, rather than realist constructs. Verisimilitude is, thus, not the goal (a realist narrative would not support, for example, Cristina falling for the man who has her husband's heart); rather, the artistic treatment seeks an emotional response from viewers, with colour instrumental in this treatment. Prieto explains that they 'designed an emotional arc for each of the stories, and whenever we went back to one, we tried to be at that place visually' (Calhoun, 2003: 1). Initially, there are clear divides in the colour schemes, in keeping with the distinct nature and feel of each character's story. Prieto reveals that:

> We divide the three stories color-wise because of the structure of the movie. There are subtle cues for the audience to know; this is Paul's world – a cooler blue; this is Jack's world – a yellow red; and this is Cristina's world – sort of in-between, with red and golden but mixed with some of the blue of Paul's world. (Hollywood Jesus, 2003)

Despite the distinct choices made, there is a degree of overlap between the colours used for the characters. Blues, oranges, and greens increasingly merge as their storylines come together, with colours the primary means of connecting the characters. Blue is used to paint Paul and Mary's world of hospitals, breathing machines, and a loveless marriage, signifying sterility on a number of levels. One example of this can be seen when Paul is about to produce a semen sample, under pressure from his wife, Mary, to give her a child before his expected death. This takes place in an impersonal room at the hospital; the whole room is bathed in a blue tint, accentuated by the blue screen of the television showing a graphic pornographic movie. This, along with the latex gloves Paul resignedly puts on, creates a highly un-erotic ambience, and hints at Mary's presumed failure to conceive. The film buys into the old romantic myth of fertility's connections to love, as it is Cristina who ultimately conceives Paul's baby, giving the film's ending a degree of hope.

The link between the two characters is made at this point, as the above-mentioned scene is followed by a cut to Cristina's arrival at the same hospital, where she will learn of the deaths of her family. The colour coding links the two scenes, as she is wearing a blue tracksuit; the television screen is mirrored by the blue computer screen that the admission nurse examines, looking for the family's details; her uniform is also the same blue shade as Paul's shirt. In addition, the use of the bleach bypass process, also applied throughout *Amores perros*, creates a desaturated, washed out look to both these scenes, and provides everything within the frames with a bluish tone. The visual connections thus enhance the thematic connections: Paul occupies a solitary space, facing death with little hope of creating new life through medical procedures; and Cristina's family has been taken from her, and her children are dead. In addition, the use of this bleach bypass process has the effect of creating a sense that this is cinema to be taken seriously, in opposition to glossy superficial entertainment, associated with much mainstream Hollywood studio production.

Blue is also the colour of death and acts as the primary tone in the pre-accident scene, suggesting both the proximity of nightfall and the fatal accident. The scene is reminiscent of another film which features blue tones associated with death, Kieslowski's *Trois couleurs: bleu* (*Three Colours: Blue*, 1993). In *21 Grams* the camera focuses on a young gardener blowing away leaves, while the sound of the collision is off camera. In the opening of *Three Colours: Blue*, the camera focuses on a young hitchhiker of similar age, and the sound of the car crash is heard before it is seen from the young man's perspective, all set to a blue backdrop of nightfall. As with *Blue*, *21 Grams* also presents the anatomy of a mother's pain after losing her family in a car accident. The intertextual reference is another example of the film's roots in the language of art and independent cinema, as is the influence of Soderbergh's *Traffic* (Soderbergh, 2000) (also edited by Stephen Mirrione), which can be seen in both the multi-stranded narrative structure and in the use of colour coding for each of the storylines.[12]

As the characters' situations change, the colours change in symbolic meaning, although they continue to link them together. Blue, for instance, is the predominant tone in the scenes in the wilderness of the New Mexican desert that Jack has gone to in exile from his family, after his release from prison.[13] Here the colour appears to signify escape from the world, and the loneliness this brings. This is where Paul and Cristina travel to in search of revenge against Jack; however, it ultimately becomes a space of closure and thus represents the possibility of new beginnings. Paul, unable to go through with murder, ultimately shoots himself, and Jack transforms from accidental killer to helper as he takes Paul to hospital. Although he dies, hope is offered in the fact that Cristina learns that she is pregnant.

Blue also features in the repeated visual motif of the black figures of birds set against a blue sky; this is an image that is a marker of poetic filmmaking, and speaks of freedom and escape from earthly troubles. The first time the image is seen (towards the opening of the film), it is set to Santoallala's sparse but melodic electric guitar notes, and the birds are flying upwards at dusk. They next appear towards the end of the film, after Paul has shot himself. In this shot it is hard to distinguish between birds and leaves, as the birds fall downwards against a blue-purple night sky with the sense that they have no inner life. This suggests Paul's imminent death, and an escape from this world. The blues of the swimming pool that Cristina swims in also link to the idea of escape, although the abandoned, empty blue pool, littered with debris, at the motel becomes a visual companion to Paul's dying moments. Thus, one tone comes to signify death, sterility, illness, and solitude, but also escape and the entry into a cosmic space, and it is used to emotionally connect Paul and Cristina.

Orange is the tone that is used to link Jack and Cristina. A burnt orange (or red golden colour, as Prieto describes it) connotes the emotional world of the family home for both Cristina and Jack. In a scene demonstrating a happy moment showing Cristina making a cake with her daughter, a light orange colour with yellow tones

5.1 Jack tells his wife about the accident in *21 Grams*

produces the required emotional warmth. Likewise, it is the predominant colour used for Jack's birthday party, to paint the warmth of friendship and his community. Significantly, the colour dulls and shifts to a more mustard yellow/green hue from just before Jack's arrival, to visually indicate the impending revelation of the tragedy, which, as will be seen, is the colour of death throughout the film. Red golden oranges are also the tones of intimacy for Jack and his wife Marianne (Melissa Leo). In the scene where he confronts what he has done and tells his wife he will turn himself in (figure 5.1), a golden hue lights their faces. It is also the tone of Marianne's hair, and is the chosen colour for key elements in the mise-en-scène: orange/red walls, a bright yellow lamp, and an orange pillow. The same tones are applied in the later lovemaking scene between them, which, although interrupted by Jack's pain at what he has done, indicates that it is the colour of warmth and intimacy.

These tones also signify compassion and serve to connect Jack and Cristina in their most abject and painful moments. Reds and yellows are visually painted onto the post-funeral gathering in Cristina's home. The walls are red and yellow, as are the colours carefully chosen for lampshades around the room. An intense golden red lights the faces of Cristina and her father, both shot in close-up as he attempts to comfort her. Colours are used to create an emotional link as a bright orange light bathes Cristina as she is taking drugs in her bathroom to escape from her pain. Red is the dominant colour in the club where Cristina goes to score some drugs; here, orange is replaced by red to indicate vice and danger, with characters illuminated by red filters, and a focus on the dealer's red dress, all of which indicate the lack of warmth in this environment.[14]

Yellows and golden orange tones are also used to paint the pain and suffering of the perpetrator of the accident, again connecting the characters emotionally. These are the dominant colours when Jack attempts to cut out his crucifix tattoo, with the, now mocking, words 'Jesus Loves You', using only the flame of a lighter and a blunt knife. An intense yellowy orange lights his face, illuminated by the white light of the flame, all accompanied by Santoalalla's sad and empathetic tango score. The tones used suggest that he has entered a state of grace, with the physical pain helping to alleviate the emotional pain. The warm colours the filmmakers bathe the characters in have the effect of inviting the audiences' compassion for both the bereaved mother and her slide back to drug abuse, and the accidental killer. It is worth noting that the use of the tango score recurs throughout the film, and is also used when Cristina is at one of her lowest points as she is retracing the sequence events that led to the death of her family, again placing them in a shared emotional space.

This orange colour palette is returned to in one of the final sequences, when Cristina confronts and attacks Jack, and Paul shoots himself; as Prieto comments, 'when they finally meet Jack, all three color schemes become more red-orange' (Calhoun, 2003: 1). This choice of colour design for the only scene in which all three characters are all in the same frame is significant.[15] It indicates that its function is to connect the characters emotionally, with the suggestion that they are sharing a common space of pain, and to seek audience sympathy for them. Sound is also important in this scene: the voices of the characters are silenced and there is a dull drone that can be likened to the sound of wind through a tunnel, reflecting the dream-like envisioning of the events, interrupted by the loud gun-shot which shocks Cristina out of her actions. It is quite an achievement that the film manages to elicit the same warmth for the accidental killer, the victim, and for Paul, the temporary beneficiary of this sequence of events. Paul, as with all Arriaga and Iñárritu's characters, is ambivalent in moral terms; he is cast in a redemptive role with regard to Cristina and Jack, but he is also a man who has left the wife who has cared for him while terminally ill, to start an affair with Cristina.

Another colour that predominates in *21 Gram*'s visual design is mustard green, and it is the most negative tone in the film. It is a sickly hue that connotes despair, loss, hopelessness, and death. The sofas and the walls are mustard green in the hospital waiting room where Mary, Cristina, her sister, and father share a space momentarily. Mary is waiting for a dying Paul to finish depositing his semen sample, and Cristina and her remaining family walk by, visibly devastated after receiving news of the fatalities. It is a tone that comes to the fore in Cristina's home after the death of her family, and fills the frames in the scene when she is washing her dead children's clothes, with her face and the walls lit a sickly, yellowish green. It is also the colour of the breathing appliance on Paul's life support machine before his heart transplant, and of the walls in the motel where Jack is staying in the wilderness, while Jack's car following the accident is lit to take on the same tone, all reflecting death in one form or another.

As with the yellows and oranges, mustard green connects Cristina and Jack emotionally, and provides a visual background to the despair that they share. When Cristina is in the club scoring drugs (figure 5.2), this is the colour of her jacket, and the grimy sink in the bathroom is also lit to take on the same tone. There is a smooth cut from the sink

5.2 Cristina in the nightclub where she goes to score some drugs in *21 Grams*

21 Grams

5.3 Jack attempts suicide in jail in *21 Grams*

to a dripping tap in Jack's prison cell, then a cut to a close-up of his face (figure 5.3), all in the same deathly colour, as are the walls of his cell.[16] This is fitting, as it is soon clear that he is in the (failed) act of hanging himself. Mustard green, then, in the cases of Cristina and Jack represents the characters' death wish as a response to the deaths that have been inflicted upon them.

The final important colour featured at specific points in the film is an intense white light. It is used with all characters, but associated particularly with Paul throughout and Jack before the accident, and provides an excellent example of how Iñárritu and Prieto generate meaning through lighting and colour, and add depth to characterisation. Prieto outlines the method used to achieve this and the intention in the scenes featuring Jack in the church. He used Rosco Soft Frost gel on the camera to whiten the windows, and explains:

> using that filter gave me an almost godly religious intensity, a sense of Jack believing in the holiness of his life's mission. On interiors, I would purposefully light Benicio with the sunlight coming through the windows but would keep it off of the person he's with. After the accident, which sparks his downfall, I stopped doing that. (Calhoun, 2003: 2)

This godly or spiritual form of lighting is used most consistently in the case of Paul (Calhoun, 2003: 2). This technique is seen in the

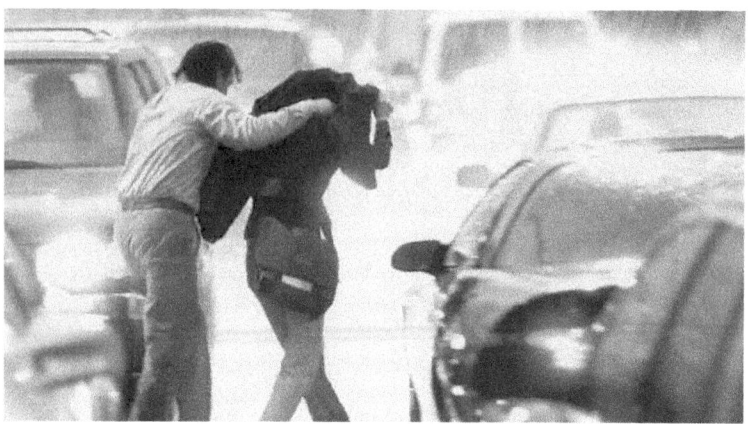

5.4 Cristina and Paul in the rain, illuminated by an intense white light in *21 Grams*

film's opening fragment as he sits on the bed next to Cristina, and accompanies most subsequent scenes in which they are together. Intense light is projected from and onto the windows when Paul first shares a space with Cristina in a pharmacy as he follows her (the first time in the syuzhet, not the fabula). The same brilliant light fills the window during their second meeting, in the café of the health club. It is even used in the street scene outside the health club when Paul offers Cristina a lift, despite the fact that it is pouring with rain (figure 5.4). A realist approach in this final example would necessitate the creation of grey, muted colours to indicate the weather, but this artistic approach succeeds in signifying the special nature of their relationship.

Throughout, the symbolic function of the use of this unnatural, otherworldly brightness is to carve out a special place for Paul within the diegesis of the film, and to provide him with a spiritual dimension. This is highlighted by Iñárritu, who has said of his protagonist, 'I needed one leader, the one who redeemed the other two' (Wood, 2006: 146). Within the narrative, Paul redeems Cristina by teaching her to love again, and by giving her a future child, and he redeems Jack through his own final sacrifice, allowing Jack to take the role of helper rather than killer.

Conclusion

What I have attempted to do in this chapter is to examine the way Iñárritu establishes himself as an international auteur through *21 Grams* and the film's paratexts, in particular the short feature *21 Grams: In Fragments*. Throughout *21 Grams*, the director and team establish signature aesthetic and narrative approaches associated with independent filmmaking. Working within specific parameters in *21 Grams* Iñárritu and team have created an independent art film, using techniques commonly associated with this mode, such as experimental camera work, time-scrambled chronological exposition, and an anti-naturalistic colour palette. The last aspect has been a focus and has been examined in some depth here. The filmmakers have thus combined original auteurist visions with an international style that is in vogue, and have demonstrated that a team of Mexican cineastes can master the codes of independent American cinema. As the director and key crew demonstrate with their subsequent film projects, and as is explored in the following chapter with reference to *Babel*, this approach can be adapted to and developed for other national and production contexts. There is an international film language which provides the grammatical foundations for types of independent film, art cinema, and 'world cinema', which also allows space for filmmakers to carve out their own distinctive voices (to continue the linguistic analogy), and that language is applied in different ways in *Amores perros*, *21 Grams*, *Babel*, and *Buitiful*.

Notes

1 Only one of the key filmmakers is North American, the editor, Stephen Mirrione. He has edited all of Iñárritu's films from *21 Grams* onwards.
2 Indiewood is the label attached to a cluster of films that challenge many classical Hollywood conventions made by studios and independent companies in the 1980s and 1990s (see King, 2005: 9–10; King, 2009).
3 For an early examination of émigrés in early Hollywood cinema see Taylor (1983).
4 For an overview of the debates surrounding definitions of the term, see Yannis Tzioumakis (2006: 1–15).
5 See also King (2005: 107), who argues that American independent cinema breaks the classical narrative structure, challenges the formal elements of classical Hollywood filmmaking, and goes 'beyond' its 'neutral' approaches to take more stylised and self-conscious options.
6 The founders (Ted Hope, Anthony Bregman, and Anne Carey) previously

worked for Good Machine, as did Linde and Schamus. It was a successful independent production company until it was bought and rebranded as Focus Features by Universal (King, 2004: 82).

7 This clearly contrasts with del Toro's roles in *Traffic* (Soderberg, 2000), in which he plays a local from Tijuana, and his performance as Che in Steven Soderberg's two films made in 2008 on the Argentine revolutionary.

8 The only Latin American reference in *21 Grams* can be found in a poem cited by Paul Rivers (Sean Penn), written by an unnamed Venezuelan poet (which a quick search on IMDB reveals to be from 'La tierra giró para acercarnos' ('The earth turned to bring us together'), by Eugenio Montejo (www.imdb.com/title/tt0315733/trivia). Nevertheless, the observations in the poem are 'universal' in nature and can be applied in many national contexts.

9 Her focus in the article is on the homepages created by Spanish directors Isabel Coixet and Álex de la Iglesia.

10 In the closing ceremony that ends the short feature, Iñárritu thanks all his cast and crew as they hold hands, before instructing them to throw the head of a white rose into the air.

11 These are terms that originate from Russian formalism; for more explanation, see Bordwell (1985: 48).

12 Both films feature Benicio del Toro. For more on *Traffic* see Shaw (2005).

13 The production notes reveal that these scenes were shot in Albuquerque, New Mexico. The producer, Robert Salerno, comments that the New Mexico settings provided 'a desert starkness, which was the big contrast from Memphis that we wanted and needed at that point in the story' (Hollywood Jesus, 2003).

14 Prieto illuminates the processes that they used to achieve this: 'The bar was totally redesigned by Brigitte Broch, our production designer, to incorporate the color of lighting we were going for. I gave it a general wash with Rosco Light Red, punctuated with Par cans containing 1.2K Firestarter bulbs; those units were dimmed down for a sort of amber color and overexposed by three stops. I contrasted that with blue-green fluorescents that were placed here and there' (Calhoun, 2003: 3). The use of red in nightclubs to connote an underworld of sin and danger is clearly a common cinematic device; perhaps the most famous examples can be found in the bar scenes in Scorsese's *Mean Streets* (1973).

15 This scene is glimpsed momentarily in the first few shots, but acquires meaning only when it is seen for the second time, near the end of the film.

16 Michael Stewart (2007: 58) argues that 'the film pushes greenish desaturation into monstrous grotesqueness ... Iñárritu makes his characters more fishy gray metal than human flesh'.

6

Babel and the global Hollywood gaze

In the previous chapters, I have explored the ways that Iñárritu has (with help from his team) applied the languages of intensified continuity or post-classical filmmaking, and the experimental form rooted in American independent cinema, and explored the links between these. *Babel* is the last of the three films of the Arriaga/Iñárritu collaboration, and, as with the previous two films, the trademark formal cinematic techniques associated with the screen writer/director and with the above-mentioned film languages are retained. Thus, *Babel* too has multiple plotlines and protagonists, and similarly rejects having a single hero; it employs extremes of lens length, and close-ups at key emotional moments, and free-ranging camera work with most of the film shot using a handheld camera.[1] Likewise, time is not presented in a strictly chronological way, although the complex scrambling of *21 Grams* is wisely avoided in what is an already complex plot structure.[2] Auteurist strategies are also developed (as discussed in the analysis of *21 Grams*) in the colour design to create a painterly work, with Brigitte Broch suggesting a range of reddish tones to visually separate countries: 'burgundy for Morocco, bright-red for Mexico, and violet for Japan' (García, 2006: 259).

As all of the above-mentioned formal aspects have been the subject of analysis in the previous two chapters, I want to develop a different focus here. Thus, I examine the ways that the Iñárritu-led outfit attempts to apply these elements to a world stage in terms of structure, themes, and locations, in an apparent 'progression' from Mexican cinema to American cinema to 'world cinema'. *Babel* sets out to be a new sort of film, one that attempts to create a 'world cinema' gaze within a commercial Hollywood framework. I examine how the team approaches this and ask whether the film succeeds in this attempt. I explore the tensions between progressive and conservative political agendas, and pay particular attention to the ways 'other' cultures are seen in a film with 'third world' pretensions and US money behind it. I frame my analysis around a key question: does *Babel* successfully create a paradigmatic 'transnational world cinema' text that decentres US hegemony, or is this a utopian project doomed to failure in a film funded predominantly by major US studios? I examine the ways in which the film engages with the tourist gaze and ask whether the film replaces this gaze with a world cinema gaze or merely reproduces it in new ways. I also explore the relationship between the director's particular vision of world cinema and suffering, and analyse the viability of this pairing.

'World cinema'

In popular imaginaries, 'world cinema' and Hollywood commercial cinema appear to be two opposing forms of filmic production, obeying different political and aesthetic laws. However, definitions of world cinema have been vague and often contradictory, while some leftist discourses have a simplistic take on the evils of reactionary Hollywood, seeing it in rather monolithic terms. A number of critics have identified the loose and, at times, contradictory thinking associated with the label 'world cinema'. For instance, in their introduction to *Remapping World Cinema*, Stephanie Dennison and Song Lim argue that when approaching the term we are confronted with 'a web of power relations and at times conflicting ideologies that defy any simplistic account on the definition or meaning of world cinema' (Dennison and Lim, 2006: 3).[3] They claim that to ask 'what is world cinema?' is, in fact, fruitless, and can never be value free (1). Like Dennison and Lim, Catherine Grant and Annette Kuhn also state that 'world cinema' is 'a catch-all term suffering from contradictions and a lack of clear definition' (Grant and Kuhn, 2006: 1). It can, they argue, be used to mean:

> all non-Hollywood or all non-First world cinemas from the most mainstream to the most-experimental ... [or] world cinema can stand simply for a global cinema that embraces all films, including those of the First World. (Grant and Kuhn, 2006: 1)

In a similar vein Dennison and Lim write of two conceptualisations of the term: 'The first regards it as the sum total of all the national cinemas in the world, and the second posits it against US or Hollywood cinema' (2006: 6).⁴ While it is, then, neither possible nor desirable to provide a definition for 'world cinema', what we can do is examine the ways in which it has been applied in practical and theoretical terms, and then consider how *Babel* and Iñárritu's sense of himself as a world cinema filmmaker fit within this.

According to Grant and Kuhn (2006: 1), in its practical usage, 'world cinema' is 'a strenuously promoted brand' that lends respectability to film festivals, DVD collections, academic courses, and academic publishing. In academia, it refers to a canon of 'great cultural texts' (1). In commerce, it has links to world music, and for Dennison and Lim (2006: 1) it is a non-Western, often counter-hegemonic cultural product. To extend ideas about the practical usage of the term to a pedagogical context, world cinema is broadly taken as a collection of national cinemas in an idealised, usually canonical syllabus for film studies. An illustration of this can be found in the *The Oxford History of World Cinema* (Nowell-Smith, 2000), hyperbolically described by its publishers on the book's cover as 'the definitive history of cinema worldwide'.⁵ In commercial terms, the types of films that are sold in the 'world cinema' section of retail outlets are national/transnational films (as I have defined *Cronos* and *Amores perros*); that is, they are rooted in a specific national context, but have the ingredients to sell in the international market.

A second strand of 'world cinema' is seen in films that seek to say something about 'the world', with a focus on relationships between citizens and transnational socio-political issues in a 'cinema of globalisation'.⁶ These texts explicitly address questions of globalisation within their narratives, central to which are the ways in which relations of power between nations and peoples are played out on screen. Some well known examples of such films are *El viaje* (*The Voyage*) (Solanas, 1992), *Dirty Pretty Things* (Frears, 2002), *In This World* (Winterbottom, 2002), *The Constant Gardener* (Meirelles, 2005), *Syriana* (Gaghan, 2005), *Blood Diamond* (Zwick, 2006), *The International* (Tykwer, 2009), and *Children of Men* (Cuarón, 2006; discussed in chapter 9). The films are often transnational in terms of production context and cast and crew.

Babel is an interesting case of a hybrid text, for while it is an example of the (commercial) cinema of globalisation, in that it engages with relations between people of the world and attempts to create thematic links between them, it also shares elements of the 'foreign' films traditionally seen as examples of world cinema. Thus, while two of the cast are global Hollywood stars (Brad Pitt and Cate Blanchett), and while the film was predominantly funded by Paramount Vantage (on which more later), it has a focus on non-English-speaking peoples and cultures (Moroccan, Mexican, and Japanese), and relies on a predominantly Mexican core team of filmmakers, and local cast and crew in the shooting locations.[7]

Babel is a film of great scale and global ambition. It tells four stories located in four countries (the USA, Mexico, Morocco, and Japan) and uses six languages (Spanish, Arabic, Berber, Japanese, sign language, and English), translated for a global audience through subtitles. The storylines are held together by an accident, as with *Amores perros* and *21 Grams*, this time caused by a bullet fired in play by two young Moroccan goatherds, Ahmed (Said Tarchani) and Yussef (Boubker Ait El Caid) (one storyline). Yussef unwittingly shoots Susan (Cate Blanchett), an American tourist, when testing a rifle, and the Moroccan storyline focuses on the aftermath of the shooting for the family. The second storyline explores the aftermath for the victims, and focuses on Susan's attempt to survive in the shack of their tourist guide, accompanied by angry and worried husband Richard (Brad Pitt). It also deals with the way in which the accident is highjacked by the US government, which takes it to be an act of Islamic terrorism against its citizens. A third storyline, linked to the US couple in Morocco, features their children in the care of Mexican nanny Amelia (Adriana Barraza) in California, and her ultimately disastrous decision to take them across the border to her son's wedding in a village near Tijuana, in the absence of alternative childcare. This results in her arrest and the immigration authority's refusal to allow her back into the USA where she had lived and worked for many years. The fourth story is set and shot in Japan, and deals with the traumas faced by deaf mute teenager Chieko (Rinko Kikuchi). This storyline has the most tenuous link with the others, as her father had, on a hunting trip to Morocco, given his Winchester rifle to his guide, the rifle that is used to shoot Susan.

Babel and Hollywood world cinema

In their discussion of definitions, Dennison and Lim (2006: 3) challenge the idea that 'world cinema' texts contest hegemonic (Western) power structures and challenge cultural norms imposed by globalisation. They question these simplistic definitions, arguing that rather than foregrounding resistance as a defining principle, more emphasis should be placed on 'the interconnectedness of cinematic practices and cultures in the age of globalisation, particularly in terms of the conditions of production and consumption' (4). They also advocate a theoretical shift from the West/Hollywood versus the rest dichotomy, and suggest thinking in terms of 'hybridity, transculturation, border crossing, transnationalism and translation' (6). This is helpful in seeing *Babel* as a new form of film, a Hollywood world cinema text. In line with Dennison and Lim's formulation, *Babel* in many ways deconstructs an America versus the rest paradigm, and is indeed characterised by 'hybridity, transculturation, border crossing, transnationalism and translation' in terms of storylines and themes, score, and cast and crew, all the while relying on US funding and the star system to make and sell the film.

The plot description outlined above points to the fact that *Babel* is a transnational film in the most obvious of ways: it has multiple locations, with different types of border crossings explicitly featured in two of the stories. It is made by a transnational director, and features transnational stars (Brad Pitt, Cate Blanchett, and Gael García Bernal).[8] It can also be seen as a film that fits within the concept of a cinema of globalisation, as explained above. *Babel* takes some of the most pressing contemporary social issues in its attempt to make a film about 'the world'; nevertheless, as befitting a Hollywood world cinema text, it privileges a North American point of view, even when it appears not to. While the film has a focus on non-Western cultures, the shadow of US socio-political concerns hangs over all of these, with the exception of the Japanese storyline. Two of the four storylines are concerned with the fates of North American characters: Susan and Richard, and, in the sections dealing with Amelia's story, their children. It can also be argued that the plot dynamic in the Moroccans' storyline is only possible and of interest because Yussef shoots a North American citizen. In addition, in terms of topics addressed, Mexican immigration to the USA and the 'war on terror' are very much North American 'global' concerns. The Japanese storyline, which focuses on teenage alienation, is presented in such a way as to make it easily accessible to Western audiences, with a focus on teen culture, including Western dance music.

The concept of a Hollywood world cinema text is also apparent from the production context. The film was a co-production involving five companies: Iñárritu's Mexican production company Zeta film; Media Rights Capital, which provided bridge financing for the project until the other companies came on board (Kerr, 2010: 44); Paramount Vantage, the specialty division of Paramount, with *Babel* the first film it produced; Anonymous Content, a production and management company that operates in the fields of film, commercials, music video, television, and talent;[9] and Central Films, a Paris-based company run by the Argentine Fernando Sulichin, which has produced films from a range of national settings. The three principal financial backers of *Babel*, Media Rights Capital, Paramount Vantage, and Anonymous Content, are all known for their mainstream/independent features, and *Babel* can be seen to fit well within this remit, despite its transnational settings.[10] The film can also be seen to prefigure a trend adopted by sectors of the US film industry in response to the conservative, belligerent administration of George W. Bush. There were a number of films made following *Babel*, such as *Syriana* (Gaghan, 2005), *In the Valley of Elah* (Haggis, 2007), *Rendition* (Hood, 2007), and *Redacted* (de Palma, 2007), that demonstrated an engagement with foreign affairs and critiqued the USA's dealings with the Arab world.

It is not surprising that *Babel*'s global reach is, in large part, conditioned by a North American perspective, given that most of the money came principally from US production and distribution companies (Paramount Vantage was the principal distributor).[11] This perspective, as well as the production context, can also explain why, in terms of its branding, the film is not found in the 'world' section on the real or virtual shelves of DVD outlets, but in the mainstream sections, featuring mainly English-language Hollywood films. It can also explain the excessive focus on Pitt and Blanchett in the marketing of the film, despite the fact that they share equivalent screen time with lesser known and unknown actors from other national contexts.

The category of Hollywood world text is also well illustrated by the fact that for the 2007 Academy Awards *Babel* was nominated in a number of the main categories, despite its multinational cast, multiple languages, and predominantly Mexican crew, presumably again as US companies were the principal producers and distributors.[12] Despite seven nominations, the only category in which it won was for Best Original Score, by Gustavo Santoalalla. This links to the way in which a 'world music' score provides the foundations for the 'world' feel Iñárritu is seeking in *Babel*. The predominant instrument in the soundtrack is the oud, described by Iñárritu as 'the musical

DNA of the picture' (García, 2006: 259). Santoalalla comments that this Middle Eastern instrument is an ancestor of the lute and the Spanish guitar, and is connected to the Japanese koto (Ordóñez and Nieto, 2007). The oud is frequently played in the same way in which the composer uses the electric guitar in previous collaborations with Iñárritu, with signature single plucked notes repeated throughout to create a simple repetitive sound that aims to link disparate stories. Here, the marriage of Eastern and Western styles achieved through the choice of instrument aims to signify the union between the characters (it is, for example, very apparent in the scene in which Richard and Susan are in the Moroccan tourist guide's shack). The notion of world music, then, helps consolidate *Babel* as a world cinema text; it is apparent, in addition to Santoallalla's score, in the use of a range of songs, from Mexican *norteño* tracks at the Mexican wedding, to Western club tracks in the Japanese section, and other orchestral compositions by globally successful Japanese musician Ryuichi Sakamoto. There is even a track (significantly sung in English) entitled 'World citizen (I won't be disappointed)' by Sakamoto and David Sylvian.[13]

Babel and the tourist gaze

Despite the Hollywood production context in which the film was made, the notion of 'world citizen' is very apposite to the intentions of the director, and Iñárritu casts himself as a world cinema filmmaker in the way that he implicitly brings his Mexican identity into play by suggesting that he can use what he calls his 'third world perspective' to make films for everyone and bring people together (Gardels, 2007). What I aim to do in this section and the following one is to explore the ways in which these seemingly contradictory elements are played out through two specific types of cinematic gazes: a tourist gaze, and a world cinema gaze.

In a sense, the project of the film is a challenge to God; it is an attempt to construct a cinematic Tower of Babel, built upon a universal language of film to unite the scattered audiences of the globe. It does this by setting out the differences between people of a range of national identities (Japanese, North American, Moroccan, and Mexican), then seeking to show them as fundamentally the same through a focus on universal human emotions. At the root of the director's ideas of filmmaking is a grandiose idea that humanity is united in suffering, and that his cinema, through a form of visual Esperanto underpinned by a globalisation of emotion, can bring people together.

Babel follows the trend favoured by Iñárritu and Arriaga for a multi-stranded narrative, but has taken this to a new global level. The film is more ambitious than many other examples of this narrative form in that it is used to advocate a utopian message about a 'world community'. It is a film with diverse locations, and no single hero, both of which mean that *Babel* has no centre, no implied unitary home, and no tour guide. Central to the idea of representing a 'world community' is the way in which members of this world are seen within the film. Iñárritu's approach aims to stand in contrast to narratives of the solitary US hero abroad that have characterised so much mainstream Hollywood filmmaking. In his words:

> Films like *Babel* can transcend the one-point-of-view formula that has reigned for so long.... It is true that the sensibility of *Babel* is that of someone from a Third World country. This film could not have been conceived or executed, and certainly would have been completely different, if it was made, say, in Switzerland or the US. (Gardels, 2007)

This 'third world sensibility' stands in opposition to a hegemonic colonial or neo-colonial position which rests on a tourist gaze, and Iñárritu acknowledges this. He has made a number of comments in interviews that show that he deliberately set out to avoid constructing this type of gaze for audiences in *Babel*. He says, 'I tried to tell the story from the point of view of the people who live in those cultures and not that of a tourist' (Mitchell, 2006).

The type of voyeurism built into viewing film, and particularly 'foreign'-language film, means that there are many links between tourism (in terms of travel abroad) and film spectatorship. A number of theorists have commented on the links between the viewing process of the tourist and the film spectator. Ellen Strain has extended the definition of the tourist gaze to include practices beyond traditionally conceived concepts of tourism, and she cites this gaze as central to cinema and television viewing, anthropological study, and reading issues of *National Geographic*, among other cultural practices (Strain, 2003: 2–3). Strain and others have also commented on the analogous practices between film viewing and tourism, and the similarities in the framing of the spectacle. So, there are parallels between the travelling shot so common in film and the view from a bus or train (Gibson, 2006: 169–170; Schivelbusch, 1986: 24; Strain, 2003: 35).

In addition, cinematic use of close-ups, long shots, and aerial shots find corresponding viewing strategies in the staging of tourist sites, with visitors encouraged to climb a tall monument for a good view, then switch to a close inspection of a map or a 'tourist object' (Gibson, 2006: 167; Strain, 2003: 33–34).

There is a power dynamic in the tourist gaze, which often rests upon an implied viewer of the developed world observing a 'third world other' or objects of another culture, frequently deemed to be more desirable than the people themselves. John Urry notes that the tourist gaze 'facilitates the world of the "other" to be controlled from afar, combining detachment and mastery' (2002: 147). Likewise, Strain talks of 'mastery through vision and aestheticized representation' (2003: 25). The foreign 'other' becomes an object of consumption, included in the price of the cinema ticket or the tour, with audiences/tourists encouraged to confuse seeing with understanding and knowing a country.

On a number of levels, *Babel* does seek to deconstruct this gaze, partly by making it the very subject of the film in the Moroccan section that focuses on Susan and Richard, the American tourists, and partly by de-exoticising characters from a range of nationalities. Nevertheless, it also employs a double strategy, as it relies on familiar cinematic tropes relating to the representation of nationals, and typical tourist landscapes in its bid to attain universal appeal, and in this double discourse we see its hybrid position as a Hollywood world cinema text. In what follows, I first consider how the tourist gaze is resisted, and then explore its hold on filmmakers through the ways in which the film fails to escape tourist landscapes.

The story that focuses on Richard and Susan explores the position of the tourist in 'third world' settings. This storyline demonstrates tropes associated with this position in order to challenge them. The two have come to Morocco to escape from the trauma of their child dying in the crib, establishing tourism as an escape from reality for wealthy Westerners, although Susan's grief is too strong to allow her to succumb to the 'pleasures' of tourism. The group they are part of is carried by coach and the film appears to share the tourist position, with film and travel practices merging, as a travelling shot reduces Moroccan women seen from the coach to veiled, shadowy, exotic figures devoid of subjectivity (figure 6.1). This contrasts with the Hollywood-centric focus on Susan, whose grief is signalled by her expressions seen in close-up (figure 6.2). Signature Prieto/Iñárritu

6.1 Moroccan women are viewed from the bus in *Babel*

6.2 The camera focuses on Susan in the tour bus in *Babel*

close-up fragment shots focus on her hands and those of Richard's finally joining to show the difficulties in their relationship and the potential for reconciliation. Morocco, then, is little more than an exotic backdrop for our two Hollywood stars enacting a bourgeois couple in crisis.

However, after it has been established, the tourist figure is literally and figuratively shot by Yussef's bullet, and the holiday location soon shifts to a very different setting. An unbearably long take marks this pivotal transformative moment, with the camera unblinkingly focusing on Susan, until the gun-shot punctuates the take. The switch from still camera position to a haze of extreme confusion filmed in close-up after the shooting signals the switch in Susan's position from holiday-maker to victim and recipient of shelter and care from the locals. Susan and Richard are taken, significantly, to the home of Mohammed (the tour guide), and now the dynamics of seeing alter, with the American couple objects of a curious local gaze. Children look through the tour guide's window at Susan lying injured on the floor of the shack, and men, women, and children stare inquisitively at Richard as he anxiously phones the American embassy for help. The images from the bus are partially inverted as they are now in the position of strange foreigners for the locals; nevertheless, the decentring of the hegemonic gaze is not complete, as the objects of the camera's gaze are predominantly Susan and Richard, with the Moroccans in supporting roles.

This can be linked to the dismantling of the power structures built into the tourist gaze. Richard and Susan learn to lose the arrogance and distance built into their position as tourists as they become dependent on the Moroccan villagers for their survival. They no longer consume them as local exotic objects, but come to forge bonds with them. One of the most powerful scenes in the film comes when the helicopter arrives and Richard tries to give Mohammed money in thanks. Mohammed pointedly refuses to take it, and Richard, moved and stunned, thanks him. No dialogue is heard and this is filmed to Santoallalla's score of strummed melodic oud. This scene illustrates Iñárritu's utopian idea of world cinema expressed through individuals from different nations coming together, united by the language of music and film, and making connections despite their governments' positions.

In this section, Iñárritu, to some extent, demonstrates his 'third world' perspective by sympathising with Moroccans and taking on aspects of Orientalism which characterise both tourist practices and the political agenda under the George W. Bush administration. Edward Said highlights America's dominance over the Orient, following from British and French colonialism (1979: 73), and in one of his categories of the term 'Orientalism' he describes it as 'a Western style for dominating, restructuring, and having authority over the Orient' (73). This is characterised by a 'relationship of power, of domination, of varying degrees of a complex hegemony' (75). Contemporary post-9/11 Orientalism takes the form of Islamophobia and paranoia, with Arabs and Muslims en masse seen to be seeking to destroy the West and target Westerners. This is effectively challenged in the film by demonstrating that the fears of the tourists and US government are unfounded, and critiquing the actions of the US authorities. Political systems are attacked by dehumanising the agents of repression, while humanising citizens from both countries. The audience never actually see US political figures, but are referred to government-dictated policy through disembodied voices on the telephone when Richard is asking them for help, and television reports. Likewise, a sense is given of Moroccan authorities who over-react by killing Ahmed, just a boy, as they are keen to appease the Americans, and show that they are dealing with 'terrorists'.

Nevertheless, to return to the idea of *Babel* as a Hollywood world cinema text, the film never fully deviates from mainstream culture in remaining within and relying on familiar and expected locations and types. Representations of places in *Babel* correspond to one of John Urry's categories of tourism, the tourist sign, whereby the sightseer seeks out typical landscapes in his/her travels (the typical English garden, the American skyscraper, the German beer garden, etc.) (Urry, 2002: 13). For Urry, 'tourists are, in a way, semioticians, reading the landscape for signifiers of certain pre-established notions or signs derived from various discourses of travel and tourism' (13). Thus, in the film the locations correspond to national stereotypes: Japan is hyper-modern, featuring the latest mobile phones, cool clubs, trendy cafés, and impressive neon bright cityscapes. Mexico is rural and poor, complete with dusty tracks and a drunken wedding with traditional *norteño* music. Morocco also conforms to type and is reduced to rocky, arid land, mountainous scenery, and poor villages. As Paul Kerr (2010: 47) observes, the film recycles 'some of the most familiar cinematic tropes' and types, including the US–Mexico border, urban Japanese teenage angst (embodied in a sexualised schoolgirl), and

Moroccan desert poverty. The colour design for each setting also reinforces the familiar and expected choice of representation of the diverse locations. Brigitte Broch, the production designer, who was behind the use of colours, explains:

> Alejandro and Rodrigo accepted that Morocco would be void of a primary red, so it would basically be a very dark, rich red and the oranges of that country in contrast to Mexico, where we decided to use a primary red color, like the red of the flag, to represent the straightforward Mexican passion. For Tokyo, we chose to use a lot of purples, pinks and fuchsias to make it look like a diluted blood of futuristic essence. (Sneider: 2007)

These colour schemes, then, link the visuals with guidebook images of each country, with modernity reserved for Japan, passion for Mexico, and underdevelopment for Morocco. The film's take on each setting is also made to conform to cultural expectations through the use of lenses, formats, and choice of film stock (Kaufman, 2006).

Thus, in the Moroccan section, although the film does take viewers to areas that are not accessible to tourists – through its focus on Yussef, Ahmed, and family, all played by non-professional actors – other aspects of the tourist gaze and the Orientalism inherent within this are reinforced. As Said (1979: 76) has observed, Eurocentric ideas of Orientalism root the Orient in inferiority and backwardness, and this is the image presented to the audiences of *Babel*. What is interesting in this section is what we do not see, and the way in which a specific geographical setting is stripped of contextual local markers. There are no signs of modernity in this representation, and no sense is given of linguistic diversity, political dissent, religion, or colonial history, despite the fact that all of these areas are significant in the country's profile.[14] The vast majority of Moroccans speak Berber as their first language, yet this is rarely spoken in the film; the fact that the characters are made to speak Arabic, a significant global language, when non-fictional Moroccan goatherds would be speaking Berber, ensures that the film is more likely to appeal to a wider audience.[15] A number of popular reviews and bloggers with knowledge of Morocco question the authenticity of this section of the film, and the erasure of linguistic and ethnic diversity. One blogger asks of the boys, 'why ... were they speaking Darija, the Moroccan dialect of Arabic, and not Tamazight, the local Berber dialect?' (York, 2007).[16] Likewise, a reviewer for *Moroccan Time* asks, 'why would boys from a village in the Atlas Mountains speak Darija, not Tamazight or Tachelheit?' (Felix,

2006). The film presents an image of a linguistically and ethnically unified country because it is not concerned with creating an authentic documentary-like portrait of rural Morocco, but seeks to present characters as archetypes that sit comfortably in a tale ultimately more concerned with representing US concerns. Thus, despite many admirable efforts to escape the tourist gaze, *Babel* ultimately relies on images of otherness as familiar to the tourist as to the film spectator.

Suffering and a world cinema gaze

These archetypal characters are connected within the text by their suffering: a reduction of heterogeneity is sought through an appeal to a universality of emotion and a globalised form of pain in a bid to create the sense of a 'world village' where we all care about each other. Iñárritu has been explicit about the role of suffering in uniting peoples from around the world. In an interview the director outlines his position:

> By filming *Babel* I confirmed that real borderlines are within ourselves and more than a physical space, barriers are in the world of ideas. I realized that what makes us happy as human beings could differ greatly, but what makes us miserable and vulnerable beyond our culture, race, language or financial standing is the same for all.... Accordingly, *Babel* was transformed into a picture about what joins us, not what separates us. (Iñárritu, n.d.)

This type of universality which rests on personal suffering is formed in the marketplace, and relies on melodramatic structures to pull in audiences. This philosophical brand of liberal universalism is dependent on a lack of self-conscious recognition of specifics of class and socio-economic realities for its commercial success, and the paradox here is that socio-economic realities are behind the reason for the negation of these. What makes us miserable and vulnerable is not the same for us all, but that credo is behind the emotional pull of *Babel* and its position in the marketplace.[17] While the film was not a hit on the scale of a Hollywood blockbuster, it was commercially successful, and from a modest budget of $25 million it made $135,330,182.[18]

Each storyline in *Babel* is built upon emotional trauma, and much of the film takes audiences outside of viewers' comfort zones. As the stories develop, the suffering of the characters intensifies and watching the film becomes an almost unbearable experience. The Moroccan boys have to face the consequences of their actions and Ahmed is ultimately fatally shot by the police in front of his brother and father. Susan's condition worsens and viewers are shown her in the degrading position of lying in her own blood and urine (although she is ultimately taken to a hospital and recovers). Amelia has a moment of pleasure at her son's wedding before she has to fight for her survival and that of the children in the desert land forming the US–Mexico border. She is ultimately caught by the police, deported back to Mexico and loses her job and her home. Audiences witness the alienation experienced by Chieko, a deaf mute teenager facing a series of humiliating rebuffs to her sexual advances, culminating in her howl of pain when faced with her rejection by the handsome police officer. The final scene in the Japanese storyline hints at reconciliation with her father as he embraces his naked daughter, but not before audiences are teased into thinking that she has thrown herself off the apartment balcony.

Thus, while connections for the characters depend on suffering, the implicit intention of the film is that audiences are connected by their ability to empathise with this suffering. An implied 'world cinema gaze' is built upon this empathy; audiences can transcend national borders and share the pain of a Moroccan family, wealthy Americans, a Mexican nanny, and a Japanese teenager. *Babel* seeks to construct a global viewer by rooting the storylines in multiple locations and reducing 'foreign' signifiers to a surface level. In this way, the imagined viewer of *Babel* is put into the spectatorial position of 'citizen of the world'. The text seeks acceptance for the foreign 'other', but this is because she/he is like us on an emotional level – whoever 'we' may be. Thus, a new gaze is posited, intended to take the place of the tourist gaze, one that I am tentatively calling a 'world cinema gaze'. This, of course, can exist only as an imagined category, and is implied rather than embodied, because, although the film may have no geo-spatial centre, actual viewers do.

This gaze is built on empathy, as a brief analysis of Rodrigo Prieto's camera work will show. The cinematographer frequently places viewers in the centre of the action through the use of the extreme close-up. Viewers are often positioned as if they are in the room or sharing the space of the characters, and any sense of distance is removed from their look. 'Imperfect' camera work mimics the eye movement of the invisible member of the group (the implied viewer), and whip pans and abrupt edits that follow conversations convert the implied viewer into one of the characters present.

In one of the most effective sequences featuring Chieko and her friends, this is illustrated very well. They first meet in a local park, where they take drugs and drink. The close-ups are so extreme that the viewer can only be in the position of one of the friends. Dreamy ambient music captures their drug-induced high, and, at one point, Chieko looks directly at the viewer (her implied friend), as she is captured by surreal camera movements on a swing. Viewers share her euphoria as, for a time, she is not limited by her disability and is able to socialise with her friends and flirt with boys like any other teenager. Audiences experience Chieko's wonder as she enters the nightclub and we switch from our perspectives (if we are hearing) to hers, as the sound of Earth, Wind and Fire's 'September' (1978) cuts in and out. She begins to dance, mimicking the other dancers' movements, and an extreme close-up of her ecstatic face (figure 6.3) allows audiences to share in her momentary joy at participating in normal rites of teenage years. However, a mood shift is indicated by extremely fast blinks/edits as light switches to black and back to multi-coloured lights (purple, red, and green feature) in synch with the hard-core club track 'The Joker' (ATFC's Aces High Remix, Fatboy Slim, 2004). This reveals, in

6.3 Chieko at the club in *Babel*

flickering shots, Chieko's best friend kissing Haruki, the boy she was attracted to, thus destroying the moment. Her come-down is seen as she walks through the silent streets of Tokyo, with the audience again in a position of her deafness, and we share the cruelty of the moment as she walks past a silent rock band busking on the streets. There is no space here for any freedom of emotional interpretation, and meaning is constructed by the camera work, lights, music, and close focus on Chieko. We are her best friend, but we can do nothing for her, as, despite the illusions of presence, we exist in entirely separate planes on opposite sides of the screen. In this way our suffering increases. This technique of the camera positioning the spectator in the centre of the action is commonly used in the film (and in the other Iñárritu/Prieto collaborations), in order for the implied deterritorialised viewer to care about all the characters and empathise with their suffering, and is central to establishing an empathetic world cinema gaze.

Babel: a politically conservative or progressive film?

While the film does, then, decentre the white male gaze of classical Hollywood cinema, does it say something meaningful about 'the world' and the connections between societies within a coherent diegesis? *Babel* is a difficult film to assess definitively in terms of conservative or radical politics. Dolores Tierney's reading of the film points to some of these difficulties. Thus, while she argues that '*Babel* broadens out the Third Worldist critiques of *Amores perros* and *21 Grams*, addressing the reality of cultural and political borders in a global sense' (Tierney, 2009: 114), she also acknowledges 'that for all its radical politics *Babel* still ends on a politically and racially conservative note: the privileged (white) family is saved/rescued and instead it is the (dark-skinned) inhabitants of the Third World who suffer or die' (114).[19]

A theoretical framework within which to examine the question of whether the film is radical and rooted in a third world perspective, as Iñárritu has claimed, can be found in Frederic Jameson's concept of cognitive mapping. For Jameson, within contemporary society (the period of late capitalism), there is a:

> gap between the local positioning of the individual subject and the totality of class structures in which he or she is situated, a gap between phenomenological perception and a reality that transcends all individual thinking or experience. (Jameson, 1990: 353)

This results in 'the incapacity of our minds, at least at present, to map the great global multinational and decentred communicational network in which we find ourselves caught as individual subjects' (Jameson, 1991: 44). This 'incapacity to map socially ... [is] crippling to political experience' and leads to individual and social alienation (Jameson, 1990: 353). Cognitive mapping can counter this through 'a pedagogical political culture which seeks to endow the individual subject with some new heightened sense of its place in the global system' (Jameson, 1991: 54).

Cultural artefacts and post-modern texts cannot represent a spatial totality, but they can be self-conscious about their failures, and in this find a political strength. Self-conscious texts, thus, need to be aware of their limitations, and *Babel* does not acknowledge any failures, remaining very ambitious, with a belief in its totalising abilities. The cultural flattening and search for a form of globalised emotion means that any meaningful political and social lines on the map which connect the characters are obscured. They are, in a Jamesonian sense, alienated from the global world in which they live. Audiences, meanwhile, are provided with false connections made through a reliance on emotional strategies of melodrama, which negate specifics of class. While the film does create sympathy for both first and third world peoples, suffering is relied on to provide the melodramatic power of the film; thus connections depend on the ability to elicit emotion from the viewer and are not rooted in social or class-based realities.

It is fruitful to look at the links that the film attempts to create and the reasons for their failure in order to examine both the alienation of the characters and the disempowering of the audience. Tourism and border crossings generate the superficial narrative connections between characters. The ill-fated hunting rifle, which accidentally injures Susan, finds its way to Morocco when Chieko's father, Yasujiro Wataya (Kôji Yakusho), gives it to his Moroccan hunting guide, who sells it on to Abdullah. Thus the rifle is initially a symbol of friendship but is ultimately an object that comes to signify US misunderstanding of other cultures. The rifle, transformed by events into a catalyst for pain, creates rather contrived connections which are not rooted in meaningful individual or socio-political relationships, while the text itself often speaks against its own purported message of individuals united in suffering. To give some examples, the narrative connects Richard to Abdullah, as both lose a son, and suffer due to the rifle;

however, these are very different characters who can never share a space due to cultural, ethnic, and class differences. Richard's son dies in individual, private circumstances, while Adbullah's son is a victim of the very public 'war on terror'. The circumstances of their grief are also very different. Adbullah will never be able to afford to travel abroad and take a holiday with his wife as Richard and Susan have done, while the loss of his son will bring financial as well as emotional hardship, as the role of children in the two societies differs greatly, with the Moroccan boys working to help support the family. The Moroccan children's lives could not be more different to the bourgeois Western experiences of Debbie and Mike.

The connections between the characters due to their suffering at the hands of the US authorities work better, however. Characters from both stories are disempowered because they cannot see their place in the world, and will never be able to forge alliances against an invisible enemy. The casting also works against the superficial narrative connections, and against the sense of a transnational world cinema viewer: Brad Pitt is one of Hollywood's leading stars, while Mustapha Rashidi is a non-professional previously unknown actor, and one can only assume that their pay cheques also differed greatly.[20] Audiences are more likely to give more value to the story interpreted by the actors with whom they are more familiar.

Chieko, as a middle-class teenage deaf-mute, also experiences the death of her mother, but in a very different way to the other characters, and she takes solace in friendship, drugs, and boys. Chieko's mother committed suicide (with the causes of her depression never explored), illustrating the fact that the deaths experienced by the characters are very distinct in nature. As the film shows very well, her sense of loss is linked to her loneliness and sexual insecurities. Her father may have provided the gun which sparks the narrative in the other plotlines, but the characters affected will never be more than a momentary, miscommunicated news item that appears on her television set. Thus, while her storyline is very powerful, no real ties link her to the others.

The narrative also attempts to connect Amelia's suffering with that of the other characters, but here, too, crucial differences are found in specific socio-cultural factors. She comes to lose the children she has brought up, ironically when she attends her own son's wedding, due to harsh US immigration policies. She does not see her place in the world, and her suffering is a result of her failure to consider the personal implications of these policies. Only when she is caught does she become one of the many *indocumentados*, and gain an awareness of socio-economic conditions and the lines which connect her to other illegal immigrants. As with the other characters, this is too late and she, like them, is disempowered by the melodramatic structures of the film, which claim the maximum of suffering by the characters and the audience.

The revolutionary, active audience demanded by 1960s and 1970s Latin American cinema has been replaced through the text by an implied weeping world cinema spectator, who can only watch in masochistic despair. The characters cannot create meaningful political alliances and find a way out of their predicaments, as there is no space for cognitive mapping within the diegesis. Thus, what is lacking in *Babel* for the connections to work is a political vision that explores the ways in which US power structures are played out in specific political contexts, rooted in class and cultural realities. Characters lack political agency and knowledge of their place in the world and are, thus, passive victims of circumstance.

Nevertheless, this emotional response is central to the positioning of the film as a liberal Hollywood/world cinema text, and to marketing strategies that accompany these labels. It is also central to Iñárritu's aspiration to be a world cinema auteur, freed from both the financial restrictions of the Mexican film industry and the limitations placed on directors of Hollywood mainstream films. Audiences are also rewarded with impressive cinematography and artistically crafted images of the multiple locations of the film world. Thus, *Babel* both deconstructs the tourist gaze and relies upon it, and creates an implied world cinema gaze that is central to the construction of a world cinema auteur, and for the marketing of the film. Nevertheless, the gaze is flawed, as it can work only through a universalist and melodramatic take on 'the human condition'. Iñárritu's dream of building a cinematic Tower of Babel is ultimately impossible. Esperanto failed as an international language as it lacked cultural and national roots, and *Babel* cannot provide a model for a new cinematic language for the same reason.

Notes

1 According to Iñárritu a handheld camera is used throughout the film with the exception of three scenes in which a dolly was used: the first scene, the final scene, and the scene where Yussef weeps over the death of Ahmed (García, 2006: 262).

2 For a discussion of the temporal dislocations in *Babel* see Deleyto and Azcona (2010: 50–56). They note the way that the film is 'not interested in simultaneity but in the networked nature of human life' (53).
3 Their solution is 'to rethink world cinema in three ways: as a discipline, a methodology and a perspective' (Dennison and Lim, 2006: 7).
4 For further analysis of concepts of 'world cinema' see Chaudhuri (2005), and Hill and Church Gibson (2000).
5 While this book provides a valuable source in terms of the quality of individual essays, and I am not looking to critique the quality of the book itself, it does give an insight into the use of the label in marketing terms (in this case in the discourse of academic publishing). There are chapters on the history of Hollywood, dominant American genres, and a number of chapters dedicated to an overview of national cinemas.
6 This term is used by Tom Zaniello (2007) and is discussed in the introduction of this book.
7 Cate Blanchett is Australian; however, like Naomi Watts, she has forged her career in the USA.
8 In a case of intertextual casting, Bernal and Adriana Barraza reform as a family unit, with Bernal playing Amelia's nephew Santiago; in *Amores perros* they played mother and son.
9 For more information about the company, see www.anonymouscontent.com/about. Like the other companies, it has produced popular independent features, including *Being John Malkovitch* (Jonze, 1999), *Nurse Betty* (LaBute, 2000), and *Eternal Sunshine of the Spotless Mind* (Gondry, 2004).
10 Some of the films Paramount Vantage produced include: *There Will Be Blood* (Anderson, 2007), *Into the Wild* (Penn, 2007), *A Mighty Heart* (Winterbottom, 2007); *No Country For Old Men* (Coen and Coen, 2007), and *The Duchess* (Dibb, 2008). Films funded by Media Rights include *The Invention of Lying* (Gervais and Robinson 2009), *Brüno* (Charles, 2009), and *Linha de passe* (Salles and Thomas, 2008).
11 For a full list of distribution companies, see IMDB at www.imdb.com/title/tt0449467/companycredits.
12 The film was entered in the following categories: Best Supporting Actress, Adriana Barraza; Best Original Score (which it won), Gustavo Santoalalla; Best Film Editing; Best Original Screenplay; and Achievement in Directing. The nominations and results are reported by Sciretta (2007). *Babel* won the award for Best Director at the 2007 Cannes Film Festival, and also won Best Picture at the Golden Globes of that year.
13 For review of the score and full listing of the soundtrack see www.filmtracks.com/titles/babel.html.
14 For a useful introduction to key issues in contemporary Morocco, see Entelis (1989).
15 I am grateful to Walid Benkhaled for this observation.
16 The blogger adds, 'Other friends have also noted the fact that much of

the dialogue sounds like English (or Spanish) translated directly into Darija – meaning, of course, that much of the Moroccan characters' speech is inauthentic' (York, 2007).

17 For an analysis of the use of melodrama in *Babel*, see Laura Podalsky (2011). She argues that the film has its roots in the Mexican tradition of melodrama, and, in contrast with my argument here, succeeds in creating transnational communities of feeling. Her paper, entitled 'Migrant Feelings', was initially presented at a panel at the 2010 Society for Cinema and Media Studies conference along with my paper on *Babel* in which I summarised some of the ideas here, and our different readings sparked lively debate.

18 'Babel', Box Office Mojo [n.d]. Retrieved from http://boxofficemojo.com/movies/?id=babel.htm.

19 For another reading that critiques the ethnic radicalism of the film, see Hassapopoulou (2008).

20 It is also significant that Pitt was active in the promotion of the film at international film festivals, and on posters and DVD covers, while, as is to be expected, the Moroccan actors were entirely absent.

PART III

Alfonso Cuarón: a study of auteurism in flux

7

Alfonso Cuarón's first films in Mexico and the USA

Sólo con tu pareja: bringing the middle classes back to Mexican cinemas

Alfonso Cuarón's filmmaking career has many parallels to that of Guillermo del Toro and Alejandro González Iñárritu. All have made a first film in Mexico, before consolidating their careers in the USA. The difference between Cuarón's trajectory and that of the other two directors is that he is the only one who has returned to Mexico to make a film – *Y tu mamá también* (2001) – and this transnational nationally successful film came after, not before, success in the USA, as were the cases with del Toro and Iñárritu. Cuarón's first film, *Sólo con tu pareja* (*Love in the Time of Hysteria*, 1991), was a national hit, but did not have the necessary ingredients or support to be a global success. The film is a light, screwball comedy which tells the story of Tomás Tomás (Daniel Giménez Cacho), a serial womaniser, who undergoes a character transformation when he is tricked into believing he is HIV positive, in an act of revenge by a doctor's assistant who is one of his conquests and victims. *Sólo con tu pareja*, along with other key films of the early 1990s, signalled a commercial turn in Mexican filmmaking, via a shift to more audience-friendly productions by serious filmmakers. In this it can be compared to other films with commercial ambitions made in that period, such as *Como agua para chocolate* (*Like Water For Chocolate*) (Arau, 1991) and *Cronos* (1993), and, a little later, *Sexo, pudor y lágrimas* (*Sex, Shame and Tears*) (Serrano, 1998).[1] This commercial turn led the way for the transnational impact of *Amores perros* and *Y tu mamá también*.

Prior to the 1990s, the national cinematic culture was divided between low-budget popular films for which commercial success rested on sex and violence (Rashkin, 2001: 14–15), and art films deemed worthy of sponsorship by the Mexican Film Institute (Instituto Mexicano de Cinematografía, IMCINE), which were not required to make big profits. Popularity was stigmatised due to the quality of the films which drew large audiences. In the words of Juan Carlos Vargas (2002), these were characterised by:

> populistic films of the lowest quality possible, repeating worn out formulas in a cinema of whorehouse themes, sexual innuendo filled comedies and narcotics dealer films, thus eliminating the possibility of a competitive commercial cinema, with a sense of worth, in a market dominated by Hollywood.[2]

The new commercial cinema was aimed at the urban middle classes, and succeeded in bringing them back into the movie theatres (Zavala, 2011), a phenomenon helped by the development of modern multiplexes in major urban centres from 1994, when the US chain Cinemark opened its first cinemas (indeed, multiplexes opened throughout modern cities in Latin America) (Ross, 2010: 74–85; Sánchez Prado, 2010). This succeeded in consolidating cinema-going as an urban middle-class activity, due to the location of the complexes in the major cities, and the fact that the rise in ticket prices was dramatic, jumping from 10–15 pesos to 40 pesos, thus putting ticket price out of the reach of those on low incomes (Sánchez Prado, 2010). Miriam Ross notes that, in most cases, throughout Latin America, piracy is the sole means for those on low incomes to gain access to films (Ross, 2010: 163).[3]

Sólo con tu pareja can be seen to have spearheaded this new direction in filmmaking that would appeal to the urban middle classes, despite the fact that it was made just before the advent of multiplex-ready cinematic products. As Miriam Haddu (2005: 79) argues, 'with *Sólo con tu pareja*, Cuarón constructs a new image of the young *chilango*, as hip, independent, fun loving and cosmopolitan; a Mexican ready for the twenty-first century'.[4] According to Lauro Zavala there are certain key thematic and formal tendencies of the best-known films of this period, most of which were produced under the nationally funded 'first director' scheme.[5] He identifies identity, eroticism, and humour as key markers of films of this period (Zavala, 2011), which, it can be argued, are traits established by the national success of Cuarón's first feature. Del Toro succeeded in reinvigorating horror for Mexican audiences and, likewise, Cuarón introduces a Mexican take on the screwball comedy to Mexican middle-class audiences with *Sólo con tu pareja*.

Ignacio Sánchez Prado (2010) makes this point, and argues that Cuarón's early film is the first example of a movie featuring the neo-liberal middle classes, citing the primacy of advertising within the narrative (Tomás is an advertising executive). In this, *Sólo con tu pareja* can be distinguished from other dominant forms, namely melodrama and social realist films. It also provides a more conservative take on sexuality, and in this it stands in contrast to more challenging representations of marginal sexuality previously seen in films by auteurist art cinema directors, such as Arturo Ripstein's *El lugar sin límites* (*Place Without Limits*, 1978) and Jaime Humberto Hermosillo's *Doña Herlinda y su hijo* (*Doña Herlinda and Her Son*, 1985) and *La tarea* (*Homework*, 1991).[6]

So, what was it about this film that managed to bring the middle classes back to the cinema? According to the screenwriter (and brother of the director) Carlos Cuarón, until this film there had not been a Mexican take on the screwball comedy, a well established and popular US genre, which cine-literate Mexican viewers would be familiar with. Both Carlos and Alfonso cite Blake Edwards's and Ernst Lubitsch's screwball comedies as sources of inspiration and say, in an interview presented among the extra features on the DVD release of *Sólo con tu pareja*, that the film was made for a contemporary urban middle-class Mexican audience. They update and localise the formula in a number of ways: they set it in Mexico City and cast local actors; they deal, albeit in a comic tone, with the subject matter of AIDS; and they feature a fair amount of nudity and sex. Finally, according to the director (DVD extras interview), they make the first mainstream film with characters speaking in Mexico City slang, *Chilango*, a practice famously continued in *Y tu mamá también*. The characters are all from a professional middle class, with a new breed of modern Mexican as the protagonist, an employee of an advertising company, whose job is to write slogans for advertisements. The characters also fit within a fair-skinned racial ideal of the Euro-Mexican, with whiteness a central component of social mobility in Mexico (Vigil and López, 2004). Darker-skinned mestizo Mexicans are almost entirely absent from this production, and appear only briefly, in the role of the folkloric mariachi bands. Indeed, the female objects of Tomás's desire, Silvia, Clarisa (figure 7.1) and Gloria (figure 7.2),[7] correspond to a fair-skinned Euro-Mexican ideal.

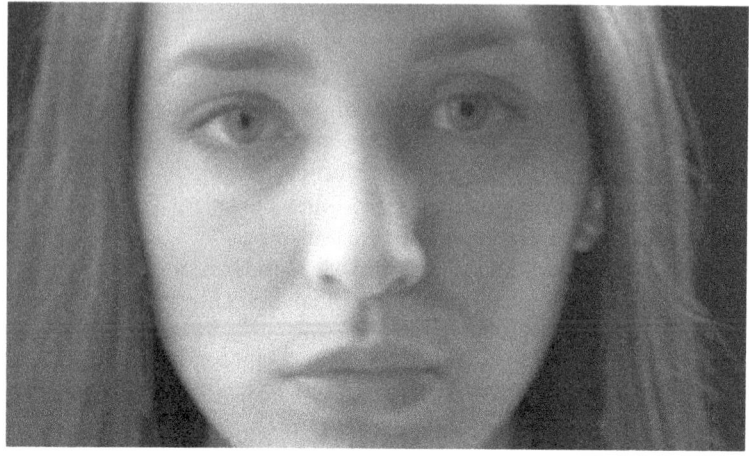

7.1 Clarisa (Claudia Ramírez), the air hostess in *Sólo con tu pareja*

7.2 Gloria (Isabel Benet), Tomás's boss and occasional lover in *Sólo con tu pareja*

Another way the film appeals to urban middle-class audiences is through the representation of women. The virgin/whore paradigm which characterised 'golden age' Mexican filmmaking has been replaced by modern, professional, independent women, who broadly correspond to a post-feminist model. Gloria and Silvia are single and live alone, and do not depend on a man for financial security, yet they are sexually liberated, as seen in their willingness to have sex with Tomás with no need for seduction on his part. Andrea Noble has commented on the centrality of the prostitute in Mexican culture, stating 'the importance of the prostitute as an enduring figure in Mexican literature and culture cannot be overstated' (Noble, 2005: 117), yet, as seen, these female characters overwrite the figure of the prostitute, with sexuality a key part of the modern female identity in the Cuarón brothers' filmic universe. This is a point made by Miriam Haddu, who notes:

> The sexually active women in *Sólo con tu pareja* are neither whores nor femme fatales, as would have been the case in the portrayal of sexual women in Golden Age urban dramas and films belonging to the *cabaretera* genre. (Haddu, 2005: 81)

Nevertheless, while Haddu argues that these representations correspond to the advance of feminism in Mexico (2005: 81), I argue they are products of a male fantasy, and cannot be seen as stemming from a feminist tradition; rather, their insatiable desires for Tomás are a product of male heterosexual wishful thinking. While they may reflect the figure of the sexually liberated working Mexican woman, neither Gloria nor Silvia is seen in a professional capacity. Clarisa's training as an air hostess is fetishised by Tomás as he voyeuristically watches her practise her safety procedures at home. Silvia unprofessionally falsifies Tomás's HIV results as an act of revenge, and Gloria is more interested in taking her employee to bed than hearing the latest slogans for 'jalapeños Gómez'.

The model of the modern, sexually active woman is given a feminist slant in *Y tu mamá también*, as will be seen, but while the creation of professional sexually liberated female characters may be post-feminist, the fact that their identities revolve around a man is pre-feminist. This is perhaps best illustrated in the fact that the woman of his dreams, Clarisa, wants to kill herself when she discovers her boyfriend has been cheating on her, and then, once her affections have shifted to Tomás (in the same day), tells him she will kill him if he leaves her. This is, of course, all at the service of humour, but the humour relies on partially supporting the Don Juan (or Don Giovanni) myth it is supposed to be deconstructing.[8] The film does partially deconstruct the figure of the hyper-sexual macho, and shows him to be both ridiculous and racked with anxiety and hypochondria; yet, every attractive woman he meets finds him irresistible and comes to place him at the centre of her world. Thus, the film appeals to a wide demographic through its representation of male and female characters by offering images of modernity that remain within safe, conservative gender paradigms.

This form of combining modernity with a conservative approach to sexuality can also be seen in the way the film represents AIDS. In the DVD extras interview with Alfonso Cuarón, the director claims that there was a serious reason for dealing with AIDS at a time when the subject was met with homophobic jokes and associated exclusively with male homosexuality. The topical nature of the film can be seen in the fact that the title was adopted from a government slogan for CONASIDA, the government-run AIDS agency in Mexico. Its slogan was 'Sólo con tu pareja o usa condón' ('Only with your partner or use a condom') (DVD extras interview). The director claims that he and Carlos wanted to show that anyone can contract the disease. This is a noble sentiment; however, in the film AIDS is a narrative device to generate humour, and no more. Tomás reveals to his doctor friend who is at a party that he has AIDS via his pager, and Silvia confesses to falsifying the result of the tests. This is one of the central comic moments in the film, as the guests at the dinner table collapse in laughter. When Tomás falsely believes he is HIV positive, his response is hardly an example to sufferers of the condition: he decides to kill himself. The humour is generated through his initial decision to put his head in a microwave, with the idea coming from a newspaper story of a 'gringa' who killed her French poodle by cooking it in the microwave. The film also does not distinguish between HIV and AIDS: when his test is HIV positive, Tomás announces that he has AIDS. The main point is that, despite Tomás's sexual promiscuity, he is not HIV positive, which rather goes against the intended message that anyone can contract the disease. The sense given is that not only has Tomás escaped unscathed from his refusal to wear a condom when having sex with countless women, but that ultimately he is rewarded with the final conquest of the woman of his dreams and marries Clarisa. This is a mainstream comedy that does not challenge gender relations or social attitudes towards HIV and AIDS.

Another area in which the film relies on a reactionary form of representation is in the portrayal of the Japanese characters, which relies on crude cultural stereotypes. Despite the fact that they are attending a medical conference, audiences only ever see them as tourists. They are frequently drunk, constantly grinning, and they take photographs of everything they see. They speak pidgin English and Japanese, and thus remain largely incomprehensible to Mexican audiences. Their only role in the narrative appears to be to generate humour through their presence: they are meant to be funny simply because they are stereotypical Japanese men.

This populist fare is scored with a classical soundtrack of Mozart's music mixed with some popular, romantic Mexican music. The cinematography and the soundtrack coupled with Tomás's escapades blend together high and low cultural formats, and raise the artistic status of a crude sex comedy. One scene which illustrates this is a wedding of an old conquest of Tomás. Here there is the only example of a long take, in the form of a tracking shot, a technique Cuarón and cinematographer Emmanuel Lubezki would develop in *Y tu mamá también* and *Children of Men*, as will be seen (chapters 8 and 9). The long take reveals children playing and running accompanied by the Mozart soundtrack; there is then a cut to Tomás having sex with the bride in her wedding dress, and one of the boys shoots his water pistol at them in a phallic gag. Mozart's score and the quality of the cinematography, which focuses on delicious-looking food and lush green vegetation, take what is rather crude in narrative terms to a higher level, and this is an approach which is applied throughout the film, through music and mise-en-scène.

The images of the city in *Sólo con tu pareja* also represent an important shift within Mexican cinema, as Miriam Haddu (2005) has argued. She notes that, until Cuarón's film, dominant representations from both the golden age to films of the 1990s focus on the *arrabales* (the slums), the poor inhabitants, and the troubles they face, while bourgeois Mexicans are the object of criticism (Haddu, 2005: 72–79).[9] In contrast, *Sólo con tu pareja* presents a modern, stylish metropolis marked by the absence of poverty in terms of both location and people. Cuarón has said that Mexico City is a character in the film (DVD extras interview), and audiences do indeed see a number of national landmarks: the Ángel de la Independencia (the Angel of

Independence), the Plaza Garibaldi, and the Torre Latinoamericana (the Latin-American Tower).[10] The fact that the Torre Latinoamericana, one of Mexico City's tallest buildings, is chosen as the site for the attempted suicide of Clarisa and Tomás is significant. As Haddu (2005: 83) argues, this choice of location allows for the numerous aerial shots which project a modern and dynamic city and speak of the development of the country, in contrast to previous representations of poverty and underdevelopment:

> The Torre Latinoamericana is one of Mexico City's largest skyscrapers and as such is symbolic of the modern nation's state of progress, and to an extent, of the capital city itself. (Haddu, 2005: 83)

However, what audiences are not shown is equally significant. There are no busy street scenes, no images of poor, urban citizens, and the affluent lifestyle of Tomás and the doctor is protected from the poverty, pollution, and over-population of the streets of Mexico City. The mise-en-scène reproduces a middle-class aspirational lifestyle. In fact, most of the shots in this film are of interiors, and most of the action takes place in Tomás's smart, modern bachelor pad, and the lush apartment of his doctor friend and neighbour, Mateo Mateos (Luis de Icaza), and his wife, Teresa de Teresa (played by the well known Mexican singer Astrid Hadad), as seen in figure 7.3.

7.3 Gloria waits for Tomás in Dr Mateos's apartment in *Sólo con tu pareja*

This is a gorgeous interior that, like the wedding scene, communicates wealth and privilege, and, as with the classical score, has the function of raising the cultural status of this bawdy sex comedy, which again explains its middle-class appeal. The look of the room, with its green walls, classical antique furnishings, golden lighting, and indoor foliage, will come to define Cuarón's style in the three films of his 'green period', *Sólo con tu pareja, A Little Princess* and *Great Expectations*, as will be seen.

In the parts I and II of this book, on del Toro and Iñárritu, I have turned to their first Mexican film to argue that they have made transnational national works that have laid down thematic and stylistic markers for their subsequent film careers outside Mexico. It is useful here to return to two categories of transnational cinema that I have outlined in the introduction to analyse the contrasts with Cuarón's first feature film. There is clearly evidence of transnational cultural influences seen in the reference to Mozart, and to Lubitsch's and Edwards's screwball comedies, while Haddu (2005: 82) cites the influence of Almodóvar's Spanish take on these comedies. Nevertheless, the film does not engage with transnational modes of narration in the way that I have described in the chapters on *Cronos* and *Amores perros*.

In order to assess the reasons for this it is useful to examine points made by Núria Triana-Toribio in her book *Spanish National Cinema*. The author identifies sex comedies as the most popular form of national filmmaking in Spain in the same period (the early 1990s) (Triana-Toribio, 2003: 152), and notes that these films, which eschewed the respected tradition of quality, did very well at the national box office, yet were not exported to foreign markets. The reasons she gives are a lack of political correctness and an unwillingness to consider art cinema audiences, to whom foreign-language releases are shown (154). Triana-Toribio states, 'these films aim to appear as resolutely Spanish as possible through a popular idiom that makes them inexportable' (154). I would argue that similar reasons can be given for the failure of *Sólo con tu pareja* to break into global markets, as seen in the film's regressive representation of women, the superficial and potentially offensive treatment of AIDS, the crude humour, and the stereotypical representations of its Japanese characters. That is not to say that some US mainstream cinema of the 1990s is not as guilty of these forms of representations; however, foreign-language releases are largely confined to art cinema circuits, and *Sólo con tu pareja* does not fit within the auteurist quality films screened at these cinemas.

The fact that the film does not employ a transnational mode of narration in that it is not suitable for art cinema programmers is also linked to the film's inability to enter transnational distribution and exhibition networks, despite the director's ambitions. This can be illustrated by the fact that Cuarón had sold the distribution rights to Miramax, which subsequently reneged on the deal (Krassakopoulos, 2007), no doubt for the reasons I have outlined above. Cuarón's reflections on the production process and the ways in which he saw this limiting the success of the film are illuminating, as they reveal the restrictions that many directors saw with national funding strategies. The film was funded by IMCINE, the Mexican film institute, as part of programmes designed to support the first work of aspiring new directors (Zavala, 2011). While these schemes are admirable in their support they offer, the model was not one that could contain Cuarón's global ambitions. He critiques what he views as IMCINE's paternalistic attitude and lack of business model, seen in its failure to connect with publicity agents (Fernández, 2001):

> Yo tenía claro que quería comercializar la película en México y en el mundo. Pero uno de los funcionarios de Imcine me dijo que yo era tonto y arrogante, porque el cine mexicano no le interesaba a nadie fuera del país. Tuvimos muchos pleitos. (Fernández, 2001)
>
> I was clear that I wanted to sell the film in Mexico and throughout the world. But one of the officials at Imcine told me that I was stupid and arrogant because Mexican cinema didn't interest anyone outside Mexico. We had many arguments. [My translation]

He reiterates the lack of commercial vision of IMCINE in a master class given to film students in Greece, and, when discussing *Sólo con tu pareja*, says, 'I wanted my films to travel. I didn't want them just to be for here. I wanted something to be part of a world community' (Krassakopoulos, 2007). According to the director, these rows resulted in him being told that if he continued to be difficult he would find it hard to work again (Fernández, 2001). As I have argued, the content of the film had as much to do with the fact that these global ambitions were not realised as the approach taken by IMCINE. Nevertheless, while the film failed to make the international impact hoped for by the director, it did pave the way to Hollywood when it was seen at the Toronto Film Festival, to which the director took it independently. Here, the film attracted the attention of agents who, once in the USA, showed it to

Sydney Pollack (the well known actor, producer, and director), and he began developing projects with Cuarón (Krassakopoulos, 2007).[11] It is worth noting that in recent years the role of IMCINE has changed, with new commercial directions introduced by our three case studies, among others. The Institute has accepted a co-habitation with private finance, and now provides partial funding to film projects which have already secured funds. Indeed, by the end of the 1990s filmmakers would not be funded unless they had raised 80 per cent of the cost of a film (Hershfield and Maciel, 1999: 289).

As was the case with *Cronos*, the film was released on DVD in 2006, also by Criterion (but only in a region 1 format), thanks to the subsequent achievements of Cuarón, who had by then directed *A Little Princess* (1995), *Great Expectations* (1998), and *Y tu mamá también* (2001), as well as *Harry Potter and the Prisoner of Azkaban* (2004). Nevertheless, despite the director's curriculum, it did not see commercial success, and at the time of writing was placed at number 6,828 in Criterion's all-time sales rank.[12] It was also released on one screen by IFC films in the USA in 2006, at the IFC Centre in Greenwich Village (Scott, 2006), and its taking amounted to a paltry $9,915 according to Box Office Mojo, illustrating that the lack of success was not due only to problems of distribution, but also to the nature of the film. In a review for *The Village Voice*, Michael Atkinson (2006) comments on the fact that the film was not released in the USA at the time it was made, and writes that 'sometimes the culture's natural selection is on the money the first time around'. He notes the sexist representations in the film, and summarises his review with the following comment: 'The film is more stale than crisp, with dialogue that is at least 50 percent old aphorisms, homilies, and clichés. The frankness and sophistication of *Y Tu Mamá* were, it seems, hard earned.'

It is interesting to compare the lack of international success of *Sólo con tu pareja* with the only globally successful film of this period, *Como agua para chocolate*, which was made in the same year as Cuarón's film, but released internationally two years later. While *Como agua para chocolate* also had a conservative approach to gender relations, the film applies the proven formulae of magical realism and fairytale romance to present a tourist-eye view of Mexico (Shaw, 2003: 36–51). With *Y tu mamá también* (the subject of chapter 8) Cuarón shows that he has learnt the lessons of failure in terms of the global distribution of his first film, thanks to increased experience and a period working in Hollywood, as will be seen.

Not such great expectations: working within the Hollywood system

Four years after making *Sólo con tu pareja*, Cuarón began his Hollywood career with *A Little Princess* (1995). With this and *Great Expectations*, made three years later, the director attempted to carve out a name for himself by forging a personal style, with the help of cinematographer Emmanuel Lubezki. Yet he was often frustrated with the lack of creative freedom, in contrast to that afforded to him when working in Mexico. In this section, through a focus on *Great Expectations*, I explore Cuarón's distinctive use of colour and mise-en-scène, and examine the purposes they serve in pursuing auteurist ambitions. I also outline the tensions generated when these ambitions come into conflict with studio pressures, and use the analysis here to set up the discussion in the following chapters, on *Y tu mamá también* and *Children of Men*, made when the director was finally able to work on internationally successful films true to the vision he had for them, and leave behind his status as director-for-hire.

Great Expectations was produced by the independent company Art Linson Productions and Twentieth Century Fox and starred Gwyneth Paltrow, Ethan Hawke, Anne Bancroft, and Robert De Niro, among others. This may have seemed like a dream for a director with the type of global ambitions mentioned above; however, the freedoms that the director had with his first Mexican film were seriously curtailed. Cuarón has commented on the difficulties experienced with *Great Expectations*, and, as is the case with all directors with auteurist ambitions, the main gripe was with the lack of creative control. As he tells George Krassakopoulos (2007): 'it was a very difficult experience because I didn't like the interference of the studio; the studio was interfering a lot and I didn't like the process. I felt like I was doing a film that I was not fully controlling.' The script was incomplete as shooting started and Cuarón did not have the input into the script that he enjoys in his collaborations with his brother Carlos. He claims that the producers disagreed with his take on the representation of class, insisted that class was not a problem in the USA, and changed the original script (Lawrenson, 2002).

This is rather a problematic omission in a text based on a novel in which class is the central theme, and the quality of the screenplay resulted in some of the less favourable reviews. The popular reviewer Roger Ebert (1998), writing in the *Chicago Sun*, comments that the screenplay by Mitch Glazer has an overemphasis on romance; in his words, 'the moment this movie declares itself as being mostly about affairs of the heart, it limits its potential'. The critic, nonetheless, praises the visual quality of the film, writing of the painterly quality in Lubezki's use of lighting. In a similar vein, Janet Maslin (1998), in a review for the *New York Times*, also praises Cuarón as a 'voluptuous visual stylist', while criticising what she sees as a weak screenplay. As noted by the critics, the director and cinematographer thus make their mark through lush visuals, expert cinematography, and the attempt to create a coherent visual style through the recurrent use of the colour green in the film. Cuarón explains that he was enticed to the project by the stars on board, such as De Niro, and tried to make the best of a bad decision: 'we started shooting and the script was not working and we started overcompensating with form, with visuals. Whatever was not in the page, we tried to convey it with visuals' (Krassakopoulos, 2007).

There is a clear visual parallel here with the mise-en-scène in Dr Mateos's apartment in *Sólo con tu pareja* (see figure 7.3), with an emphasis on the colour green, an opulent and lush decor, and cluttered rooms filled with antiques, despite the fact that the scene in *Great Expectations* represents wealth in decay.

There is not space for a full analysis of *A Little Princess*, but it is worth mentioning that this film shares many aspects of the look that Cuarón and Lubezki had cultivated in their earlier two films. The children all wear green uniforms in the boarding school, the walls are all painted green, and there are many examples of highly stylised interiors (figure 7.4). This is a film that exudes quality, and the effect achieved is that of a classic children's novel (*A Little Princess* was written by Frances Hodgson Burnett) in the hands of a master filmmaker.

It is interesting to examine Cuarón's decision to use a green colour palette for his first three films – *Sólo con tu pareja*, *A Little Princess* and *Great Expectations* – as it can illuminate his auteurist ambitions, and the desire to make a mark within studio constraints. In an interview he has said the following:

> something what [sic] we had in common in these films is that everything was green. In those first three films, everything, absolutely everything, costumes, props, everything was absolutely green and that was part of enhancing that universe. (Krassakopoulos, 2007)

However, what constitutes 'that universe' is less clear; Cuarón himself has said that he does not know what the colour stands for, other than

7.4 Sara Crewe's (Liesel Matthews) room is magically transformed in *A Little Princess*

the fact that it conveys a strong emotion. The colour green was chosen by chance for a television programme he was filming for *La Hora Marcada*, a show for Mexican television (Krassakopoulos, 2007).[13] While this was an unconscious choice, he and Lubezki then chose it deliberately for the next three films. Of this the director says, 'Why? I don't know. I just know that each color carries an emotion and for us that was the kind of emotional palette that we wanted' (Krassakopoulos, 2007). This vagueness is also conveyed in the interview with Alfonso Cuarón on the DVD extras for *Sólo con tu pareja*. Here, he simply says that he did not feel comfortable with any colour other than green, while his brother Carlos compares this choice of colour palette with Picasso's periods determined by colour, and says the only reason for it is the whim of the director. The reference to Picasso is revealing, as it points to the supposition that this colour was chosen consistently due to auteurist motivations. What is most likely is that Cuarón and Lubezki were seeking to cultivate an identifiable style in projects in which they had limited creative input, following the making of *Sólo con tu pareja*. The fact that the use of this colour was abandoned with the filming of their autonomous text *Y tu mamá también* and with their auteurist project *Children of Men*, in which there was no studio interference, illustrates this point neatly.

All of this supports the idea of Cuarón as unable to escape the status of director-for-hire in his Hollywood career prior to the return to Mexico, and his need to make a film that had an authorial stamp on it beyond a sophisticated use of mise-en-scène. *Great Expectations* can be seen as a prestige picture that belongs somewhere between Iñárritu's independent feature *21 Grams* and del Toro's more mainstream and commercial *Hellboy II*.[14] This is largely thanks to the classic status of Dickens's source text and the visual style cultivated, yet this is not a film which the director can be proud of, as seen through his statements in interviews and discussion of the conflicts that occurred while making it.

It is not without significance that class becomes a central concern of *Y tu mamá también*, and, as will be seen in the following chapter, the director takes an entirely different stylistic approach to filmmaking in that film. This career choice demonstrates a paring down of finance and scale in return for the artistic freedom to make a personal film. It is enlightening to make comparisons with the trajectories of Iñárritu and del Toro, as it demonstrates the importance of establishing an auteurist identity *before* seeking work in the US film industry if a director is to be allowed to consolidate that identity with his/her subsequent films. In contrast to Cuarón, Iñárritu had his big global hit before seeking work in the USA, and he thus had a higher status, which allowed him to retain directorial independence, and secure a contract with the independent production company Focus Features for *21 Grams*. However, like del Toro, Cuarón's Mexican debut produced a film that was too little known, and in Cuarón's case too lightweight, to allow him this type of independence. Also, as with del Toro, this status would have to be won with a Spanish-language film made away from Hollywood structures.

Looking at their respective trajectories from this careerist point of view, *Y tu mamá también* becomes Cuarón's equivalent to del Toro's *El espinazo del diablo*. Commercial ambitions thus take Cuarón to Hollywood, but auteurist ambitions are behind his return to Mexico, where he can make a film with complete creative freedom. It can be argued, following this, that the director was awarded the degree of independence he had with *Children of Men* thanks to *Y tu mamá también*, as here he proves that he can make a commercially viable independent film that plays very well on the art cinema circuit.

Notes

1 *Sexo, pudor y lágrimas* broke all box office statistics up to that point for a Mexican film. It took in excess of 118 million pesos (around $11.8 million) and had an audience of five million (Vargas, 2002); this figure is likely to be much higher with piracy taken into account.
2 'Narco cinema', which focuses on the exploits of drug dealers and traffickers, is a good example of popular national cinema: it is a low-budget form outside of global film circulations models; see Williams (2011).
3 Ross (2010: 156–170) has an excellent analysis of piracy in South America.
4 *Chilango* is a slang term used to refer to those who are from or live in Mexico City.
5 Key films of the 1990s cited by Zavala and made under this scheme include, alongside *Sólo con tu pareja*, *La mujer de Benjamín* (Carrera, 1991), *Mi querido Tom Mix* (Agraz, 1992), *Novia que te vea* (Schyfter, 1994), *Cronos* (del Toro, 1993), *Tequila* (Gámez, 1994), *Un beso a esta tierra* (Goldberg Lerner, 1994), *Dos crímenes* (Schneider, 1995), *Entre Pancho Villa y una mujer desnuda* (Berman and Tardán, 1995), *Sobrenatural* (Gruener, 1996), *Bajo California: el límite del tiempo* (Bolado, 1999), *Santitos* (Springall, 1999), *Del olvido al no me acuerdo* (Rulfo, 1999), *Rito terminal* (Urrutia Lazo, 1999), and *Sexo, pudor y lágrimas* (Serrano, 1998).
6 More positive, confident representations of homosexuality can be seen in the recent work of Julián Hernández.
7 It is worth noting that Gloria's surname is Gold, which suggests that she is Jewish, although this identity is not alluded to beyond her surname.
8 Cuarón explains in 'Making *Sólo con tu pareja*' among the DVD extras that one of the inspirations for the original idea came from Mozart's Don Giovanni. Mozart's comic opera is about the eponymous promiscuous nobleman who is dragged to Hell after refusing to change his womanising ways. In Cuarón's commercial domestic feature, Tomás is saved from this, changes his ways, and has his happy ending with Clarisa.
9 Some golden age films from the *arrabal* genre which Haddu cites are *Nosotros los pobres* (*We the Poor*, 1948), *Ustedes los ricos* (*You the Rich*, 1948), and *Pepe el toro* (*Pepe the Bull*) (1953), all directed by Ismael Rodríguez. Films from the 1990s she mentions include *Lolo* (Athié, 1991), *Angel de fuego* (*Angel of Fire*) (Rotberg, 1992) and, later, *De la calle* (*Streeters*) (Tort, 2001).
10 In keeping with the crude tone of much of the film, a drunken Dr Mateos celebrates the fact that the statue of the Angel of Independence is the only angel 'with boobs'. He says this in English for the benefit of his Japanese guests.
11 The film was shown internationally only at the time of release at the Toronto and Chicago Film Festivals. See IMDB (www.imdb.com/title/tt0102958/releaseinfo).

12 Information taken from www.dvdempire.com/exec/v4_item.asp?item_id =1184495.
13 Cuarón made six or seven shows for *La Hora Marcada*, a Mexican take on the US series *The Twilight Zone*, that the makers termed the Toilet Zone because of the low budget ('Making *Sólo con tu pareja*'). Interestingly, del Toro also directed several episodes between 1986 and 1989, as IMDB reveals (www.imdb.com/name/nm0868219/#Director).
14 I am grateful to the series editors, Núria Triana Toribio and Andy Willis, for this point.

8

Cuarón finds his own path: *Y tu mamá también*

The only film over which Cuarón had full creative control before making *Y tu mamá también* (2001) was *Sólo con tu pareja* (*Love in the Time of Hysteria*, 1991); both films were co-written with his brother Carlos Cuarón. As seen, *Sólo con tu pareja* is a domestic film, a national film that lacked the backing and the ingredients to become a global success. Nevertheless, what Cuarón learnt from the experience of the filmmaking and the production, distribution, and exhibition processes is that, with the right kind of film, and a new marketing strategy, the middle classes can continue to be lured back to the cinemas in large numbers, while foreign audiences can also be targeted.

This was achieved by applying and developing some of the key elements of *Sólo con tu pareja* to his next Mexican film, *Y tu mamá también*, namely a focus on sex, a comic critique of the excesses of Mexican machismo, and the incorporation and reworking of generic tropes. Importantly, experience taught Alfonso and Carlos to lose some of the more politically incorrect elements, which would deter investment from international sales agents with an eye on potential foreign-language/art cinema film audiences. The one-dimensional, sex-obsessed female characters of the earlier film are dispensed with, and the film features Luisa (Maribel Verdú), whose gynocentric manifesto replaces the teenage, male manifesto of Tenoch (Diego Luna) and Julio (Gael García Bernal). The exclusively 'white' focus on the bourgeois characters of *Sólo con tu pareja* is also, to a degree, decentred through the camera's focus on the 'other', mestizo Mexico; while the characters' failure to see this Mexico becomes a central theme of the film. To this was added a focus on youth culture, the sexual allure of the rising stars García Bernal and Luna, and the established Spanish actress Maribel Verdú.

What is perhaps central when considering the international appeal of the film is that it presents a traveller-friendly view of Mexico that corresponds to expectations of the commercial end of the foreign-language film market. With *Y tu mamá también* Cuarón had finally made a Mexican film that could be sold both nationally and in the global market, and, along with *Amores perros*, it became the stand-out Mexican box office hit of the start of the twenty-first century. No Mexican film, aside from *Rudo y cursi* (*Rough and Corny*) (Carlos Cuarón, 2008), has seen the type of global success achieved by these two films, perhaps because Iñárritu, Cuarón, and del Toro, whose transnational travels have taught them how to create globally marketable products, have not since returned to make films in Mexico.

The fact that *Y tu mamá también* was made after experiences in the USA, where Cuarón directed *A Little Princess* (1995) and *Great Expectations* (1998), is also important to consider when looking at the new directions taken by the film. It can be seen as a reaction against working practices he had to adopt within the American film industry, and it both undermines and borrows from US culture, seen in the simultaneous subversion and dependence on tropes of US road movies and sex comedies. In contrast to the large industrial context and big production values of his US films, *Y tu mamá también* is an intimate film, with a small, tight cast and crew, and the process of making the film is described by the director as 'like going on a road trip with your family' (Basoli, 2002: 30). This allowed the director the type of control not permissible within an American studio film. In another interview, Cuarón summarises the difference clearly:

> In Hollywood every crew member's job is specialised – you have a guy who's in charge of placing an ashtray, and he's the best in the business – but here there was a degree of improvisation. And the other big difference here was that I was also the producer, which left me free to make every decision. (Lawrenson, 2002)

Interestingly, Cuarón claims an auteurist status with his return to Mexico, by not continuing in the tradition that he had established for himself, as no clear artistic identity had emerged beyond a lavish and stylish use of mise-en-scène in the director-for-hire role he had with *Little Princess* and *Great Expectations*. In *Y tu mamá también* the focus on the colour green was dispensed with, as were some of the dominant modes of Hollywood filmic storytelling he had mastered while working in the USA. In an interview he talks of his desire to reject dominant mainstream cinematic techniques he had previously used, such as dollies, dissolves, and close-ups, to make a more documentary, realist-style film (Fernández, 2001). The implication of the choice of such an approach is that there is a truthful vision of Mexico which the director will reveal to audiences all over the world, an idea I return to and question.

Based on techniques developed with *Y tu mamá también* and continued with *Children of Men* (2006), Cuarón has become known as a director who favours long takes, and, with the help of his director of photography, Emmanuel Lubezki, has carved out his auteurist reputation on the basis of this approach to editing. This stands in contrast to his Hollywood features, *A Little Princess*, *Great Expectations*, and *Harry Potter and the Prisoner of Azkaban*, in which conventional continuity editing is rigorously applied, with average shot lengths of 5–6 seconds (Udden, 2009: 29), well within the norm for most mainstream filmmaking. This drastically alters in *Y tu mamá también*, which has average shot lengths of 19.6 seconds (Udden, 2009: 29).[1]

Cuarón's comments on the filmmaking process in the production notes of *Y tu mamá también* reveal a conscious decision to react against his previous Hollywood films as part of an attempt to regain directorial control and identity:

> What I really felt like doing was a movie that was completely different from what I've been doing, something that came from a more realistic reference point. So I decided to change my point of view on everything – from the way the story is told to the way it should look. I'd been talking to 'el Chivo' (cinematographer and long-time collaborator Emmanuel Lubezki) about making something like this ever since we finished shooting GREAT EXPECTATIONS.[2]

In addition to long takes, *Y tu mamá también* is characterised by a camera that deviates from expected paths and wide panoramic shots of the landscape, with Cuarón and Lubezki developing a new personal style that they carry over to *Children of Men*. James Udden argues convincingly that the long take is key to raising the status of the director to auteurist levels, and has more to do with this than a Bazinian quest for phenomenological reality (Udden, 2009: 27).[3] He notes that, following the tradition of art cinema directors such as Michelangelo Antonioni, 'the long take occasionally has emerged as a marker of aesthetic and authorial distinction even within the Hollywood system' (27), where it has been embraced by directors such as Paul Thomas

Anderson and Gus Van Sant (39–40). Thus, for Cuarón this approach to shooting and editing was favoured to recast himself as an auteur. Publicity material by *Children of Men*'s producers Universal Pictures chose to announce Cuarón as director of *Y tu mamá también* rather than mention his role with his previous US, more commercial films. The fact that a major studio chose to highlight this low-budget feature over his big Hollywood films shows that the choice to make a personal Spanish-language film with complete creative control had enhanced the director's status. This stylistic approach to editing adopted by Cuarón and Lubezki has become the foundation on which they are choosing to build their auteurist reputations. Early press reports on their new film *Gravity*, in post-production at the time of writing (March 2011), and due for release in 2013, indicate that the opening sequence will be a single take 20 minutes long (Roary, 2010).

Despite the distinction I have made between films such as *Y tu mamá también* and *Great Expectations*, there is a clear relationship between director-for-hire and auteurist projects: the opportunity to return to Mexico and make a relatively well funded film within a Mexican context was possible only due to the contacts Cuarón had made in the US film industry. In the next section of this chapter I examine the production context of the film and the reliance on North American funding secured via these contacts, which ensure global distribution. In the following section I consider the implications of this through an exploration of the relationship that the film has with the genre of the road movie, and examine the way in which generic tropes are used to present an auteurist vision of Mexico suitable for export through transnational distribution channels. I end with a discussion of the gender politics of the film through a discussion of the character of Luisa, and consider her as a post-feminist character central to the global success of the film.

Producing a global Mexican film

Iñárritu with *Amores perros* demonstrated the successful adoption of a private financial model which allowed the directors to aim for a transnational reach for their films made in Mexico, something not achieved, at that point, to any significant degree with state-funded films. All three directors in this study are director producers, and their role is as much about marketing and selling their products as about making films, hence the documented frustration of Cuarón and del Toro with the limited ambitions of the Mexican Film Institute (Instituto Mexicano de Cinematografía, IMCINE), their later reliance on private production companies, and the fact that Iñárritu bypassed IMCINE altogether.[4] *Y tu mamá también* was produced by the company Anhelo Producciones co-founded by Cuarón and Jorge Vergara, a prominent Mexican businessman. This provided sufficient funds to make the film and launch an ambitious marketing campaign. As Ernesto Priego explains, the promotional campaign helped ensure the domestic success of the film:

> A whole marketing package was put together: a sharp, cool promotional campaign inspired by British film design, including ads and billboards absolutely everywhere, from bus stops, metro stations and public transportation to every imaginable free space in the already-overcrowded, 20 million-plus city of Mexico. (Priego, 2002)

The $5 million budget for the film, while miniscule by Hollywood standards, was on the high side for Mexican features, and the investment on promotion paid off. The film broke existing box office records for a domestic film and was screened at 250 theatres, where it took $2.2 million in its first week (García Tsao, 2001b). The Mexican film critic Leonardo García Tsao notes that this was despite the refusal of the authorities to grant the film an under-18 certificate, although the film was aimed at teenagers. Nevertheless, the controversy generated a good deal of free publicity and under-18s were able to gain entry to the film due to lax admission practices (García Tsao, 2001b). Vergara did not play an active role in the filmmaking process, aside from providing the funds; nevertheless, the film's production notes are enlightening when considering the relationship between the co-producer and film:

> Born in Guadalajara, Jalisco, this businessman and industry visionary founded the Omnilife de Mexico S.A. in 1991, a company that has grown rapidly and has been a model of quality.
> The company creates products for healthy living, using the latest technology. It later became GrupoOmnilife, one of the 250 most important companies in Mexico.
> Vergara met Alfonso Cuarón in 1999 and wanted him to direct a corporate promotional movie for the more than one million distributors of Omnilife's products. However, Alfonso was more interested in filming a screenplay, Y TU MAMÁ TAMBIEN, which he wrote with his brother, Carlos. Upon reading the script, Jorge proposed that they begin production right away.

> Jorge has always guaranteed Alfonso complete freedom as a director, the best production quality possible and freedom from interference or censorship by Vergara. (Production notes)

This reads as promotional material for Vergara and his company, and it becomes clear that financing *Y tu mamá también* could serve as an act of profile raising and indirect advertising that was even more effective than having this Hollywood-endorsed director make a promotional movie for his company, Omnilife. The businessman, through his role as producer, associated himself with the fashionable world inhabited by Cuarón, and the film's stars, Bernal, Luna, and Verdú, an association which helped promote his company. This was highlighted by the fact that he has a small cameo in the film, as Mexican President at the wedding scene, as the director tells us in the extras on the DVD package ('Audio Interview with Director Alfonso Cuarón'). The impact of this private sponsorship on the film is not directly obvious; however, the production context of a film is central to an analysis of the political nature of the text. This is especially significant with a film which purports to critique bourgeois values and neo-liberalism, and to show the 'other' (mestizo) Mexico. I will argue below that the film adopts a soft brand of corporate anti-globalisation; that is, it presents a broad, unfocused critique of the greater evils of globalisation, while seeking to become a global product.[5]

The film did become a global product thanks to the fact that, from its inception, its international sales were to be represented by the US independent company Good Machine International. Cuarón explains that they recouped funds before exhibiting the film as they had pre-sold it to Good Machine (Fernández, 2001). Indeed, the film was conceived through discussion with the director and Ted Hope, the co-founder of the US company (Production notes). Thus, both production funding and access to transnational distribution and exhibition networks were taken care of before the film was even made, ensuring that the most common reason for Mexican films failing to break into the international market was avoided. It is worth noting that David Linde of Good Machine was the film's executive producer, and that he and his other partners at the company, James Schamus and Ted Hope, went on to form Focus Features, the production and distribution company with which Cuarón, del Toro, and Iñárritu's own production company, Cha Cha Cha, reached a $100 million deal for a five-film package. Iñárritu, as noted in chapter 5, also forged an effective working partnership with Linde and Schamus in the making of *21 Grams*. This clearly demonstrates the importance of a reliable track record and personal contacts when forging directorial careers, and consolidates the sense of collaboration between the Mexican directors.[6] In the USA, distribution rights were sold to the auteurist independent New York-based distribution company IFC; in Mexico they were bought by the transnational corporation 20th Century Fox, and in the UK the rights were bought by the independent company Icon (Minns, 2001). *Y tu mamá también* was distributed to forty countries (Vargas, 2002) and made in excess of $13.62 million within the USA (Miller *et al.*, 2012).

Miller *et al.* (2012) explain that the film quickly went beyond traditional Latino outlets in the USA, thanks to the fact that IFC is a subsidiary of the Cablevision cable television company and had connections with Bravo and the Independent Film Channel, where the film was promoted. There was an aggressive marketing campaign, with posters and television and radio advertisements, and prominent figures associated with the film toured with it; these include Cuarón, García Bernal, Diego Luna, and Salma Hayek, a prominent Latina star and fantasy figure for Tenoch and Julio within the narrative. Thus, Good Machine and subsequently IFC did an extremely effective job, and their role in making this a transnational film cannot be downplayed.

In the discussion of *El laberinto del fauno* in chapter 3, I examine the ways that the film challenged simplistic associations of foreign-language film with art cinema, and explore the development of commercial popular art cinema. The same analysis can be applied to *Y tu mamá también*, and, indeed, to *Cronos* and *Amores perros*, with the shift away from rules governing art cinema production central to the commercial trajectory of these films. This can be illustrated through comments made by Bob Berney, then senior vice-president for marketing and distribution for IFC:

> The film broke away from the foreign-language market and showed that a Spanish-language film is not a foreign-language [movie] in the US. The film became a crossover mainstream film with all the major theater chains wanting to play it. (Cited in Miller *et al.*, 2012)

The concept that it is not a foreign-language film refers to the sizeable Latino/Latin American Spanish-speaking population in the USA. It is interesting to note the similarity in tone used by Berney (by this time working at Picturehouse), a major figure in US independent film, when discussing the approach used to market *Pan's Labyrinth* (see pp. 77–78).⁷

Y tu mamá también and the road movie

As demonstrated by del Toro, the incorporation of generic tropes is central to creating crossover films, and genre is one of the key factors in explaining the global circulation of films. Ezra and Rowden (2006: 6) cite Jigna Desai, who states that 'those films most likely to circulate transnationally are those that are more "Western friendly", adopting familiar genres, narratives, or themes in their hybrid productions' (Desai, 2004: 45). This is an argument developed by Luisela Alvaray, who, through the frame of genre, explores the relationship between national cinema and international success. She states, 'Filmmakers in Latin America are considering elements of genres – or a combination thereof – as shortcuts to tell autochthonous stories. And producers are using crossover genres to appeal to wider audiences' (Alvaray, 2011).⁸ *Y tu mamá también* is one of the first Latin American films to demonstrate the global potential of an auteurist Spanish-language film which uses genre to gain an entry pass into global distribution circuits. It is not without significance that one of the other best-performing Latin American films internationally was *Diarios de motocicleta* (*The Motorcycle Diaries*) (Salles, 2004), which also relies on a road movie format.

While *Y tu mamá también* is a genre film that came into being partly thanks to US financial muscle, it is also a reaction against the Hollywood studio films and working practices that Cuarón had experienced while in the USA, as seen. How do these apparently opposing forces play out in the film text itself? The key to the answer to this question lies in the treatment of generic components, and in the film's appropriation and subversion of these. *Y tu mamá también* is a form of Mexican road movie that is as much about what the characters do not see as what they do. In addition, it both takes elements from and subverts the teen sex comedy, with the boys' macho posturing unmasked, and their inexperience and latent homosexual desires revealed. The film, then, disrupts generic conventions while taking pleasurable aspects of them: namely sex and scenery. My emphasis in this section is on the road movie, as this is the dominant form which structures the narrative and into which are incorporated elements of the teenage sex comedy, through the focus on the protagonists, Tenoch and Julio.⁹

A key element of road movies noted by critics is that they can be seen as allegorical, in that they often aim to say something important about a nation. In the introduction to *The Road Movie Book*, Cohan and Hark (1997: 3) observe that road movies use 'the road to imagine a nation's culture', with the genre linked very specifically to a US identity (2). They argue that 'the road movie provides a ready space for exploration of the tensions and crises of the historical moment during which it is produced' (2), with more such films appearing during periods 'of upheaval and dislocation' (2). This desire to present the nation is a central feature of *Y tu mamá también*, which aims to reveal the 'real' Mexico, and places the country at the centre of what has been a dominant North American genre, rather than having Mexico as the romanticised space to which US road novel/movie characters seek to escape – for example in *On the Road* (Kerouac, 1957), *Easy Rider* (Hopper, 1969), and *Thelma and Louise* (Scott, 1991).[10]

In his book *Driving Visions: Exploring the Road Movie* (2002), David Laderman identifies other central features of the US road movie. He argues that the road movie is known for its 'cultural critique and rebellion against conservative social norms' (1). This stems from the fact that the genre originated with the counter-culture, and books such as Kerouac's *On the Road*, and films such as *Bonnie and Clyde* (Penn, 1967) and *Easy Rider*. Nevertheless, the films are also characterised by a 'tension between rebellion and conformity' (20). Laderman and others (Corrigan, 1991; Cohan and Hark, 1997; Stringer, 1997) note that conservative values are most often manifested with regard to gender relations, and Laderman explains that 'most road movies ... retain a traditional sexist hierarchy that privileges the white heterosexual male in terms of narrative and visual point of view' (20), with characters unable to escape from the prevailing social values that they carry within themselves. Women are often simply objects of desire, and female characters and homosexuals are generally relegated to secondary roles, at least until the advent of *Thelma and Louise*, and in a Mexican context *El jardín del Edén* (*The Garden of Eden*) (Novaro, 1994), and independently produced gay road movies from the 1990s such as *My Own Private Idaho* (Van Sant, 1991) and *The Living End* (Araki, 1992).[11]

With these key characteristics of the road movie in mind, I will approach my reading of Cuarón's take on the genre through, in the next section, an examination of the image of Mexico that the film presents, and the cultural critique offered by the film and the forms

Y tu mamá también

this takes, and, in the following section, the role of Luisa, and her destabilising effect on the boys' masculinity. The analysis will always be framed within a focus on the ways in which Cuarón endeavours to make a Mexican film for both the domestic and the global market.

In plot terms, *Y tu mamá también* is very simple. Two teenage boys, Tenoch (Diego Luna) and Julio (Gael García Bernal), are on summer vacation, in between high school and university, and they spend their time smoking marijuana, going to parties, and trying to seduce other teenage girls, as their girlfriends have decided to spend their summer in Italy. At the wedding party of Tenoch's sister, they meet Luisa Cortés, the wife of Tenoch's older cousin, Jano. In an act of boyish bravado they tell her they can show her the most beautiful beach in Mexico, which they give the made up name Boca del Cielo (Heaven's Mouth). On discovering her husband's infidelity, and, unbeknownst to the audience, her terminal cancer diagnosis, she takes the boys up on their offer. They hastily borrow Julio's sister's car, a 1983 Le Baron station wagon they have named Betsabé ('Audio Interview with Director Alfonso Cuarón'), and the road trip to the paradisiacal beach begins. We thus have all the ingredients for a Mexican road movie, and the format for the exploration of the features outlined above.

The journey takes them through Mexico, from the capital, Mexico City, through tiny, sleepy towns to their ultimate goal of La Boca del Cielo (which they are astonished to find is a real beach), found in the state of Guerrero, on the Pacific Coast. The digressive journey structure allows the Cuarón brothers (and Lubezki) to make an allegorically based film that presents a specific vision of Mexico. The above-mentioned 'tension between rebellion and conformity' sustains the narrative: the boys are members of their own gang, the Charolastras, and they have created their own manifesto, which they believe to be transgressive, but which is rooted in contradictions and flaws, rests on patriarchal values, and is ultimately overturned by Luisa's feminist manifesto.[12] The woman in this film thus shifts from being an object of desire to a dominant force who sees the boys initially as sexual objects, and temporarily (for the duration of the trip) makes them reconsider their values. Heterosexuality is also central to the boys' identities, and this is called into question.

The familiar tropes of the road movie are, thus, all present in *Y tu mamá también*; however, there are some important challenges to traditions established within the genre as developed in the USA which allow Cuarón to carve out an auteurist presence. This is seen in the re-centring of Mexico and the privileging of the feminine world of Luisa, and in the attempts to destabilise the white male heterosexual gaze by turning the camera away from the boys at key moments and having a voice-over run counter to their vision of the world. In interviews, Cuarón cites Godard's *Masculin/féminin* (1966) as the source for the idea of using the narrator's voice-over (Basoli, 2002: 27), and he states that he wanted a poster of the film for Tenoch's girlfriend's bedroom, but as it did not arrive he chose a poster of the film *Harold and Maude* (Ashby, 1971) (Lawrenson, 2002). It is worth noting that a poster of the Colombian novelist Gabriel García Márquez features on the wall. These references to auteurist cinema and classical literature also highlight the director's cultural literacy and authorial ambitions, despite the fact that the texts referenced have little in common with Cuarón's.

In terms of approach and aesthetics, there are also identifiable ways in which the director lays out his authorial stall by marking out his film as something new and original. This, along with the generic factors, is also key to international success, as auteurism is the central factor for buyers of foreign-language films and programmers of art cinemas, where Cuarón's film was shown (Wood, 2011). There is an interplay between discovery and familiarity central to the film's commercial viability and crossover status, and the image of rural Mexico presented both to urban Mexicans and to international audiences is a combination of the new and the recognisable. Laderman (2002: 1–2) writes that 'road movies aim beyond the borders of cultural familiarity, seeking the unfamiliar for revelation, or at least for the thrill of the unknown'. Yet Cuarón, by rooting his film in Mexico while aiming for a global audience, needs to present enough elements of the country that are familiar to foreigners to not alienate international film viewers, all the while giving them a sense of adventure and revelation.

Mexico in *Y tu mamá también*

The sense of discovery is found in the way that audiences are given the impression that they are accessing an insider's view of Mexico, through the journey with the protagonists and through the narrator's commentary, which can be thrilling to foreign audiences, who can experience virtual travel without having to leave their hometowns.[13] Yet this image of the country goes hand in hand with a reassuringly familiar Mexico. To a large degree the film presents a vision of the country that is sought out by tourists: Mexico is one of the top tourist destinations for its North American neighbours, and most do not head to the capital city but to seaside locations such as Acapulco and Cancún. Consequently, the drive through the country in search of an idyllic beach will resonate with many US citizens and city dwellers across the world who associate Mexico with holidays.

There are many images that are almost too obviously Mexican. Thus, the film is punctuated with mariachi bands, desolate yet beautiful scenery, and stunning beaches, while local traditions, such as villagers seeking donations for their beauty queen, are presented for the viewers' pleasure. There are also the requisite social signifiers that are internationally associated with Mexico: namely, corrupt politicians, student demonstrations, and a heavy police presence.[14] In addition to this, the characters' names provide audiences with a list of some of the most famous figures from Mexico's history, although these names must be seen as ironic, and have no bearing on the characters themselves, with none sharing attributes of conquerors, the heroes of the War of Independence, or the revolutionary leaders they are named after.[15] Thus, non-specialist viewers do not have to trouble themselves with complexities of Mexican history, but feel reassured by the familiar names, while Mexicans and those with knowledge of Mexican history can share an in joke.

This familiar Mexico shown to viewers merges with a journey of discovery through the voice-over, which disrupts any form of escapist fantasy, and which, in contrast to the traditional voice-over of a travelogue, does not tell viewers what they can see, but tells them what they cannot. Nevertheless, as is common to road movies, beauty and a sense of escape are central to the narrative: audiences are shown the delights of the paradisiacal beach of Heaven's Mouth, alongside the characters, even as tourism itself becomes the object of critique for the film through the narrator's revelation of the fate of Chuy, the characters' personal tour guide, as I discuss below.

In many respects *Y tu mamá también* presents a guided tour of Mexico, as Nuala Finnegan (2007: 30) has argued, a tour that is off the beaten track, with a guide ever present in the form of the 'omniscient' narration, voiced by Daniel Giménez Cacho, Cuarón's protagonist in *Sólo con tu pareja*. In this way the filmmakers address the audience with the implied promise that they can show us a Mexico just out of tourists' reach: the audience is thus constructed as a traveller, who is not shown Mexico through the eyes of the teenage boys, but rather the Mexico outside their field of vision. This is rather muddled by the fact that Tenoch and Julio also represent a part of Mexico, and, on one level, come to stand for an under-developed nation in the process of growing up. Cuarón explains:

> Thematically this is a movie about seeking one's identity and it's a journey. You have two teenagers who are seeking validation as adults and there's the woman's journey. She's seeking her identity as a free woman. Alongside them there's this country, Mexico, which in my view is a teenage country trying to find its identity as a grown-up country. That was our premise. (Basoli, 2002: 26)

This clearly had particular resonance within the timeframe in which the film is set. This is revealed at the end of the film when audiences are told of the first defeat of the Institutional Revolutionary Party (Partido Revolucionario Institucional, PRI), in seventy years, locating the film in 2000.[16] Thus, the teenagers are intended to represent an urban Mexico, but they are also blind to their own country, seen in the representation of the 'other', rural Mexico. The sense given, then, is that there is a subjective and objective reality, to both of which this film will give viewers access.

The allegorical ambitions of the film are made clear in interviews with the director in which he repeats the assertion that *Y tu mamá también* is intended to show the 'real' Mexico. In one example Cuarón tells María Delgado during a public interview at the 'BAFTA Goes to Mexico' event in London in 2007, 'not only was Mexico put in [sic] the map but, also, it was shown as it is without filters or make-up' (Delgado, 2007). He argues that the filming techniques developed between himself and Lubezki sought to reflect this, and can be seen in the use of a distant camera, long takes, and long shots aimed to ensure that characters were not favoured over the environment (Delgado, 2007). This is attempted principally by contrasting the subjective and 'objective' points of view. In addition to this, the camera wanders off, as if bored with the exploits of the protagonists, to focus on matters of greater import, seen, for instance, in a long tracking shot of Tenoch's mestiza nana/maid, Leo, who comes up the stairs to bring him a sandwich and to answer the phone for him, ringing by his side and which he had been ignoring, thus exposing a clear class and ethnic divide.[17]

A realist vision is, then, constructed through narration and image, and, at the same time, a traditional understanding of the road movie narrative format, which aligns point of view with the protagonists, is challenged. Of course, the relationship between the real and realism is notoriously slippery, and directors' assertions should not be taken at face value. Indeed, it can be claimed, as does the Mexican critic Leonardo García Tsao (2001b), that the film rests on a tourist vision, while Priego (2002) questions the notion of truthful representations of Mexico by arguing that they rest on social stereotypes and caricatures. The image of Mexico is indeed carefully manufactured and, despite the totalising sense given through the two narrative positions, relies on a partial political and social vision that rests on an easily digestible and transportable image of the country. This is an image which allowed it to be the global hit that *Sólo con tu pareja* never was.[18]

The nature of this vision can be revealed through an exploration of the 'objective' voice-over and the realist camera work. In many cases, the narrator reports on an event that has happened of supposed social import, while the camera focuses on the landscape and signs of the happening, such as a cross to mark the deaths from a road accident. At times, the dialogue of the three principal characters is heard over images of the dry, natural landscape, which stands in contrast to their conversation within the car, usually focusing on sex and their exaggerated abilities as lovers. The frivolity of their conversation is highlighted by the way in which the car is dwarfed and they are not the object of the camera's gaze (figure 8.1).

8.1 The car is dwarfed by the landscape in *Y tu mamá también*

At other times, the camera focuses on police detentions and arrests, not usually noticed by the two boys who are telling stories of the way they pleasure their girlfriends and are thus too wrapped up in myths of their own masculinity to pay attention to the outside world. The other technique used to present the other, 'objective' Mexico is for the sound of the first level of the diegesis to be cut (the world of the protagonists), while the narrator's voice provides a commentary for events that are outside the field of vision, and either occurred in the past or are about to occur. This functions much like a filmmaker's commentary in a DVD package, and in this way acquires additional resonance and the weight of 'truth' and omniscience. Indeed, the narrator's voice comes to be associated with the voice of the director guiding us towards what is 'important'. Many of these commentaries accompany long unedited shots of the landscape, which brings us back to the earlier point made by James Udden about the cultivation of auteurist vision through the long take, while such shots also add to the sense of a truthful vision in the way they appear to present Mexico with little manipulation in the form of editing.

Events recounted by the narrator cannot be known to the three travellers, and despite the focus on death, poverty, and corruption, these events seem rather haphazard and lack a coherent vision. They include deaths on the road ten years previously, following the crash of a truck carrying chickens, the death of a bricklayer in Mexico City after being hit by a bus (the narrator informs viewers that he did not use a pedestrian bridge to get to work, as this would take too long, thus exposing poor town planning), and even the fatal fate of pigs that invade the Boca del Cielo beach. Audiences are also told of the hypocrisy of the President through the voice-over as he leaves the wedding of Tenoch's sister: one day he visits citizens to express his indignation at a massacre and deny the involvement of the state governor, and the next day flies to an international conference on globalisation in Seattle. While the implication of the guilt of his governor is never stated, it is clearly implied, and he chooses profile-raising trips abroad over investigation of domestic human rights abuses. Finally, the narrator tells audiences of the fate of Chuy, the fisherman who, with his family, takes Tenoch, Julio, and Luisa under his wing and provides them with tours of Boca del Cielo, as well as food and drink. The narrator informs audiences that, in the future:

> He will never fish again. Chuy and his family will have to leave this place to give way to the construction of an exclusive hotel.... Chuy will try to

give a boat service to tourists, but will be blocked by the Acapulco boat owners union, protected by the Tourism Council. Two years later he will end up as a janitor in the hotel and will never go fishing again.

This intervention provides the most directly political commentary within the film, and is a critique both of the way 'development' leaves behind local employees, and of local trade unions and their crushing of individual entrepreneurism.

A number of critics have noted that the technique of the wandering eye or straying camera, combined with the voice-over, creates a sense of a deeper, more political vision of Mexico that stands in contrast to the world of the boys and Luisa (Acevedo-Muñoz, 2004; Finnegan, 2007; Noble, 2005). While this is certainly the case, it is interesting to analyse the nature of this political vision, and here I return to the idea of a soft leftist form of corporate anti-globalisation adopted by a film with powerful financial backers, and ambitions in the global market. The film's use of the narrator to undercut the protagonists' point of view appears to challenge their partial view, yet its apparent totalising vision is strangely limited and fragmented. What is apparent in the narrator's account is the seemingly random nature of the events chosen, which display small instances of social critique and yet are lacking in a defined or coherent political message. The narrator refrains from anything other than a neutral tone, merely informing the audience on the events selected, and equal weight seems to be given to road accidents, presidential corruption, job losses, and even the fate of the pigs which invade the beach.

These narrative interventions are also digressions, and the camera always comes back to the three protagonists, their banter, the boys' clumsy sexual exploits with Luisa, and their evolving relationships. Landscape passes by, as do the faces of the mestizo characters they encounter; yet the focus on teenagers remains the central feature of the film (figure 8.2), even as it is being critiqued through its juxtaposition with more serious concerns. In the tradition of the US teen sex comedy, the world of the teenagers is what generates most humour and amusement for the viewers, all while the vision of the outside world presents the requisite edification expected by art-house audiences, and raises the status of the film in auteurist terms.

When considering the political vision of the film, it is as significant to consider what is not shown or commented on. Audiences are told that Julio's sister lends her brother the car for five days with the condition that she can have it for the following three weeks to take food,

8.2 Julio, Tenoch, and Luisa in the car in *Y tu mamá también*. Julio teases Tenoch about using prostitutes

medicine, and other provisions to Chiapas. However, no more explanation or context is given for the Zapatista rebellion in Chiapas, which constitutes Mexico's largest social upheaval and popular struggle of the recent historical period; indeed, the Zapatista revolutionaries and their cause go unmentioned.[19] While Mexican audiences and those familiar with Mexican politics would pick up the fleeting reference to Chiapas, and the revolutionary cause, it would be entirely lost on most foreign viewers. It is also noteworthy that Julio's sister, who is politically active and studying political science, is a marginal character, and is only glimpsed once, at a student demonstration. Spanish speakers can see from the placards that the demonstrators are calling for free state education, but this scene is only 23 seconds long, and no explanation of the protest is given. The following scene returns to the focus of the film: the boys are shown having fun in a supermarket, preparing for their trip by buying teenage 'essentials' such as crisps, beer, and condoms. The film is not, then, concerned with organised political protest, and not simply because this is not of interest to Julio and Tenoch, as it is also largely bypassed by the narrator.

In addition, no real poverty is seen. Further, while state oppression is hinted at, in the prominence of the police presence, no explanation is given for the arrests made by the police, and the audience is left as ignorant as the boys as to why arrests are being made. The boys do pay attention, at one point, when people are stopped by drug patrols, as this will affect them, but an overall sense of the film's vision of the police is lacking from this. Even in the more overt political moments, such as in the commentary on the President and Chuy's loss of employment, seen above, it is unclear what the 'message' of the film is. Viewers are left with a soft leftist notion that there are victims of globalisation and modernity; yet no alternatives are suggested, and no particular group is held accountable. A comment by Cuarón when interviewed about *Y tu mamá también* illuminates this point:

> Saying 'I'm against globalization' or in Mexico saying 'I'm against modernity' is like saying 'I'm against the law of gravity.' You can be against them but there's no way around them. The question now is how to democratize globalization and modernity in Mexico, and I think that's a big challenge not only in Mexico but also in the world. (Basoli, 2002: 26)

It is particularly significant that there is no mention of North American tourists, who would, of course, be the main residents at the hotels which have put Chuy out of business. Ernesto Acevedo-Muñoz (2004: 47) states with regard to this, 'this sequence is arguably analogical of the negative impact of the yearly invasion of American college spring-breakers to Mexico's coastal resorts, from Cancún to Cozumel, to Puerto Escondido'. However, US audiences would never feel implicated in Chuy's fate, as the film makes no reference to these 'spring-breakers' or to North American tourists. Indeed, I would argue that a film with global ambitions and dependent on US funding has deliberately sought to downplay any criticism of Mexico's northern neighbours.

Cuarón is, in fact, reacting against a traditional view of political cinema and he has commented on his dislike of the politically driven filmmaking that dominated the culture at film school (Fernández, 2001). Elsewhere, the director rejects the idea of the Latin American political film associated with the 'new' Latin American cinema of the 1960s and 1970s, stating 'I don't really like [sic] when political statements drive a film. Everything is political', and he adds that he prefers to express a political view through 'emotional experience' (Basoli, 2002: 27). The film seeks connections between the world outside the car window and that within the car, by suggesting that Tenoch and Julio, and the urban upper and lower middle classes

8.3 Luisa with Mabel and family in *Y tu mamá también*

they represent, need to see their country and the issues affecting rural Mexico if they are to effect any changes. However, the precise nature of the key issues and an appropriate response are uncertain. No genuine rebellion against the status quo is suggested by the film, as no alternative is offered.

Ultimately, the white privileged gaze of the city dwellers is maintained, as, while viewers do see the 'other', mestizo Mexico, their emotional energy is taken up with the teenagers and Luisa. There is very little narrative interaction with the 'other' Mexicans, who are all there to serve the protagonists or to give a snapshot of the Mexico that is outside the car window. This is illustrated in the idyllic final images of Luisa and Chuy's family (figure 8.3), whom she chooses to remain with. These scenes suggest that Luisa joins their family unit, thus breaking through national and ethnic boundaries. Here again, what audiences are not shown is significant: Luisa is dying of cancer, although we see her only as a Spanish beauty in good health. Cuarón may well assert that Luisa 'muere tremendamente feliz' ('Luisa dies tremendously happy') (Fernández, 2001), but what remains unspoken and unfilmed is that Mabel, Chuy's wife, will have to nurse this stranger who has decided to spend the remainder of her life with them, before spending her final four days in a hospital (we learn of the final days when Tenoch recounts the facts of Luisa's death to Julio at the end of the film). *Y tu mamá también*'s relationship with the real is, then, filtered through an awareness of commercial imperatives. Despite the claims of realism and the realist techniques, seen in the use of the long shot, the wide panoramic shots, the incorporation of 'real' Mexicans, and the rejection of a subjective narration, the text offers a filmic imagining of a country that will sell to foreign audiences in similar ways as a holiday to Mexico booked with an independent tour guide, with the promise of an insight into the 'real' Mexico a central part of the draw of the film. Poverty, death, corruption, and social unrest (as well as pigs) may be part of the landscape of the film, but it was a domestic and international hit thanks to its focus on sun, sea, sex, stars, and sentiment for its generation of pleasure.

Here's to the clitoris!

While the political vision in *Y tu mamá también* is, then, rather safe and does not challenge its position as a popular commercial text, there is a more progressive dimension to the film which, as with *El laberinto del fauno*, lies in the gender politics (with Maribel Verdú featuring in both films) and, in this case, form of (post-)feminism it espouses.[20] This is seen in the representation of Luisa, a sexually liberated woman who calls into question the power and sexuality of the next generation of young men, but whose power is limited to the sexual sphere. This, rather than threaten the marketability of the film, also fits well within contemporary discourses in Mexico, the USA, and other developed countries, and thus works to enhance, rather than dilute, the film's global commercial potential.

Ernesto Acevedo-Muñoz (2004: 40) notes that 'films since the 1990s have either allowed women to render "another" view or have revised, satirized, and even reinvented the meaning and position of women in Mexican cinema'. This can be seen in films such as *Danzón* (Novaro, 1991), *Angel de fuego* (*Angel of Fire*) (Rotberg, 1992), *Novia que te vea* (*Like a Bride*) (Schyfter, 1994), and *Nadie te oye: Perfume de violetas* (*Violet Perfume: Nobody Hears You*) (Sistach, 2001), to name a few early examples,[21] and the trend continues with *Y tu mamá también*. In its privileging of the feminine, the film also links to one of the most successful feminist US road movies, *Thelma and Louise*, and in its questioning of a secure heterosexual space it has connections to the previously mentioned US gay indie road movies of the 1990s.

The primary function of Luisa, in addition to providing sexual allure through the performance of Verdú, is to call into question the foundations of Mexican machismo, as Acevedo-Muñoz (2004) has argued. Her Spanish identity is significant, not in the way she re-colonises the country, as her surname, Cortés, teasingly implies, but in the way she is conceived of as an (older) outsider who refuses to play by the gender rules of teenage Mexican dating. Her casting also, of course, helped promote the film in Spain and other Hispanic countries, as she is a well known Hispanic star.[22]

Luisa overturns and destabilises the boys' performances of masculinity and their insecure teenage identity, which hinges on sexual conquest and sense of ownership over their girlfriends. Luisa initiates sex with both of them, and reworks traditional power relationships, while revealing their failures as lovers, and refusing any attempts they make of controlling her. She replaces their teenage manifesto, with its focus on personal freedom, pop music, drugs, masturbation, sex, and fidelity (of the girls), with her own female manifesto. She forms this personal manifesto as a response to their rivalry and (unspoken) anger that she has used both of them as sex objects. Luisa's rules insist on the abnegation of their macho identities, and the assertion of her dominance over them: there is to be no fighting, no further sex with her, no stories about their girlfriends; she chooses the music, while they have to cook, do the manual work, and cannot contradict her or push her (as Julio has just done). They accept all of this, as to be abandoned by the older, attractive Spanish woman would be more of a challenge to their sense of self than to accept her rules.[23] Their performances of heterosexual masculinity depend upon a female figure needed in the on-going construction of their masculinity.

Once Luisa has established a female order of control, she is free to break some of her rules. She does in the final scenes reinitiate sexual relations with the boys, but this is only after she has established a 'clitoral' order to overturn a phallic order. In a drunken final dinner, she jokingly reveals the failings of their lovemaking, and attempts to teach them the secrets of the clitoris, and the importance of knowing how to give women good oral sex. She tells them, 'you have to make the clitoris your best friend'; Julio then calls for a round of applause for the clitoris, and they all make a toast to it. This new order appears momentarily to liberate the boys from their machismo: they toast

Y tu mamá también

the Italians who are 'screwing their girlfriends', and laugh at the fact that they have slept with each other's girlfriends. Here, the title of the film is explained, as Julio says to Tenoch, 'y tu mamá también' ('and your mother too'), revealing that he has had sex with his friend's mother while she was cleaning his aura. This temporary disruption of the phallic order sets the scene for the threesome that follows, and, along with the alcohol, provides the space for the boys to have a sexual encounter with each other.

The female empowerment in the film, then, takes a predominantly sexual form and is not threatening to men, but rather invites them to become better lovers and be more considerate of women's needs. It thus fits within a post-feminist discourse which holds sway in many twenty-first-century urban centres around the world. It also creates the commercially desirable space for plenty of sex. The homosexual encounter is a momentary event, repudiated the next day by the boys, who never speak of it, and whose friendship is terminated. Luisa points towards the potential for reconstructing masculine identities, but, in the tradition of the road movie, Tenoch and Julio are returned to the conservative social order once the trip is over. It is also noteworthy that, despite the significant amount of heterosexual activity shown in the film, the encounter between the two friends is not shown, beyond a single kiss, and sex between the two is implied but not confirmed. For Cuarón, homosexuality is not a defining label for the boys, and they are not gay; rather, sex between them is a natural act which their prejudices do not allow them to accept (Fernández, 2001). This is an interesting, potentially radical concept; however, the fact that this natural act remains unseen, when there are a number of scenes featuring them engaged in heterosexual acts, does limit the progressive potential of the film, as not only do the boys recoil from the idea of homosexuality, but so, it appears, do the filmmakers.[24] Once again, this situates *Y tu mamá también* as a commercial foreign-language film that sought to reach as wide an audience as possible.

Conclusion

Y tu mamá también is, along with *Children of Men*, one of Alfonso Cuarón's most important films. Although it pales in comparison with films such as *Harry Potter and the Prisoner of Azkaban* and *Great Expectations* in terms of profit generation, it was a break-through film in that it allowed Cuarón to be taken seriously as an auteurist director, who, along with del Toro and Iñárritu, has managed to break down marketing and exhibition barriers for foreign-language films. The director achieved this by incorporating a personal style into a generic tradition, and presenting Mexico in a new way to both domestic and international audiences. The film combines a fine balance between progressive and conservative elements in terms of its politics and its representation of sexualities, while its representation of landscape and national identities is not to do with 'truth', but rather to do with the economic systems that they are part of.

Notes

1 Udden (2009: 29) notes, 'The longest take in the film, the last meal among the three main protagonists, lasts almost seven minutes uninterrupted by the reputed machinations of editing'.
2 Production notes at www.cinema.com/articles/812/y-tu-mam-tambien-production-notes.phtml.
3 Udden explains Bazin's ideas on pp. 34–35 of his article.
4 Maciel (1999: 220–227) outlines the problems faced by IMCINE from 1994 to 1997.
5 The notion of corporate anti-capitalism was sparked by a spate of films which achieved commercial success while attacking the sins of global capitalism. See Brook (2010) for discussion of this. See K-punk (2010) for an analysis of this debate in relation to James Cameron's *Avatar* (2009).
6 For more on Good Machine, Linde, and Focus Features, see the press release from Universal Pictures 'Universal Studios Promotes Marc Shmuger to Chairman and David Linde to Co-Chairman, Universal Pictures' at www.prnewswire.co.uk/cgi/news/release?id=166436.
7 Picturehouse folded when Warner Brothers took over New Line Cinema, and with it Picturehouse, a company put together by HBO and New Line Cinema to release specialty films. Berney went on to form a new company called Apparition in 2009, but left in May 2011 (see Fritz, 2009, 2010). He has since been hired as president of theatrical distribution for GK Films for its new project Film District, 'which will function as an acquisition, distribution, production and financing company with plans to release between four and eight wide commercial releases per year' (Kilday, 2010).
8 The Mexican films Alvaray discusses are *Niñas mal* (Sariñana, 2007), *Viaje redondo* (Tort, 2009), the romantic comedy *Cansada de besar sapos* (*Tired of Kissing Frogs*) (Colón, 2006), the horror film *Km 31: Kilómetro 31* (Castañeda, 2006), and the comedy *Matando cabos* (Lozano, 2004). I am grateful to the author for sending me her article prior to publication.
9 The road movie is an unusual genre in Mexican film. The other

Y tu mamá también

best-known Mexican road movies are *El jardín del Edén* (*The Garden of Eden*, 1994), directed by María Novaro, and *Viaje redondo* (*Round Trip*, 2009), directed by Gerardo Tort and scripted by Beatriz Novaro, who also wrote the screenplay for *El jardín del Edén*, although neither has had the success of Cuarón's film. *Viaje redondo* has been successful in Mexico, but has not been released internationally (Alvaray, 2011).

10 This is an element which Laderman sees (referring to *Thelma and Louise*) as illustrative of the exoticising tendencies of the genre (2002: 193).
11 For a detailed analysis of the advent of gay road movies in the 1990s, see Robert Lang (1997: 330–348).
12 Audiences never find out exactly the meaning of 'charolastra'; the boys tell Luisa it is a combination of the Mexican words for space and cowboy, but they also say it came from one of their friends misunderstanding the English lyrics to a song.
13 For a discussion of the relationship between film and a tourist gaze, see chapter 6, in which I apply these concepts to *Babel*.
14 Nuala Finnegan (2007: 33) has a different take on these signifiers of Mexico, and argues that they are parodic.
15 Priego (2002) notes that, 'significantly, the last names of all the characters are clear, almost too obvious references to famous protagonists of Mexican history: Tenoch's last name is Iturbide, whereas Julio's is Zapata. Their respective girlfriends are Ana Morelos and Cecilia Huerta; Tenoch and Julio's best friend is Saba Madero, Luisa's last name is Cortés, and Tenoch's indigenous housemaid is Leodegaria Victoria'. He goes on to explain who all these figures are. For more on the significance of the names see Acevedo-Muñoz (2004).
16 The election was won by Vicente Fox, leader of the National Action Party (Partido Acción Nacional, PAN), Mexico's conservative party.
17 This technique is referred to as the 'straying camera' by Andrea Noble (2005: 143) and as 'the wandering eye' by Acevedo-Muñoz (2004: 42).
18 Other critics have noted that the soundtrack is also key in appealing to a global youth market (Finnegan, 2007; Priego, 2002). Finnegan (2007: 32) notes that 'fashionable Western and Mexican artists feature on the soundtrack including Frank Zappa, Brian Eno, Natalie Imbruglia, La Revolución de Emiliano Zapata, Flaco Jiménez, and Café Tacuba'.
19 See note 21 in chapter 4 (p. 113), on *Amores perros*, for more on the Zapatistas.
20 In *El laberinto del fauno* Verdú's character, Mercedes, is a key figure in the rebellion and supplies provisions to the Maquis and provides them with crucial information, before she actively joins them.
21 On women's filmmaking in Mexico see Rashkin (2001).
22 Maribel Verdú has a rich filmography; early on in her career she became known for her sexually daring roles in films such as *Amantes* (*Lovers*) (Aranda, 1991), and *Huevos de oro* (*Golden Balls*) (Bigas Luna, 1993). Del

Toro cast her against type as Mercedes in *El laberinto*. For her full filmography, see hwww.imdb.com/name/nm0893941.
23 All of this does invite an Oedipal reading, but this would take me on a different analytical journey.
24 This stands in contrast to other gay representations in Mexican cinema, including *Doña Herlinda y su hijo* (*Doña Herlinda and Her Son*, 1985), by the well known filmmaker Jaime Humberto Hermosillo, and more recently the films of Julián Hernández.

9

Children of Men: the limits of radicalism

Children of Men (2006) is Alfonso Cuarón's greatest filmic achievement to date and constitutes an auteurist statement in the way that it demands that its director be taken seriously. It addresses weighty issues and sets out to provide an account of the most pressing problems facing humanity: environmental destruction (symbolised by infertility), mass migration, and the tyranny within democratic states. It has its own specific look and applies a grimy desaturated realist aesthetic to a fantasy premise: the fact that the earth's inhabitants can no longer have children. It also develops innovative filmic techniques, and Cuarón and his cinematographer, Emmanuel Lubezki, chose to use unusually long takes for action sequences, which in Hollywood films are characterised by increasingly rapid editing (Bordwell, 2002a). All of these factors made *Children of Men* stand out and brought it critical acclaim. They also brought the film high-profile nominations, including a number for the 2007 US Academy Awards. Although *Children of Men* did not win any Oscars, the nominations helped to raise the international profile of both Cuarón and Lubezki as serious filmmakers, while the latter won Outstanding Achievement in Cinematography in Theatrical Releases from the prestigious American Society of Cinematographers.[1]

The most fruitful focus for an analysis of *Children of Men* shares key elements of the approach I have taken in the chapters on the two other global break-through films by Mexican directors in 2006, del Toro's *El laberinto del fauno*, and Iñárritu's *Babel*. Thus, I explore the ways in which Cuarón's work challenges a number of notions relating to how film has been understood. I consider the relationship between the national, the transnational, and the global in terms of production context, cast and crew, and text; I examine the ways in which the film transcends generic and industry boundaries, and consider the ways in which it takes from, yet rejects, conventions from genres such as sci-fi, political thrillers, disaster movies, and social realist filmmaking. In the final section, I return to the question posed in the introduction to the book and explore the tensions between social and political forms of filmmaking and industry demands, and consider the limits of radicalism in a commercial film text funded in large part by Universal Studios. I examine the political vision presented with the film, and the relationship between this and the ideas developed through Cuarón's accompanying documentary, *The Possibility of Hope*, which is available on the DVD and Blu-ray extras package.

Children of Men: a paradigmatic transnational film

Children of Men is an ideal model case study for a transnational film, and meets the criteria in the majority of the categories that I have identified in the introduction as most pertinent to attempts to theorise transnational cinema. The film relies on transnational modes of production, distribution, and exhibition; it fits within my conceptualisation of the cinema of globalisation, and shares the concerns of exilic and diasporic filmmaking of the position of migrants. It also employs transnational modes of narration. In addition, *Children of Men* features globally famous stars (the American Julianne Moore and the British Clive Owen), and it is made by a transnational director who has made films in a number of national settings and under differing production contexts. In my approach throughout this chapter I follow Higbee and Lim's notion of critical transnationalism in that my readings aim to be 'attentive to questions of postcoloniality, politics and power, and [consider] how these may, in turn, uncover new forms of neo-colonialist practices in the guise of popular genres or auteurist aesthetics' (Higbee and Lim, 2010: 18).

So, to explore the first category set out in the introduction – of modes of production, distribution, and exhibition – the dominant role of Universal Pictures in the marketing and distribution of *Children of Men* in the theatres, and on DVD and Blu-ray by Universal Home Entertainment, assures its position in the international market. The hands-on production work was carried out by two smaller companies, US-based Strike Entertainment Production, and the UK-based company Hit and Run Productions. Hilary Shor, the co-founder of Hit and Run, had brought the rights to the P. D. James novel *The Children of Men* (1992), and agreed to work with the producer Marc Abraham of Strike Entertainment when he approached her with a view to adapting the book (Visual Hollywood, 2006a). Cuarón brought the financial muscle of Universal into the equation when he agreed to take on the project, and Universal took on the costs of marketing and distribution, usually in excess of costs of production (Udden, 2009: 42).

The film has been highly acclaimed in critical terms, although it was not particularly successful at the box office. As James Udden (2009: 42) notes, 'the film is an undeniable aesthetic success, but hardly an economic one'. It had a number of prestigious award nominations and prizes, and critics' polls rate it consistently highly.[2] Despite this, from a production budget of $76 million the film grossed just under $70 million worldwide according to Box Office Mojo. The losses are, however, not large in film economic terms, and also only relate to figures at the box office, not DVD or Blu-ray sales of the film. It can be seen to have garnered kudos and been reputation enhancing for Universal, and, in this light, it is possible to argue that *Children of Men* has been a successful film for the studio.

The involvement of Universal appears to rest on a combination of the transnational auteur status of the director and his bankability. Cuarón notes that Universal initially rejected the project as it 'was too weird for them at the time', and that they only came on board once the director had completed *Harry Potter and the Prisoner of Azkaban* (Krassakopoulos, 2007), and proven his commercial worth.[3] It is interesting, nonetheless, that *Children of Men* was sold via the association of Cuarón with his best-known Mexican film, *Y tu mamá también*, with Universal seeking the status that this film had brought the director.

The film is also an example of transnational filmmaking in terms of cast, crew, and subject matter. This Anglo-American co-production cannot be easily defined as a British or US film: it is based on the 1992 novel of the same name by the British author P. D. James; like the novel, it is set in England and features a mainly British cast, with the exception of Julianne Moore; it includes a range of languages spoken by the immigrant community ('the Foogies'), although English dominates; and it addresses global issues and references wars in which there has been both US and British involvement, specifically the Iraq and Afghan conflicts.[4] The screenplay was co-written by the American Tim Sexton and the Mexican Alfonso Cuarón, who also directed it; the cinematographer was the Mexican Emmanuel Lubezki, while other key crew members such as the production design team were principally British.⁵

Children of Men purports to be a film about the state of the world, and addresses some of the most serious issues of our time through an imagining of a dystopian near future (it is set in 2027). In this, it is an example of the 'cinema of globalisation', and it can also be seen as a world cinema text as applied in my reading of *Babel*: that is, an example of films which 'seek to say something about "the world", with a focus on relationships between citizens and transnational socio-political issues' (see p. 137). This is a film which takes migration and the mistreatment of refugees as a central theme and in this covers what for a number of critics is a defining element of a transnational film text. For Ezra and Rowden, for instance, a focus on displaced persons is central to their understanding of transnational cinema (2006: 7). Higbee and Lim also note that one of the main approaches to 'transnational cinema relates to work on diasporic, exilic and post-colonial cinemas, which aims, through its analysis of the cinematic representation of cultural identity, to challenge the western (neo-colonial) construct of nation and national culture' (2010: 9).

An overview of the plot illustrates this concern with the wrongs of the world and the representation of a nation whose borders have been permeated despite human rights abuses committed against refugees. The film rewrites James's novel, which is a profound meditation on the spiritual dimensions of an infertile world and does not have the same focus on issues of globalisation and migration. Cuarón's film tells the story of Theo Faron (Clive Owen).⁶ Theo is an unimportant bureaucrat working in the Ministry of Energy (in the novel he is a history professor), yet, ironically, he is entirely lacking in energy, and is a depressed alcoholic. The world that he inhabits at the opening of the film is a small enclave within the fascist state of Britain, which attempts unsuccessfully to close its borders to a growing influx of migrants (Foogies) seeking refuge from a post-apocalyptic world, thus demonstrating the impossibility of the fortress nation state and by implication a purely national cinema. Western supremacy is also challenged by the fact that the only known pregnant woman in the land is an African migrant. The production notes outline the environment in which the action takes place:

> Lengthy wars, some of them fought with nuclear arms, have decimated much of the planet; Africa has been devastated by a nuclear war and Kazakhstan has been rendered uninhabitable by Russian nuclear attacks.

Children of Men

> Global pollution levels have soared and have caused irreparable damage to the global environment. Immense terrorist attacks have ravaged cities on every continent, and major cities such as New York, Geneva, Moscow and Tokyo have been wrecked by acts of nuclear terrorism. As a result of these combined catastrophes, tidal waves of refugees have been created. (Visual Hollywood, 2006c)

Women are inexplicably infertile (In contrast to the novel, in which men are infertile), and this is a world without children, which serves as a metaphor for the destruction of any promise of a future caused by the man-made catastrophes outlined above.

The plot hinges on the fact that the symbolically named Kee (Claire-Hope Ashitey), an African 'Foogie', is pregnant. Theo's ex-partner Julian (Julianne Moore) is the leader of a revolutionary group known as the Fishes and contacts Theo, ostensibly to ask him to help secure transit papers to the coast, where the mythical 'Human Project' (a utopian resistance group about which little is known) will be met and where Kee will be safe, but also because she trusts him more than her co-fighters. They are helped en route by Theo's best friend, Jasper, a retired political cartoonist (Michael Caine), and hampered by the Fishes, led by Luke (Chiwetel Ejiofor), who assassinate Julian and aim to use Kee and her baby for their political purposes. Their other main adversaries are the brutal British authorities, who associate Kee and Theo with the Fishes and are searching for them. As Cuarón has noted (Voynar, 2006; Wagner, 2006), there is an emphasis on the context of the action, and, to use the words of the high-profile cultural theorist Slavoj Žižek, 'the background persists' (from the interview with Žižek on the DVD and Blu-ray extras package). Much of the film is set in a war zone, aside from the few protected spaces of privileged London. Ubiquitous posters and television adverts call on all British citizens to 'REPORT ALL ILLEGAL IMMIGRANTS' and 'report any suspicious activity', while there are numerous images of caged immigrants, arrested Foogies with hoods on their heads, in images referencing Abu Ghraib prison in Iraq, and prisoners at Guantánamo Bay, the US military base in Cuba. The final section of the film takes place at Bexhill, which has been converted into an immigrant ghetto, and is characterised by squalor, violence, and political demonstrations.

The sense that this is an important film about 'the world' has been reinforced by other comments on the film by Žižek, who casts it as an important cultural document for our times. To give one example, he opines:

I think that this film gives the best diagnosis of the ideological despair of late capitalism. Of a society without history, or to use another political term, biopolitics. And my god, this film literally is about biopolitics. The basic problem in this society as depicted in the film is literally biopolitics: how to generate, regulate life. (Žižek, 2007)

My assessment of Cuarón's political vision of the world as presented in his film will be discussed in the section below, that is, how he proposes to solve the problem the film raises, but for now the point I am making is that with *Children of Men* the director has raised his auteurist profile by making a serious filmic statement about 'the world', in the format of an engaging feature film.

This leads to the next aspect of transnational filmmaking illustrated in the film: the transnational mode of narration it employs, that is, globally accessible cinematic storytelling devices. These can include: classical Hollywood narrative approaches still widely applied throughout the world today; the stylistics associated with a new international film language, termed 'intensified continuity' by David Bordwell (2002a) and analysed in chapter 4 in the reading of *Amores perros*; and intertextual borrowings and reworkings from recognisable genres, as seen in the analysis of the films of Guillermo del Toro (part I of this book). *Children of Men* has a different approach to filmmaking, yet still utilises a transnational mode of narration recognisable to global viewers. This approach centres on the application of several features, all of which are at the service of auteurism, notions of film as art, and the search for commercial success. These include the use of the long take, a documentary-style social realist take on a sci-fi premise, as well as tropes taken from action-adventure films and the chase movie.

Thus, Cuarón takes a hybrid transgenre approach in the sense that the film applies conventions and tropes from a number of genres and merges them together. The most commented upon stylistic feature applied by Cuarón and his director of photography, Lubezki, is the use of the long take. This is also the element most discussed by Cuarón himself in interviews (von Busack, 2007; Wagner, 2006), and it is this aspect that the respected British critic Jonathan Romney singles out in a review for *The Independent*. He notes, 'it was certainly the year's most stunningly directed film; get the DVD and study the four-minute, single-take, in-car sequence about 40 minutes in. You'll gasp' (Romney, 2006). This, as seen, is taken as a mark of a certain type of art cinema filmmaker, and is associated with consecrated auteurs such as Andrei Tarkovsky, Alexander Sokurov, Michelangelo

Antonioni, Kenji Mizoguchi, and Michael Haneke, as well as North American filmmakers such as Orson Welles and Robert Altman.

I have argued in the previous chapter that the adoption of the long take in *Y tu mamá también* helped to shift Cuarón's reputation from that of a competent director-for-hire who was developing his own style to an auteurist director. This is consolidated with the release of *Children of Men*, even when post production techniques are used to artificially create the effect of the long take by rendering cuts invisible (Seymour, 2007; Udden, 2009). The film's average shot length is slightly over 16 seconds, just under that of *Y tu mamá también* at 19.6 (Udden, 2009: 30), although this stands out more in an English-language film co-produced by Universal than in an independent Spanish-language film. The long take, combined with the use of the handheld camera, as well as establishing the director as a respected filmmaker, also links to notions of the truth in a similar way to that argued in the previous chapter, in that reality does not appear to have been interfered with and the filming gives the impression of simply reporting what is there.[7] In the words of the director, his aim was:

> not to use editing or montage, trying to seek for an effect [sic]. It is to try to create a moment of truthfulness, in which the camera just happens to be there to just register that moment. So that leads into the long shots. Because then you just register the moments as they go. (Voynar, 2006)

This sets up an intriguing paradox, as the near-future setting of the film and the notion of universal infertility would suggest that *Children of Men* belongs within the fantasy genre. Nevertheless, highly complex special effects are masked to suggest the authenticity of the newsreel or the footage associated with embedded journalists in warzones. Long takes are on several occasions created in post-production and are carefully staged. This is the case with two of the most commented upon sequences in the film: the scene in which Theo, Julian, Luke, Kee, and Miriam (Julian's midwife, played by Pam Ferris) are attacked while driving, and the scene in the refugee camp/ghetto/prison when Theo is separated from Kee and her baby and attempts to find her amid the warfare which has broken out. As James Udden points out, 'the now famous scene in the automobile took two months to plan, eight days to shoot on *three* separate locations', and six separate sections were all amalgamated into a single artificial long take by digital means (Udden, 2009: 31).[8] Within this long tracking shot, which appears hyper-realist to the viewer, the real motorbikes driven by the Fishes who assassinate Julian are swapped for digital bikes in the moment of the crash, while the baby in the camp scene is a digital baby (Seymour, 2007).

An article in the technical film magazine *FX Guide* reveals the following complex process of achieving the long-take scene in the car:

> The car ended up being a special purpose car, built with a rig developed by Gary Thieltges of Doggicam Systems. It was piloted by a stunt driver lying near flat in front with space for another at the other end when driving in reverse. The car 'shell' was mounted to appear normal but with a complete rig overhead allowing the director and DOP [director of photography] to travel along above the actors. (Seymour, 2007)

These effects are entirely undetectable to audiences. This is clearly not the case with the digital images placed on billboards and on buses around a grimy London captured with dull colours that create a futuristic version of contemporary life.[9] The point here is that what appears to be a text utilising an imperfect cinema style, with just a few muted futuristic effects, is highly contrived, dependent on a large budget, and produces a fusion of film languages with which viewers will readily identify.

This combination of big-budget effects with a guerrilla filmmaking approach, seen in the way the filmmakers give the impression of capturing the action as it happens, on handheld cameras, makes *Children of Men* genre defying. Yet these are transnational narrative modes we know how to read. Viewers are familiar with the newsreel-style footage from such global news channels as Al Jazeera, CNN, Sky, BBC 24, Euro News, the Japanese NHK World TV, the Chinese CCTV-9, France 24, and Russia Today. Images of war and refugees form the regular diet for viewers of these channels.[10] Cuarón deliberately creates a film language based on a visual style that contemporary viewers know very well from media imagery. As he has said in an interview:

> the rule #1 in this film is that whatever we see has to have a visual reference of stuff that now has become part of human consciousness. It's an iconography that mostly came out of the media. (Murray, n.d.)

This is also a point the director emphasises in the production notes: 'We don't have one iconic element in the film that is not from the present' (Visual Hollywood, 2006a), and he directed the art department to create images from his 'own file of photographs from Iraq, Sri

Lanka, Northern Ireland, the Balkans, Somalia, Chernobyl' (Murray, n.d.). The film's engagement with images from the contemporary news media can be illustrated from the screengrabs in figures 9.1–9.3.

Nevertheless, most audiences do not go to the cinema or watch a DVD or Blu-ray disc to see a slightly fictionalised version of the news; most want a good story and enough recognisable features from filmic popular culture to confirm that this is a movie. There are of course tropes associated with big-budget movies that generate pleasure and conform to audience expectations. As the director relates in an interview, Iñárritu critiqued an early version of the film for its lack of human interest (Wagner, 2006), central to successful feature films. According to Cuarón, his Mexican colleague noted that '"this isn't a movie, it's an essay. Where are your characters?" Before, I was so concerned about putting together the film's universe that, in a way, I was too distracted from character' (Wagner, 2006). The finished version certainly has a focus on the hero, as well as using conventions from other popular genres. Thus, *Children of Men* is part social-realist film documenting human rights abuses of migrants, but it is also a disaster movie, and an action-adventure/chase movie with a hero who can save the day. Cuarón explains:

9.1 A member of Homeland Security keeps guard over imprisoned Foogies in *Children of Men*. The focus on the elderly German-speaking woman is a clear reference to holocaust imagery

9.2 Miriam is captured by security forces in *Children of Men*. Her image here references the photographs of hooded prisoners from Abu Ghraib, as also noted by Arlen Parsa (2006) in her discussion of the political references of the film

9.3 Theo and Kee make their way through the Muslim uprising in *Children of Men*

'I found this premise [the concept of the infertility of the human race in the near future] was an amazing opportunity to talk about the present day, using the excuse that it's set in the "near future." I didn't want to do a film about the future – I wanted to do a film about the present, and the circumstances today that are crafting our future.' He quickly adds, 'This isn't science-fiction – it's a chase movie, set in 2027.' (Visual Hollywood, 2006a)

Here, the director makes a grand declaration regarding his film being about the present and the future state of the world, while also appealing to mainstream film-goers. Clive Owen's Theo may be the only hero who spends the majority of a movie in flip-flops, but he still metaphorically saves the world, and is involved in a number of highly charged chase scenes, a standard element for action-adventure films. These scenes take the focus away from a journalistic approach to war, as the audience, at all times, roots for the fictional hero, and is antagonistic towards both the British security forces, who are violent and racist, and the Fishes, whose goals are lost in their acts of mindless violence. In contrast to the films by Arriaga and Iñárritu, this film does not substantially deviate from the model of the single action hero common in much mainstream global cinema. Theo goes on a personal journey throughout the film and awakens from his existential torpor until he accepts the trials of the archetypal hero. Although he does die at the close of the film, this is not until he has saved Kee and her baby and ensured that they reach the Human Project's ship, the *Tomorrow*, thus guaranteeing the requisite happy ending for films with commercial pretensions.

What Cuarón has achieved with *Children of Men* is to bring these different narrative forms together in one text. In this way, the use of features from a number of genres means that it sits somewhere between commercial popular drama and independent film, in spite of its production context. It is useful here to return to Chris Holmlund's definition of independent filmmaking applied to the reading of *21 Grams* (p. 117), in which she highlights 'social engagement and/or aesthetic experimentation – a distinctive visual look, an unusual narrative pattern, a self-reflexive style' (Holmlund, 2005: 2). All of these aspects can be applied to *Children of Men*, regardless of the Universal logo on all the promotional material. While James Udden rejects the category of 'independence' for the film precisely due to Universal's involvement, preferring to see it as 'a prestige picture with Oscar potential' (Udden, 2009: 29), a number of those involved with the production call up the concept and align it with auteurism. In other words, the suggestion is that the film belongs in an independent category because it is the product of a singular vision. Of Cuarón, Julianne Moore comments:

> I think he's extraordinary. He has a tremendous imagination and a keen sense of how to tell a story visually. On this film, we sometimes worked with very little lighting, using a lot of handheld or a steadicam – almost like an independent film. (Visual Hollywood, 2006b)

The same production notes have the producer Hilary Shor comment on the 'independent' style Cuarón chose for *Children of Men*, while pointing out that the director 'sees things that nobody else involved with the film sees' (Visual Hollywood, 2006a). This auteurist vision is also flagged up by Clive Owen, who says 'Alfonso is one of the few directors who has the vision to take on a movie like this and do a completely unique thing with it' (Visual Hollywood, 2006b). This, of course, comes from promotional material, and the cast and crew interviewed are more likely to flag up the serious artistic elements than discuss the more commercial aspects mentioned above. The transnational modes of narration in *Children of Men* are from a range of forms and film languages which are not usually brought together in one text. The film combines approaches that borrow from news reporting of conflict, documentaries that rely on social realist aesthetics, with mildly futuristic effects, and action-adventure chase scenes, all of which place this text between commercial big-budget and independent filmmaking.

The political vision in *Children of Men*

As has been established above, *Children of Men* is a transnational film in a number of key senses; however, what has not been established is what this means in political terms. As Mette Hjort (2009: 15) has observed, 'there is nothing inherently virtuous about transnationalism and there may even be reason to object to some forms of transnationalism'. This section takes a lead from this point and considers whether the commercial aspects compromise the radicalism of *Children of Men*; it interrogates the seemingly progressive nature of the film and aims to elucidate Cuarón's political vision as presented in the film.

In the chapters 7 and 8 I critiqued aspects of the representation and politics of two of Cuarón's previous films: *Sólo con tu pareja* and

Y tu mamá también. *Children of Men* is a film that appears to take a big leap in a new, more radical direction by tackling the most pressing issues of our age: wars, environmental disasters, and migration as a result of the previous two. However, despite some shifts in position necessitated by the subject matter, I argue that there are some parallels in the political positioning of the director, which may not be immediately obvious.

Cuarón has highlighted the importance of the relationship between character and environment in the film, and argues that the same approach exists in *Children of Men* as with his Mexican hit. In an interview he comments:

> We used the cameras in the same principle as in *Y TuMamá* [*También*] ... we decided social environment is as important as character, so you don't favor one over the other. That means going loose and wide. The camera doesn't do close-ups. Rather than make tension between the character and the environment, you make the character blend in with the environment. (Von Busack, 2007)

This does have the effect of successfully highlighting the inequalities between the privileged 'Green Zone', as Cuarón (using Naomi Klein's term) has called the parts of England that belong to UK citizens (von Busack, 2007), and the ghettoised, hellish reality of the Foogies (see below for Klein's involvement in this project). Nevertheless, the privileged gaze is that of the documented white British male (Theo), while the Foogies are reduced to their status as victims and their experience homogenises them. White Europeans share cages with Africans and Arabs, and this creates some dramatic images and demonstrates effectively how the experience of being a migrant in a post-apocalyptic world has an equalising function (see figure 9.1). In spite of this, these characters are, in the main, passive figures who are only heard begging or crying. Arabs are reduced to becoming signifiers of militant Islam; they are witnessed chanting en masse 'Allahu Akbar' as they march through the streets once the uprising has begun. The only Foogie who is a significant character is Kee, yet, as Sayantani DasGupta (2010: 187) argues, she has 'little agency or voice, and thereby [the film] reduces her almost entirely to her reproductive and symbolic role', as fertile African earth mother. DasGupta even describes her as a 'sort of walking womb'.[11] Kee always defers to Theo after her initial mistrust and never acts without him guiding her. She is, to a degree, infantilised and passes from the care of Julian and Miriam, to the care of Theo, and on to the white men (and no women are seen) on board the *Tomorrow*.

It is also interesting to observe who the villains and heroes are of this film. Cuarón makes much in interviews of the fact that this is a film that attacks the totalitarianism lurking behind democratic facades. In one example he notes:

> Many of the stories of the future involve something like 'Big Brother,' but I think that's a 20th century view of tyranny. The tyranny happening now is taking new disguises – the tyranny of the 21st century is called 'democracy.' I found that a very interesting concept to look at in Children of Men. (Visual Hollywood, 2006a)

This is a fresh take on political filmmaking, which generally prefers to show fascistic dictatorial states under the control of a single ruler, for example in *Downfall* (Hirschbiegel, 2004), and *The Last King of Scotland* (Macdonald, 2006). It also presents an auteurist spin on the novel, which features a dictator, Xan, cousin of Theo, as ruler of this totalitarian England. The leaders of the filmic future England are faceless, aside from the Minister for Arts, Theo's cousin in this version, who is rather benign, if ineffectual. The system itself is at fault, implicitly supported by citizens clinging to their privileges in a world falling apart. The truly bad characters are the one-dimensional representatives of the armed forces and the Homeland Security forces, who detain, torture, and abuse the Foogies to protect these citizens and keep the foreigners out of their Green Zones. In a typical exchange, after Theo pretends Kee has wet herself when her waters break, a thuggish security officer responds with 'you fucking people disgust me', before slapping Miriam and taking her off the bus, after which a black hood is placed on her head (see figure 9.2). The news footage approach, with its dull colours accompanied by the aforementioned long takes in the camp scenes, presents the fiction as truth and gives the sense that we are watching actual instances of abuse. Audiences are struck by the irony of the voice on the loudspeaker in the refugee camp which announces 'Britain supports you and provides you shelter; do not support terror'. It is clear that the terror is inflicted by the representatives of Homeland Security, not the migrants (interestingly, Homeland Security is in fact the name of the US anti-terrorist agency).

This all presents an anti-establishment message and addresses the current mistreatment of some categories of migrants in British society, where asylum seekers (both adults and children) are locked up in detention centres resembling prisons (Verkaik, 2010). Effectively, all the overseas wars the British have historically been involved with come home to threaten the domestic security of its citizens in an act of transnational karma. Nevertheless, the representations of the treatment of Foogies in *Children of Men* comment on a global rather than national situation, seen in the use of iconography from a range of conflict zones, as described above.[12] The fact that the film intends to make a comment on worldwide transnational phenomena is also reinforced in the global images highlighted in the documentary made to accompany the feature film, *The Possibility of Hope*, as will be seen in the next section.

The critique of the democratic modern state and the focus on the condition of migrants is, thus, called attention to by the text and its paratexts. Nevertheless, there is another central aspect of the film about which very little has been said by either Cuarón or critics. I am referring here to the lack of attention paid to the revolutionaries, the Fishes, who share the villain status in the film with the authorities. The Fishes are a nasty organisation whose political aims are invalidated by the fact that they are brutal, murderous, lacking in all compassion, and, along with the British forces, are behind the terror condemned by the film. Luke, their leader, arranges for the assassination of their erstwhile leader, Julian, presumably because she has rejected a more violent path. The shot through the head is shocking to the audience, for a number of reasons: there is little dramatic build-up to the act; viewers do not expect the highest-profile star of the film (Julianne Moore) to be dispatched so early in the narrative; and the technique of the long shot allows viewers no reprieve from the impact of the killing as they watch her bleed to death. It is also the only event in the film up to this point which elicits an emotional response from Theo, who privately breaks down and weeps in the following scene. The emphasis on shock and empathy for the protagonist highlights the identification cultivated for Theo; audiences endorse his decision to part with the Fishes and rescue Kee as he makes the discovery that they have killed their own leader.[13]

Luke and his co-fighters' acts of cruelty are shown to the audience through the point of view of Theo; in another example, they needlessly murder the other hero of the film, Jasper, as Theo watches on helplessly. Their only interest in Kee's baby is in how it will serve their political goals and the revolution. Less attention is paid to these political goals, which in themselves are noble: the protection and demand for equality and full legal rights for Foogies. Nevertheless, Cuarón's thesis, through his portrayal of the Fishes, is that radical political groups are morally bankrupt, as ideology has replaced compassion. In a telling scene amid the chaos and destruction of the Foogie camp, after the uprising has started, Luke asks Theo, 'How can it be peaceful when they take away your dignity?', and he adds of the baby, 'we need him, Theo'. Theo calmly responds, 'It's a girl, Luke'. This shows the differing positions of the two: Luke sees the baby as nothing more than a political signifier, and for him the child is a weapon in the war, hence the assumption of masculinity. Theo, in contrast, sees the humanity in the birth of a baby girl, and chooses a peaceful route represented in the Human Project, to whom he delivers Kee and baby Dylan.[14] The audience is given within the narrative only the option of accepting the route represented by Theo – they are not shown the possibilities of the Fishes' position. The birth of a child to a Foogie could significantly help the cause of persecuted migrants, and thus their cause does have humane potential. Nevertheless, audiences are not presented with this option, because the Foogies' politics are not given any space within the narrative and are eclipsed by their violence. In addition, no other valid resistance movement is shown. We do see the Muslim uprising as background to Theo and Kee's escape in the refugee camp/prison, but its goals or agenda are never established, and members are indistinguishable from each other (see figure 9.3).

While I have found no comments by Cuarón relating to the Fishes, the position they represent appears to be encapsulated by his use of the term 'ideology'. The director's statements in the production notes are revealing:

> In the end, Children of Men isn't so much about humanity being destructive – it's more about ideologies coming between people's judgment and their actions that is at work in this story.... These complex issues are being thought about in America and Europe, and looked at very differently – how are immigrants, refugees, asylum seekers going to be treated? This is something happening now – the near future is now. I think all of us working on the film thought that you have to get the human experience to get to the social and political – it's something that needs compassion more than an ideology. (Visual Hollywood, 2006a)

The nature of the ideology which the director rejects is not mentioned, yet I would suggest from the film's vision of the revolutionaries that the implicit reference is to Marxism. The film appears to take a post-modern view of the rejection of ideology, linked to the concept of the failure of metanarratives, such as Marxism, monotheistic religions, and the Enlightenment, to make sense of the world (Lyotard, 1984). For Daniel Bell, the end of ideology is the 'exhaustion of old political passions' (Bell, 1992: 266), and the political passions of the Fishes are certainly rejected as a source of hope in *Children of Men*.

I have in the previous chapter documented the director's aversion to overtly politically filmmaking, and, despite the subject matter, this aversion is also evident in *Children of Men*. While the film presents a dystopian picture of contemporary society through an exaggerated imagining of today's social problems projected on to the near future, the main political opposition represented in the film is seen as morally rotten, and rooted in senseless violence. Hope is found through the individual hero, and the embracing of romantic ideals such as love and compassion. Individual transformation is thus placed more highly than an ideological political revolution. The Human Project remains in the realms of myth, and although it is revealed to be real enough at the end of the film to offer a happy ending and a form of resolution and hope, the audience knows almost nothing about them, beyond the fact that the members have a sanctuary in the Azores. In addition, the hero is painted in a deliberately apolitical way. He agrees to help the Fishes only because Julian asks him to and he clearly still has feelings for her. He continues to help Kee because he is in awe of her pregnancy, and pointedly rejects the political cause of the Fishes.

Another approach to Cuarón's film is taken by Kirk Boyle (2009), who argues that *Children of Men* is a politically radical text in the way in which it 'invites us to identify with those who are critical of [Naomi Klein's] ... disaster–capitalism complex', of which more shortly. However, while there are subversive elements in the film, seen in the critique of the state and treatment of migrants, the privileged status of the white male hero is retained and no credible political solution is offered. The reliance on individual escape and a happy ending fits within commercial filmic codes, while hope in a utopian and individualistic form is not part of a radical political project.

The Possibility of Hope and a political vision

It is interesting that the filmic text and the comments by the director work to reject a politically revolutionary solution to the problems posited when two of the best-known proponents of *Children of*

Men, Slavoj Žižek and Naomi Klein, are highly political opponents of capitalism and in favour of action to destroy certain capitalist institutions, of which more below. What I will do in this concluding section is examine the documentary that accompanies the film on the DVD and Blu-ray releases of Children of Men, The Possibility of Hope, and explore its relationship to the film. I consider the function of a documentary which features some of the most popular academics in their fields. A full analysis of the documentary and the position of each of the cultural critics merits a chapter in its own right, which I do not have the space for here. Thus, after some discussion of this particular form of paratext, I focus on the nature of the documentary, and consider the vision of the world which it shares with Children of Men. I go on to discuss some important divergences with regard to the political visions of Naomi Klein and Slavoj Žižek.

The Possibility of Hope was not produced by Universal, but by Cuarón's own production company, Esperantoj; this, and the fact that it is a documentary, would seem to suggest that it can be a more radical text than Children of Men. The documentary includes the views of a number of well known theorists and there are many complex ideas about the present condition of our planet, with a focus on migration and environmental disaster. In contrast to Guillermo del Toro, Cuarón does not provide lengthy director's commentaries on his films, and prefers to discuss them with the popular media. Responding to this question in an interview he explains, 'In an interview, you can respond, and then be quiet. In a commentary, you have to keep talking. And what's that saying? It's better to be quiet than let people think you are stupid' (Wagner, 2006). The Possibility of Hope does aim to provide an alternative form of commentary on Children of Men; as Cuarón has said, 'it's like a documentary approach to what the film is about' (Murray, n.d.).

The film features spoken views of media-friendly writers and academics, and combines these with images of poverty and disaster from many regions of the world, as well as with some images of the earth reproduced from NASA Johnson Space Center (always used when the author of the Gaia books, James Lovelock, is speaking). The interviewees are the Slovenian cultural theorist Slavoj Žižek, the Canadian author and anti-globalisation activist Naomi Klein, the Franco-Bulgarian philosopher and theorist of literary narrative theory and cultural history Tzvetan Todorov, the Italian human geographer Fabrizio Eva, the Dutch sociologist of human migrations Saskia Sassen,

Children of Men

the British environmental theorist James Lovelock, and the British economist John Gray. Accompanying images include signs of global warming, such as ice melting in the Arctic, large congested crowd scenes, piles of trash, images of the sea, mountains, and parched arid land, many of which are filmed with a shaky handheld camera reminiscent of the camera work of Rodrigo Prieto. The sense conveyed here through the images and the international (albeit 'Western') theorists is that of mapping the world and providing an overview of its current problems, along with a warning of what is to come. This all works to endorse the vision of the feature film. There are also scenes from the film chosen to illustrate some of the speakers' views, which have the function of enhancing the realist/'factual' nature of the film, connecting it with the documentary and ensuring that it is not considered as a fantasy product.

All the thinkers, in one way or another, then, confirm the image of the future of our planet that is created in *Children of Men*. In the first section of the documentary, which is given the subheading 'Reality', Žižek is filmed making the following comments:

> Hegel in his aesthetics says that a good portrayal looks more like the person who is portrayed than the person itself. A good portrayal is more you than you are yourself. And I think this is what the film does with our reality.

As well as offering a statement pointing to the deep truths within *Children of Men*, the reference to the feature film so early on in the documentary helps to connect the ideas in the fictional form to those of *The Possibility of Hope*. Some of the views offered by the interviewees include the rise of environmental migration and civil wars (Sassen); the idea that governments are spreading the concept of fear in order for citizens to accept human rights abuses against 'the other' (Klein); the need to make connections between the brutality of the authorities and the existence of social inequalities (Sassen); the existence of gated privileged communities for the rich and separate, run-down deprived areas, and the conflict this brings (Žižek, Klein, Sassen); and the mistreatment of immigrants, who are dehumanised in the wealthy countries they escape to (Sassen). The next section, 'Fever', speaks of environmental disaster through global warming (Lovelock, Gray); the prediction that the rate of disasters will increase due to (neo-liberal) economic structures (Klein); and mass migration and 'climate apartheid' due to the spread of large infertile regions

(Lovelock, Klein). All the voices come together towards the end with a variation on the same message of future climate chaos; Žižek, for instance, calls for the need to wake up to the truth of global warming. The documentary follows the structure of the film in the sense that the final section is entitled 'Hope'. Eva speaks of a utopian possibility (as does *Children of Men*). He calls for an 'aspacial solution', in which borders no longer function and 'space has to lose meaning as a guarantor of rights'. Žižek suggests that hope can be found when despair, along with the fact that we are 'in deep shit', is recognised. Gray, in a similar vein, rejects the type of hope which is blocking out reality. Todorov suggests that there is something in human nature which will save us as (and in this he echoes the film's ending) it is in our nature to protect babies, for we know that we can survive in the future only if we protect the weaker ones. Žižek brings the two formats together metaphorically by providing the penultimate comment to *The Possibility of Hope* with a view of the ending of *Children of Men*. He commends 'this wonderful metaphor', of the rootless boat floating around, and notes, 'this meaning of renewal means you cut your roots'. As he is speaking, there is a clip from the film of this final scene, when Kee her baby and a dying Theo float towards the *Tomorrow*.

What is apparent from Cuarón's companion piece is that these revered theorists present a coherent picture of what the problems are, which matches the vision in *Children of Men*, but there are, I would argue deliberately, no references to any larger political agendas or political dogma. This means that most viewers, regardless of political allegiance, would find themselves in agreement with their views in the documentary. They can, thus, be seen to entirely support Cuarón's message in his feature film, through their assessment of the ills of the world and the nebulous notions of hope. In what follows, I examine more closely some of the political views of two of the most prominent supporters of the director, Žižek and Klein, to examine their relationship with the politics of *Children of Men*. There is a greater focus on Klein, as she has much more coherent ideas of direct action as a response to the wrongs of capitalism. In addition to his intervention in the documentary, Žižek has also provided a fuller six-minute commentary on the DVD/Blu-ray release in which he explains his ideas on the film and uses this as an opportunity to expound some of his views. The text can also be found in the article entitled 'The Clash of Civilizations at the End of History' (Žižek, 2006). Klein has collaborated with Cuarón following the release of *Children of Men*. Kirk Boyle (2009) notes that, on her website, Klein writes of how she sent the director a copy of her book *The Shock Doctrine: The Rise of Disaster Capitalism* (Klein, 2007), because 'I adore his films and felt that the future he created for *Children* was very close to the present I was seeing in disaster zones'. She later collaborated with Alfonso and his son Jonás to make a short film entitled *The Shock Doctrine*, directed by Jonás and written by Naomi and Alfonso, to promote her book and her website.[15]

What interests me here is the divergence in approaches between the political vision laid out in *Children of Men* and that of Cuarón's two most high-profile intellectual supporters. Slavoj Žižek advocates radical politics and has caused controversy for his 'idiosyncratic hybrid of Hegelian dialectics, Althusserian Marxism and Lacanian psychoanalysis' (Homer, 2001). While there is not the space to develop the complexity of his views here, I will focus on his declarations at the Marxism 2009 conference, now publicly available on YouTube.[16] In his speech, Žižek states that overcoming capitalism is the ultimate goal of a revolutionary, and anything short of this, such as a liberal desire to keep capitalism with a human face, is not valid for radical leftists. He outlines an 'apocalyptic zero-point' vision of the present, and speaks of ecological breakdown, slums, biogenetic reduction of humans to manipulatable machines, and the digital control of our lives. *Children of Men* does present a filmic model of the catastrophic state of the world that Žižek speaks of, despite the different envisioning of a solution, and perhaps this is why the Slovenian theorist hails the text and chooses to ignore the rejection of an overtly political model.

Naomi Klein also promotes a radical political vision in her writings and activism. In *The Shock Doctrine* (one of her best-known books), she develops a very specific thesis, rooted in the rejection of neoliberal economic models. Her vision of the world is strikingly similar to Cuarón's in the feature film; however, while he does not consider economic causes for his apocalyptic vision, or endorse any collective political response, Klein's book does both. In chapter 20, entitled 'Disaster Apartheid: A World of Green Zones and Red Zones' (2007: 406–422), the author describes the separate worlds of the privileged and the dispossessed, and explains how the privileged buy their way out of conflict and environmental disaster. She notes, 'the green zone emerges everywhere that the disaster–capitalism complex descends, with the same start partitions between the included and the excluded, the protected and the damned' (414). According to Klein, disaster capitalism, or, as its supporters would prefer, free market economics, is built on the theories of Milton Friedman, the academic behind the economic policies of right-wing leaders such as Pinochet, Thatcher, and Reagan, and advocates (to simplify) the decreased intervention of the state in regulating society and increased privatisation. Klein's thesis is that shock tactics are employed by Friedman's political disciples, such as the creation of wars, and the opportunistic manipulation of environmental disasters (such as Hurricane Katrina) in order to make citizens accept a form of deregulated capitalism.

Her final chapter suggests the end of disaster capitalism through the direct action of protesters, and through the election of (usually leftist) governments which attack neo-liberal economic policies, and she cites the examples of President Lula Da Silva in Brazil (451), the re-election of the Sandinista leader Daniel Ortega in Nicaragua (452), Rafael Correa in Ecuador (452), Evo Morales in Bolivia, Hugo Chávez in Venezuela (452), and Hezbollah in Lebanon (459–462). Klein has also long been associated with anti-globalisation protests and her best-selling book *No Logo* (2000) gives voice to key ideas of anti-globalisation campaigners; indeed, she has become a leading figure within the movement (Segerstrom, 2010).

So, to highlight the divergence between Cuarón's film and the ideas of Žižek and Klein, capitalism itself is not a target of *Children of Men*, and the economic roots of the disaster facing the world are unstated. The causes of the problems are deliberately vague and derive from ecological factors. This is seen in a line from a joke Jasper tells Theo, which is the only moment in the film that obliquely and dismissively addresses the causes of infertility. He says, 'Why can't we make babies anymore? Some of them say it's genetic experiments, gamma rays, pollution, same old, same old'. In addition, the main form of direct action, witnessed in the film through the revolutionary group the Fishes, is strongly condemned, as described above. This group is the closest in contemporary society to anti-globalisation campaigners, who are heroes for Klein, yet villains of this piece, due to their representation as violent thugs.

As Žižek argues, *Children of Men* is effective as a key document for our times in a number of ways: it critiques incisively the fear generated within democracies towards the 'other', and reveals the way this fear is harnessed by democracies to commit human rights abuses (in the film, against the Foogies). For these reasons it is clear

Children of Men 223

why, for the Slovenian critical thinker, the film provides a diagnosis of the sickness within our society. It also beautifully demonstrates Klein's vision of red (war) and green (gated) zones. But this is also a film which obeys many key rules of commercial cinema, and in its adherence to these rules it dispenses with a radical political vision, as I have argued.

As a film part funded by Universal Studios as well as other smaller but established production companies, it is, of course, a product of global capitalism.[17] This is the paradox at the root of the creative industries: cultural artefacts often gain their power from critiquing the system, yet they, particularly films with large budgets, are an essential part of global economic systems. *Children of Men* is not a revolutionary film; while it provides a degree of social commentary, it avoids political and ideological answers to the issues that it raises. It presents a romantic individualist solution to humanity's problems, and is thus a successful and entertaining mainstream film.

Notes

1   For a full list of nominations and awards won, see IMDB at www.imdb.com/title/tt0206634/awards.
2   This is corroborated by the compilation of reviews on the metacritics website (www.metacritic.com/movie/children-of-men/critic-reviews).
3   According to IMDB, *Harry Potter and the Prisoner of Azkaban* grossed over $795 million worldwide from a budget of $130 million (http://pro.imdb.com/title/tt0304141).
4   'Foogies' is the term used in the film for refugees; 'foogies' is the spelling in the shooting script released by Universal (http://awards.universalpictures.com/ChildrenofMenFinalShootingScript.pdf).
5   The production designer, Jim Clay, and set designer, Jennifer Williams, are both British; see the DVD bonus disc, 'Futuristic Effects', for interviews with them. For an interview with Sexton on how he teamed up with Cuarón in Mexico, see Hyoguchi (n.d.).
6   The novel has him as Theo Faren.
7   In this the film borrows from the aesthetics of documentary news reporting in a similar way to *District 9* (Blomkamp, 2009), another film with a sci-fi premise that uses a hyper-realist approach.
8   Udden (2009: 32) also explains post-production processes used for the faux long take in the camp scene.
9   All of this technical work was given to specialist film effects companies; most were produced by Double Negative (DNeg), a sizeable outfit with

eighteen members of staff (Seymour, 2007), while the digital baby had the dedicated attention of Framestore CFC (Seymour, 2007). For a detailed reconstruction of the digital creation of the baby, see the feature on the bonus DVD package 'Visual Effects: Creating the Baby'.

10 For a list of global news channels shown by one of the largest digital channel providers, see 'The Sky TV Channel List' at www.skyuser.co.uk/forum/sky-sky-tv/12103-sky-tv-channel-list.html.

11 I would like to thank the author for sending me a copy of her chapter.

12 In an interview (von Busack, 2007), Cuarón also makes reference to the treatment of Mexican migrants to the USA, and laments the building of a wall between the two countries to keep out Mexicans while the USA celebrated the fall of the Berlin Wall.

13 The murder of Julian can also be seen as a figurative killing of the novel and an assertion of authorship, as Julian was the character in the novel who was pregnant, and Kee did not exist.

14 Dylan was, significantly, the name of Theo and Julian's son who died, and is also significantly a boy's and a girl's name, symbolising possibility for the whole world. There could also be a reference to Bob Dylan, famous for his protest songs and for the promotion of peace.

15 It was produced by the UK company Renegade Pictures and was commissioned by the publishers Penguin. At the time of writing it could be accessed on YouTube at www.youtube.com/watch?v=aSF0e60O_tw. A longer documentary based on *The Shock Doctrine* was co-directed by Michael Winterbottom and Mat Whitecross (2009), and presents an effective summary of Klein's ideas in the book.

16 At www.youtube.com/watch?v=_GD69Cc20rw.

17 This is also true of this book, as even academic books, which generally sell few copies, would not be accepted by publishers were they not likely to make some profit.

Conclusion

Between them, Guillermo del Toro, Alejandro González Iñárritu, and Alfonso Cuarón have made films that have been taken as Mexican, mainstream Hollywood, US independent, British, and Spanish, while Iñárritu's *Babel* further complicates national classifications. As they have moved between national spaces, they have disregarded established borders of genres and classifications, and have, each in his own way, taken from and rewritten the horror movie, the fantasy film, political filmmaking, the road movie, and the sci-fi film, creating hybrid forms which are often branded through the auteurist names of the directors. Their films have caused critics to rethink other classificatory borders, such as those which separate art cinema and independent cinema from commercial mainstream filmmaking, and those which separate world cinema from US cinema. This study has explored the many ways in which del Toro, Iñárritu, and Cuarón have both followed and rewritten the film industry rule book.

Throughout, I have taken auteurism as a flexible label, constructed by texts, paratexts, and critical discourses, as well as an individual director's career path. Thus, del Toro distances himself from *Mimic*, rarely mentions *Blade II*, and declares himself most proud of his Spanish-language films, and inserts as many stylistic markers as possible in *Hellboy II*, while using interviews and 'making of' featurettes to claim ownership over the film, and generate a star presence. Iñárritu managed to transform himself from Mexican director to American independent auteur with his second film, through its artistic, experimental nature, the cast he has endorsing him, and the backing of 'independent' US studios. With *Babel* he again makes a transition, to a 'world cinema' auteur, a position consolidated with his latest film, *Biutiful*, set in Barcelona, starring one of Spain best-known actors,

Javier Bardem, and with a focus on immigrant communities. Cuarón, following the domestic success of *Sólo con tu pareja*, was, in turn, cast as a solid director who could take on high-quality studio projects such as *A Little Princess* and *Great Expectations*. However, he did not earn his auteur credentials until he directed *Y tu mamá también*, the film which afforded him the opportunity to make *Children of Men* (but not before directing *Harry Potter and the Prisoner of Azkaban*). While the three directors throughout their careers have sought an auteurist status, they have also sought to advance their careers and find work as directors, goals which do not always complement each other.

Intrinsic to auteurism is the development of an individual style, forged in the cases of del Toro, Iñárritu, and Cuarón with strong working relationships with their teams and, in particular, their respective cinematographers, Guillermo Navarro, Rodrigo Prieto, and Emmanuel Lubezki. In this book I have demonstrated each director's style and approach in the films. Thus, I have explored del Toro's visual motifs and thematic tropes, and the rich treasure chest of cultural references with which he fills his filmic world. I have examined Iñárritu's particular take on the human condition, told through his interpretation of contemporary narrative modes associated with intensified continuity. I have traced Cuarón's evolution from a director seeking to cultivate his own look through a rich mise-en-scène to a proponent of the long take and serious social issues. I have examined the uses of colour palettes in the cases of all three, and demonstrated how, in their own ways, they have relied on colour to create artistic visual worlds and stamp a painterly seal on their films.

Despite the artistic differences and diverse approaches to filmmaking, there are many connections and points in common between del Toro, Iñárritu, and Cuarón. One of the most obvious is that they have a sense of collective identity and friendship rooted in their Mexican backgrounds, in spite of or perhaps because of their transnational trajectories. They appear in interviews together, and have together lobbied influential bodies within the Mexican film industry, in an act of support for filmmaking in Mexico, as outlined in the introduction. This not only illustrates the ways in which they work together, but also helps explain their cinematic globe trotting, as there have not been the funds in their home country to support their filmmaking ambitions. Only Cuarón has returned to film in Mexico following success in other national contexts, and only for a single film before making his Harry Potter film and *Children of Men*. They have

Conclusion

all worked throughout their careers to position themselves as global filmmakers, as these words of Cuarón illustrate:

> I have a huge appreciation of backgrounds. What I have a problem with is borders. The language of cinema is cinema itself: it doesn't matter whether it is filmed in Spanish or English or French or Japanese. The same goes for the people who make it. Yes, I'm a film-maker from Mexico. But I also belong to the world (Cuarón, 2007)

This could have been spoken by any one of the three, and all have made similar comments in interviews.

They are all filmmakers from Mexico, but they do not, in the totality of their filmmaking, represent Mexican cinema. The response of those who reacted against del Toro representing Mexico for *El laberinto del fauno* in the foreign film category in the Academy Awards of 2006, as opposed to Juan Carlos Rulfo's documentary about construction workers, *En el hoyo* (*In the Pit*, 2006) is, then, perfectly understandable.[1] Mexican directors making films in Mexico and featuring Mexican stories include Carlos Carrera, Busi Cortés, Fernando Eimbcke, Julián Hernández, Jorge Michel Grau, María Novaro, Carlos Reygadas, Dana Rotberg, Juan Carlos Rulfo, Marisa Sistach, Guita Schyfter, and Francisco Vargas, many of whom have enjoyed varying degrees of transnational circulations. This is not a criticism of del Toro, Iñárritu, and Cuarón, but rather a recognition that, despite the importance of *Cronos*, *Amores perros*, *Sólo con tu pareja*, and *Y tu mamá también*, they are no longer making Mexican films, even when taking into account all the complexities surrounding national labels that this book has engaged with. This is not to say that this cannot change, although declarations such as those cited above by Cuarón suggest that this is unlikely.

They are all canny enough to know that they have been able to leave behind the limited funding possibilities afforded to filmmakers who have stayed in Mexico only by making the right contacts, and in this they have worked together to cultivate relationships with key players within the US film industry. The research for this book revealed a few recurring names of individuals and production and distribution companies. These are: Ted Hope, David Linde, and James Schamus, all key players with the independent production company Good Machine, which went on to become Focus Features, the independent arm of Universal Studios. Good Machine, Focus Features, and Universal have all supported the three directors in mutually beneficial relationships. To give some examples, the international sales of *Y tu mamá también* were taken care of by Good Machine; Focus Features distributed *21 Grams*; Universal distributed *Children of Men*, and was the principal producer of *Hellboy II*. Focus is also the production and distribution company with which Cha Cha Cha entered a five-film package deal worth $100 million (discussed in the introduction). It is also worth noting that Canana Films, the Mexican company formed by actors Diego Luna and Gael García Bernal, along with producer Pablo Cruz, has made a similar deal with Focus Features (Independent Film, 2005).[2]

As well as working with some of the same people and companies, they have also worked on each other's projects, as has been seen in a number of examples throughout the book. To give a few reminders, Iñárritu advised Cuarón on *Children of Men*, del Toro advised Iñárritu and helped with the editing on *Amores perros*, Cuarón's company co-produced *El laberinto del fauno*, while del Toro is named as associate producer on *Biutiful*. In the words of Cuarón:

> Fortunately the three of us are good friends. We developed our films at the same time and we have always loved to collaborate, to stick our forks in each other's salad. So I feel as close to Alejandro and Guillermo's films as I do to my own. (Cuarón, 2007)

This collaboration is reflected in the parallels in their career trajectories: each of the directors had a breakthrough film in the same year – 2006 – in terms of establishing their international auteurist status. For del Toro it was *El laberinto del fauno*, for Iñárritu it was *Babel*, and for Cuarón it was *Children of Men*. Each film deals with serious issues in aesthetically innovative ways; each achieved international recognition, and received passionate critical responses. This recognition is illustrated in the fact that all three received nominations for the 2007 US Academy Awards, which cemented the sense of a collective identity and global auteur status, seen in the use of the term 'the three amigos' in the international media. Indeed, Cuarón has spoken of the three as 'sister films' (Voynar, 2006).

Throughout my readings of the key texts, I have paid attention to the political visions of each director. While these are informed by individual world views, there are also parallels in this area, which, as I have sought to demonstrate, are linked to the films' commercial aspirations. These broadly fit into a liberal leftist position, which eschews both reactionary and radical political positionings. Thus, I

Conclusion

have shown how *El laberinto del fauno*'s interpretations of the early Franco period correspond to fairy tale and fantasy requirements of happy endings, and demonstrated that the film fails to engage with the social realities of the defeat of the Republican forces. The more radical political element can be found in its feminist centring of Ofelia within the text. With regard to Iñárritu, I argued that the social and political critique of George W. Bush's 'war on terror' is diluted by the US-centric viewpoint of *Babel* and its failure to fully engage a world cinema gaze.

In the case of Cuarón, the director's first film was argued to be rather sexist, and to rely on crude representations of sexuality, and stereotypical portrayals of its Japanese characters. In turn, I noted the centrality of the white privileged gaze of the protagonists and commented on the 'othering' of mestizo rural Mexico, although I argued that it does present an effective critique of macho Mexican privileged culture. Finally, I presented the view that both *Y tu mamá también* and *Children of Men* reject a leftist revolutionary political position, preferring to advocate personal transformation. In this the films have clear parallels with *Amores perros*, which, through the character of el Chivo, critiques revolutionary groups and their actions, as I have argued elsewhere (Shaw, 2003).

Del Toro, Iñárritu, and Cuarón are multilingual directors who have learnt to speak a number of the international languages of filmmaking.[3] Their success in winning funding from large North American companies appears to point to new ways of theorising cultural power relationships between the USA and Mexico. I want, however, to end this study with some thoughts, questions, and tentative answers in relation to concepts of power. Although the success of three Mexican directors in the global film market is cause for a degree of celebration, can we also argue that the hegemonic structures of the US film industry are as powerful as ever? The trajectories of my case studies demonstrate that both state and private components of the Mexican film industry have not been able to accommodate the ambition of its three best-known directors, and they have, like so many migrants, gone to the north to improve their working conditions, although, of course, on an entirely different level to illegal immigrants in low-paid work. While our directors foreground the independence associated with their auteurist status, and have made films in Spain and the UK, and elsewhere, can we not argue that their success partly rests on the fact that they have become fluent in American languages of cinema (whether that be in the discourses of fantasy/horror, or American independent or popular filmmaking)? Their Mexican backgrounds and literacy in film cultures from around the world have allowed them to reinterpret and provide an original take on these languages and acquire auteurist identities; however, they have, in all but one case, earned handsome profits for their US paymasters.[4] Even del Toro's *El laberinto del fauno* would not have the high profile it has without the involvement of the US distributors Picturehouse. Thus, while traditional formulations of cultural imperialism are being rewritten, new configurations are emerging.

Notes

1   See note 14, chapter 3 (p. 91).
2   Luna and Bernal are favourite actors of the directors and in large part owe their global success to their collaborations with Iñárritu and Cuarón. They both appeared in *Y tu mamá también*, and Carlos Cuarón's *Rudo y cursi*, while Bernal has featured in two of Iñárritu films, *Amores perros* and *Babel*.
3   In this they can be compared to Walter Salles and Fernando Meirelles from Brazil.
4   The exception is *Children of Men*, discussed in chapter 9.

Filmography

The following information is taken from IMDB and Box Office Mojo. This filmography has selected key information for the feature films directed by the directors, and films they have acted as producers for. The box office information is included only where worldwide statistics are available; to include US sales available from the website Box Office Mojo can be misleading as it is too partial. This information also does not include DVD, Blu-ray and television sales, which are central when considering re-releases of the directors' early films following commercial success, such as *Cronos* and *Sólo con tu pareja*. Box office information is presented where available in the chapters on the films.

Guillermo del Toro

Cronos, 1993 (Mexico)
Producers: Arthur Gorson, Bertha Navarro, Alejandro Springall
Production companies: CNCAIMC, Fondo de Fomento a la Calidad Cinematográfica, Grupo Del Toro, Guillermo Springall, Iguana Producciones, Instituto Mexicano de Cinematografía (IMCINE)
Budget: $2,000,000
Screenplay: Guillermo del Toro
Cinematography: Guillermo Navarro
Art direction: Brigitte Broch
Editor: Raúl Dávalos
Music: Javier Alvarez
Leading players: Federico Luppi (Jesús Gris), Ron Perlman (Angel de la Guardia), Claudio Brook (Dieter de la Guardia), Tamara Shanath (Aurora), Margarita Isabel (Mercedes)

Mimic, 1997 (USA)
Producers: Ole Bornedal, Harvey Weinstein
Production companies: Dimension Films, Miramax Films
Budget: $25,000,000
Box office: $25,480,490
Screenplay: Matthew Robbins, Guillermo del Toro
Cinematography: Dan Laustens
Art direction: Tamar Deverell
Editor: Peter Devaney Flanagan, Patrick Lussier
Music: Marco Beltrami
Leading players: Mira Sorvino (Dr Susan Tyler), Jeremy Northam (Dr Peter Mann), Josh Brolin (Josh Maslow), Giancarlo Giannini (Manny)

El espinazo del diablo (The Devil's Backbone), 2001 (Spain, Mexico, USA)
Producers: Augustín Almodóvar, Rosa Bosch, Bertha Navarro
Production companies: El Deseo, Tequila Gang, Anhelo Producciones, Sogepaq, Good Machine
Budget: $4,500,000
Screenplay: Guillermo del Toro, David Múñóz, Antonio Trashorras
Cinematography: Guillermo Navarro
Art direction: César Macarrón
Editor: Luis de la Madrid
Music: Javier Navarrete
Leading players: Eduardo Noriega (Jacinto), Marisa Paredes (Carmen), Federico Luppi (Casares), Iñigo Garcés (Jaime), Fernando Tielve (Carlos), Junio Valverde (Santi)

Blade II, 2002 (USA)
Producers: Jon Divens, Peter Frankfurt, Andrew J. Horn, Patrick J. Palmer, Wesley Snipes
Production companies: New Line Cinema, Amen Ra Films, Marvel Enterprises, Imaginary Forces, Justin Pictures, Linovo Productions, Milk and Honey, Pacific Title, Art Studio
Budget: $54,000,000
Screenplay: David S. Goyer
Cinematography: Gabriel Beristain
Art direction: Elinor Rose Galbraith
Editor: Peter Amundson
Music: Marco Beltrami
Leading players: Wesley Snipes (Blade), Kris Kristofferson (Abraham Whistler), Ron Perlman (Reinhardt), Leonor Varela (Nyssa), Thomas Kretschmann (Damaskinos), Luke Goss (Jared Nomak)

Filmography

Hellboy, 2004 (USA)
Producers: Lawrence Gordon, Lloyd Levin, Mike Richardson
Production companies: Dark Horse Entertainment, Lawrence Gordon Productions, Revolution Studios
Budget: $66,000,000
Box office: $99,414,250
Screenplay: Guillermo del Toro, Peter Briggs (based on the *Dark Horse* comic books by Mike Mignola)
Cinematography: Guillermo Navarro
Editor: Peter Amundson
Music: Marco Beltrami
Art direction: James Hanbidge
Leading players: Ron Perlman (Hellboy), John Hurt (Professor Trevor 'Broom' Bruttenholm), Selma Blair (Liz Sherman), Rupert Evans (John Myers), Karel Roden (Grigori Rasputin), Jeffrey Tambor (Dr Tom Manning), Ladislav Beran (Kroenen), Doug Jones (Abraham 'Abe' Sapien)

El laberinto del fauno (*Pan's Labyrinth*), 2006 (Spain, Mexico)
Producers: Alvaro Augustín, Alfonso Cuarón, Guillermo del Toro, Bertha Navarro, Frida Torresblanco
Production companies: Estudios Picasso, Tequila Gang, Esperanto Filmoj, Sententia Entertainment, Telecinco
Budget: €13,500,000
Screenplay: Guillermo del Toro
Cinematography: Guillermo Navarro
Art direction: Eugenio Caballero
Editor: Bernat Vilaplana
Music: Javier Navarrete
Leading players: Ivana Baquero (Ofelia), Sergi López (Captain Vidal), Maribel Verdú (Mercedes), Ariadna Gil (Carmen), Doug Jones (Pan/The Pale Man), Alex Angulo (Doctor), Federico Luppi (King)

Hellboy II: The Golden Army, 2008 (USA)
Producers: Lawrence Gordon, Lloyd Levin, Mike Richardson
Production companies: Dark Horse Entertainment, Lawrence Gordon Productions, Relativity Media, Universal Pictures
Budget: $72,000,000
Screenplay: Guillermo del Toro, Mike Mignola
Cinematography: Guillermo Navarro
Editor: Bernat Vilaplana
Music: Danny Elfman
Art direction: Peter Francis, John Frankish
Leading players: Ron Perlman (Hellboy), John Hurt (Professor Trevor

'Broom' Bruttenholm), Selma Blair (Liz Sherman), Jeffrey Tambor (Dr Tom Manning), Doug Jones (Abraham 'Abe' Sapien), Luke Goss (Prince Nuada), Anna Walton (Princess Nuala)

Guillermo del Toro as (co-)producer

Carrera, C. (Director) (1998) *Un embrujo*. Mexico: Salamandra Producciones, Tequila Gang

Cordero S. (Director) (2004) *Crónicas (Chronicles)*. Mexico, Ecuador

Bayona, J. (Director) (2007) *El orfanato (The Orphanage)*. Spain: Esta Vivo! Laboratorio de Nuevos Talentos, Grupo Rodar, Rodar y Rodar

Martínez, A. (Director) (2008) *Cosas insignificantes (Insignificant Things)*. Mexico, Spain: Manga Films, Tequila Gang, Warner Bros Pictures

Cordero, S. (Director) (2009) *Rabia (Rage)*. Mexico, Spain, Colombia: WAG, Departamento de Cultura del Gobierno Vasco, Dynamo, Euskal Irrati Telebisa (EITB), Instituto de la Cinematografía y de las Artes Audiovisuales (ICAA), Montfort Producciones, Telecinco Cinema, Tequila Gang

Morales, G. (Director) (2010) *Los ojos de Julia (Julia's Eyes)*. Spain: Antena 3 Films, Canal+ España, Catalan Film and Television

Nixey, T. (Director) (2010) *Don't Be Afraid of the Dark*. USA: Central City Studios

Miller, C. (Director) (2011) *Puss in Boots*. USA: Dreamworks Animation

Yuh, J. (Director) (2011) *Kung Fu Panda 2*. USA: Dreamworks Animation

Alejandro González Iñárritu

Amores perros, 2000 (Mexico)

Producers: Alejandro González Iñárritu, Martha Sosa
Production companies: Altavista Films, Zeta Film
Budget: $2,000,000
Screenplay: Guillermo Arriaga
Cinematography: Rodrigo Prieto
Editors: Luis Carballar, Alejandro González Iñárritu, Fernando Pérez Unda
Music: Gustavo Santoalalla
Production design: Brigitte Broch
Art direction: Melo Hinojosa
Leading players: Gael García Bernal (Octavio), Goya Toledo (Valeria), Emilio Echevarría (El Chivo), Vanessa Bauche (Susana), Alvaro Guererro (Daniel), Gustavo Sánchez Parra (Jarocho), Adriana Barraza (Octavio's mother)

21 Grams, 2003 (USA)

Producers: Roberto Salerno, Alejandro González Iñárritu
Production companies: This Is That Productions, Y Productions, Mediana Productions

Budget: $20,000,000
Screenplay: Guillermo Arriaga
Cinematography: Rodrigo Prieto
Editor: Stephen Mirrione
Music: Gustavo Santoalalla
Art direction: Brigitte Broch
Leading players: Sean Penn (Paul Rivers), Charlotte Gainsbourg (Mary Rivers), Naomi Watts (Cristina Peck), Benicio del Toro (Jack Jordan), Melissa Leo (Marianne Jordan)

Babel, 2006 (US, France, Mexico)

Producers: Steve Golin, Jon Kilik, Alejandro González Iñárritu
Production companies: Media Rights Capital, Paramount Vantage, Anonymous Content, Central Films, Zeta Film
Budget: $27,000,000
Box office: $132,700,000
Screenplay: Guillermo Arriaga
Cinematography: Rodrigo Prieto
Editor: Douglas Crise, Stephen Mirrione
Music: Gustavo Santoalalla
Art direction: Brigitte Broch
Leading players: Rinko Kikuchi (Chieko Wataya), Brad Pitt (Richard Jones), Cate Blanchett (Susan Jones), Gael García Bernal (Santiago), Mustapha Amhita (Mohammed), Said Tarchani (Ahmed), Boubker Ait El Caid (Yussef), Mutapha Rashidi (Abdullah), Amelia (Adriana Barraza), Kôji Yakusho (Yasujiro Wataya)

Biutiful, 2010 (Mexico, Spain, USA)

Producers: Fernando Bovaira, Sandra Hermida, Alejandro González Iñárritu, Jon Kilik, Ana Ruark
Production companies: Menageatroz, Mod Producciones, Focus Features International, Televisión Española (TVE), Televisió de Catalunya (TV3), Ikiru Films
Budget: not ascertained
Box office: $25,147,786
Screenplay: Alejandro González Iñárritu, Armando Bo, Nicolás Giacobone
Cinematography: Rodrigo Prieto
Editor: Stephen Mirrione
Music: Gustavo Santoalalla
Art direction: Brigitte Broch
Leading players: Javier Bardem (Uxbal), Maricel Alvarez (Marambra), Eduardo Fernández (Tito), Ruben Ochandiano (Zan), Cheng Tai Shen (Hai), Luo Jin (Liwei), Hanna Bouchaib (Ana), Guillermo Estrella (Mateo), Ana Wagener (Bea), Karra Elejalde (Mendoza)

Alejandro González Iñárritu as (co-)producer (feature films)
21 Grams, *Babel* and *Biutiful* (see above)
Cuarón, C. (Director) (2008) *Rudo y cursi* (*Rough and Corny*). Mexico: Focus Features International, Universal International Pictures, Canana Films

Alfonso Cuarón

Sólo con tu pareja (*Love in the Time of Hysteria*), 1991 (Mexico)
Producer: Alfonso Cuarón
Production companies: Fondo de Fomento a la Calidad Cinematográfica, Instituto Mexicano de Cinematografía (IMCINE), Sólo Películas
Screenplay: Alfonso Cuarón, Carlos Cuarón
Cinematography: Emmanuel Lubezki
Editors: Alfonso Cuarón, Luis Patlán
Music: Carlos Warman
Production design: Brigitte Broch
Leading players: Daniel Giménez Cacho (Tomás Tomás), Claudia Ramírez (Clarisa), Gloria (Isabel Benet), Mateo Mateos (Luis de Icaza), Dobrina Liubomirova (Silvia), Astrid Hadad (Teresa de Teresa)

A Little Princess, 1995 (USA)
Producers: Delisa Cohen, Mark Johnson
Production companies: Warner Bros Pictures, Mark Johnson Productions, Baltimore Pictures
Budget: $17,000,000
Screenplay: Richard Lagravenese (from novel by Frances Hodgson Burnett)
Cinematography: Emmanuel Lubezki
Editor: Steven Weisberg
Music: Patrick Doyle
Art direction: Tom Duffield
Leading players: Liesel Matthews (Sara Crewe), Eleanor Bron (Miss Minchin), Liam Cunningham (Captain Crewe/Prince Rama), Vanessa Lee Chester (Becky), Rusty Schwimmer (Amelia), Arthur Malet (Charles Randolph), Errol Sitahal (Ram Dass), Taylor Fry (Lavinia)

Great Expectations, 1998 (USA)
Producers: Art Linson, John Linson
Production companies: Art Linson Productions, Twentieth Century Fox Film Corporation
Screenplay: Mitch Glazer
Cinematography: Emmanuel Lubezki
Editor: Steven Weisberg
Music: Patrick Doyle, Ron Wasserman

Art direction: John Kasarda
Leading players: Gwyneth Paltrow (Estella), Ethan Hawke (Finnegan Bell), Hank Azaria (Walter Plane), Chris Cooper (Jo), Anne Bancroft (Ms Dismoor), Robert De Niro (Prisoner /Lustig)

Y tu mamá también, 2001 (Mexico)
Producers: Alfonso Cuarón, Jorge Vergara
Production companies: Anhelo Producciones, Besame Mucho Pictures
Budget: $5,000,000
Screenplay: Carlos Cuarón, Alfonso Cuarón
Cinematography: Emmanuel Lubezki
Editors: Alfonso Cuarón, Alex Rodríguez
Art direction: Diana Quiroz, Miguel Angel Alvarez
Leading players: Maribel Verdú (Luisa), Diego Luna (Tenoch), Gael García Bernal (Julio)

Harry Potter and the Prisoner of Azkaban, 2004 (UK, USA)
Producers: Chris Columbus, David Heyman, Mark Radcliffe
Production companies: Warner Bros Pictures, 1492 Pictures, Heyday Films, P of A Productions
Budget: $130,000,000 (estimated)
Box office: $796,688,549 (worldwide)
Screenplay: Steve Kloves (from the novel by J. K. Rowling)
Cinematography: Michael Seresin
Editor: Steven Weisberg
Music: John Williams
Production design: Stuart Craig
Art direction: Andrew Ackland-Snow
Leading players: Daniel Radcliffe (Harry Potter), Emma Watson (Hermione Granger), Rupert Grint (Ron Weasley), Robbie Coltrane (Hagrid), Michael Gambon (Professor Dumbledore), Alan Rickman (Professor Snape), Gary Oldman (Sirius Black), Maggie Smith (Professor McGonagall)

Children of Men, 2006 (USA, UK)
Producers: Marc Abraham, Eric Newman, Hilary Shor, Iain Smith, Tony Smith
Production companies: Universal Pictures, Strike Entertainment, Hit and Run Productions
Budget: $76,000,000
Box office: $68,327,768 (worldwide)
Screenplay: Alfonso Cuarón, Timothy J. Sexton, David Arata, Mark Fergus, Hawk Ostby (from the novel by P. D. James)
Cinematography: Emmanuel Lubezki

Editors: Alfonso Cuarón, Alex Rodríguez
Music: John Tavener
Production design: Geoffrey Kirkland, Jim Clay
Art direction: Ray Chan
Leading players: Clive Owen (Theo Faron), Julianne Moore (Julian Taylor), Michael Caine (Jasper Palmer), Chiwetel Ejiofor (Luke), Claire-Hope Ashitey (Kee), Pam Ferris (Miriam)

Alfonso Cuarón as producer (feature films)

Rudo y cursi (see above)
El laberinto del fauno (see above)
Mueller, N. (Director) (2004) *The Assassination of Richard Nixon*. USA: Anhelo Producciones, Appain Way, Esperanto Filmoj.
Crónicas (see above)
Y tu mamá también (see above)
Sólo con tu pareja (see above)

General filmography

Agraz, C. G. (1992) *Mi querido Tom Mix*. Mexico: Fondo de Fomento a la Calidad Cinematográfica, Gobierno del Estado de Zacatecas, Instituto Mexicano de Cinematografía (IMCINE).
Alfredson, T. (2008) *Låt den rätte komma in* (*Let the Right One In*). Sweden: EFTI, Sandrew Metronome Distribution Sverige AB.
Almodóvar, P. (2006) *Volver*. Spain: Canal+ España, El Deseo, Ministerio de Cultura.
Almodóvar, P. (2009) *Los abrazos rotos* (*Broken Embraces*). Spain: Universal Pictures International (UPI), Canal+ España, El Deseo.
Altman, R. (1993) *Short Cuts*. USA: Fine Line Features, Spelling Films International, Avenue Pictures Productions.
Amenábar, A. (1997) *Abre los ojos* (*Open Your Eyes*). Spain: Canal+ España, Las Producciones del Escorpión, Les Films Alain Sarde.
Anderson, P. T. (1999) *Magnolia*. USA: Ghoulardi Film Company, New Line Cinema, Magnolia Project.
Anderson, P. T. (2007) *There Will Be Blood*. USA: Ghoulardi Film Company.
Aragón, M. G. (1978) *El corazón del bosque* (*The Heart of the Forest*). Spain: Arandano.
Araki, G. (1992) *The Living End*. USA: Cineplex Odeon Films, Desperate Pictures, October Films.
Aranda, V. (1991) *Amantes* (*Lovers*). Spain: Pedro Costa Producciones Cinematográficas, Televisión Española.
Arau, A. (1992) *Como agua para chocolate* (*Like Water for Chocolate*). Mexico: Arau Films Internacional, Aviacsa.

Filmography

Armendáriz, M. (2001) *Silencio roto (Broken Silence)*. Spain: Oria Films.
Aronofsky, D. (2000) *Requiem for a Dream*. USA: Artisan Entertainment, Thousand Words, Sibling Productions.
Arriaga, G. (2008) *The Burning Plain*. USA, Argentina: 2929 Productions, Costa Films, Parkes/Macdonald Productions.
Ashby, H. (1971) *Harold and Maude*. USA: Mildred Lewis and Colin Higgins Productions, Paramount Pictures.
Athié, F. (1991) *Lolo Mexico: Centro de Capacitación Cinematográfica (CCC)*.
Audiard, J. (2009) *Un prophète (A Prophet)*. France: Why Not Productions, Chic Films, Page 114, France 2 Cinéma.
Auster, P. and Wang, W. (1995) *Blue in the Face*. USA: Miramax Films, Internal Films.
Balagueró, P. and Plaza, P. (2007) *[Rec]*. Spain: Castelao Producciones, Filmax, Televisión Española, Canal+ España, Generalitat de Catalunya.
Balagueró, P. and Plaza, P. (2009) *[Rec] 2*. Spain: Castelao Producciones, Filmax, Generalitat de Catalunya.
Bayona, J. (2007) *El orfanato (The Orphanage)*. Spain: Esta Vivo! Laboratorio de Nuevos Talentos, Grupo Rodar, Rodar y Rodar.
Berman, S. and Tardán, I. (1995) *Entre Pancho Villa y una mujer desnuda (Between Pancho Villa and a Naked Woman)*. Mexico: Televicine, Televisa.
Bigas Luna, J. J. (1993) *Huevos de oro (Golden Balls)*. Spain: Antena 3 Televisión, Filmauro, Hugo Films.
Blatty, W. P. (1980) *The Ninth Configuration*. USA: Ninth Configuration.
Blomkamp, N. (2009) *District 9*. USA, New Zealand, Canada: TriStar Pictures, Block/Hanson, WingNut Films.
Bolada, C. (1998) *Bajo California: el límite del tiempo (The Limit of Time)*. Mexico: Instituto Mexicano de Cinematografía (IMCINE), Sincronía.
Boyle, D. (1996) *Trainspotting*. UK: Channel Four Films, Figment Films, Noel Gay Motion Picture Company.
Browning, T. (1931) *Dracula*. USA: Universal Pictures.
Buñuel, L. (1950) *Los olvidados (The Young and the Damned)*. Mexico: Ultramar Films.
Buñuel, L. (1962) *El angel exterminador (The Exterminating Angel)*. Mexico: Producciones Gustavo Alatriste.
Buñuel, L. (1965) *Simón del desierto (Simon of the Desert)*. Mexico: Sindicato de Trabajadores de la Producción Cinematográfica (STPC).
Buñuel, L. (1970) *Tristana*. Spain, Italy, France: Epoca Films, Talía Films, Selenia Cinematografica.
Burton, T. (1989) *Batman*. USA: Warner Bros Pictures, Guber-Peters Company, PolyGram Filmed Entertainment.
Cameron, J. (2009) *Avatar*. USA: Twentieth Century Fox Film Corporation, Dune Entertainment, Ingenious Film Partners, Lightstorm Entertainment.
Camus, M. (1978) *Los días del pasado (The Days of the Past)*. Spain, Argentina: Impala.

Cann, B. (2000) *Crónica de un desayuno* (*A Breakfast Chronicle*). Mexico: Instituto de Cinematografía (IMCINE), Tabasco Films, Argos Cine.
Carot, M. and Jeunet, J. (1995) *The City of Lost Children*. France, Germany, Spain: Club d'Investissement Media, Eurimages, Studio Image.
Carrera, C. (1991) *La mujer de Benjamín*. Mexico: Centro de Capacitación Cinematográfica (CCC), Estudios Churubusco Azteca, Fondo de Fomento a la Calidad Cinematográfica.
Castañeda, R. (2006) *Km 31: Kilómetro 31*. Mexico: Lemon Films, Filmax, Salamandra Films.
Chaffey, D. (1963) *Jason and the Argonauts*. UK: Columbia Pictures Corporation, Morningside Productions.
Charles, L. (2009) *Brüno*. USA: Everyman Pictures, Four By Two, Capital Media Rights.
Coen, E. and Coen, J. (2007) *No Country For Old Men*. USA: Paramount Vantage, Miramax Films, Scott Rudin Productions.
Colón, J. (2006) *Cansada de besar sapos* (*Tired of Kissing Frogs*). Mexico, USA: Miravista, Santo Domingo Films, Salamandra Films, Elisa Salinas, Bazooka Films.
Columbus, C. (2002) *Harry Potter and the Chamber of Secrets*. USA, UK, Germany: 1492 Pictures, Heyday Films, Miracle Productions.
Cronenberg, D. (1983) *Videodrome*. Canada: Canadian Film Development Corporation, Famous Players, Filmplan International, Guardian Trust Company, Victor Solnicki Productions.
Cronenberg, D. (1986) *The Fly*. USA: Brooksfilms.
Crowe, M. (2001) *Vanilla Sky*. USA: Paramount Pictures, Cruise/Wagner Productions, Vinyl Films.
Cuarón, A. (2007) *The Possibility of Hope*. USA: Esperanto Filmoj, New Wave Entertainment.
Cuarón, A., Cuarón, J. and Klein, N. (2007) *The Shock Doctrine*. USA, UK, Canada: Esperanto Filmoj, Klein Lewis Productions, Penguin Books.
Cuarón, C. (2008) *Rudo y cursi* (*Rough and Corny*). Mexico: Focus Features International, Universal International Pictures, Canana Films.
Curiel, F. (1962) *Los autómatas de la muerte*. Mexico: Estudios América, Producciones Corsa.
Curiel, F. (1963) *Neutrón contra el Dr Caronte*. Mexico: Estudios América, Producciones Corsa.
De Palma, B. (2007) *Redacted*. USA, Canada: Film Farm, HDNet Films.
Dibb, S. (2008) *The Duchess*. UK, Italy, France: Paramount Vantage, Pathé, BBC Films.
Egoyan, A. (1994) *Exotica*. Canada: Alliance Entertainment, Ego Film Arts, Miramax Films.
Erice, V. (1973) *El espíritu de la colmena* (*The Spirit of Beehive*). Spain: Elías Querejeta Producciones Cinematográficas.

Filmography

Fincher, D. (1999) *Fight Club*. USA: Fox 2000 Pictures, Regency Enterprises, Linson Films.
Fisher, T. (1957) *The Curse of Frankenstein*. UK: Hammer Film Productions.
Fisher, T. (1958) *Dracula*. UK: Hammer Film Productions.
Fisher, T. (1961) *The Curse of the Werewolf*. UK: Hammer Film Productions.
Fleming, V. (1939) *The Wizard of Oz*. USA: Metro-Goldwyn Mayer.
Fons, J. (1995) *Callejón de los milagros (Midaq Alley)*. Mexico: Alameda Films, Consejo Nacional para la Cultura y las Artes (CONACULTA), Instituto de Cinematografía (IMCINE).
Frears, S. (2002) *Dirty Pretty Things*. UK: BBC Films, Celador Films, Jones Company Productions.
Gaghan, S. (2005) *Syriana*. USA: Warner Bros Pictures, Participant Productions, 4M.
Gámez, R. (1994) *Tequila*. Mexico: Clasa Films Mundiales.
Gervais, R. (2009) *The Invention of Lying*. USA: Warner Bros Pictures, Radar Pictures, Media Rights Capital.
Glatzer, R. and Westmoreland, W. (2006) *Quinceañera (Echo Park, L.A.)*. USA: Cinetic Media, Kitchen Sink Entertainment.
Godard, J. (1966) *Masculin/féminin (Masculine/Feminine)*. France: Anouchka Films, Argos Films, Sandrews.
Goldberg Lerner, D. (1994) *Un beso a esta tierra*. Mexico: Jago Productions.
Gómez Reja, A. (2004) *21 Grams: In Fragments* (Documentary, DVD extras). USA: Universal Studios Home Entertainment.
Gondry, M. (2004) *Eternal Sunshine of the Spotless Mind*. USA: Focus Features, Anonymous Content.
Grau, J. M. (2010) *Somos lo que hay (We Are What We Are)*. Mexico: Centro de Capacitacion Cinematografica (CCC).
Gruener, D. (1996) *Sobrenatural (All of Them Witches)*. Mexico: Televicine.
Haggis, P. (2004) *Crash*. USA, Germany: Bob Yari Productions, DEJ Productions, Blackfriars Bridge Films.
Haggis, P. (2007) *In the Valley of Elah*. USA: Warner Independent Pictures, NALA Films, Summit Entertainment, Samuels Media, Blackfriars Bridge Films.
Haneke, M. (1994) *71 Fragments of a Chronology of Chance*. Austria: Wega Film, Zweites Deutsches Fernsehen (ZDF), arte Geie.
Haneke, M. (2005) *Caché (Hidden)*. France, Austria, Germany: Les Films du Losange, Wega Film, Bavaria Film.
Hanson, C. (2002) *8 Mile*. USA: Imagine Entertainment, Mikona Productions.
Hermosillo, J. H. (1985) *Doña Herlinda y su hijo (Doña Herlinda and Her Son)*. Mexico: Clasa Films Mundiales.
Hermosillo, J. H. (1991) *La tarea (Homework)*. Mexico: Clasa Films Mundiales.
Hessler, G. (1973) *The Golden Voyage of Sinbad*. USA: Columbia Pictures Corporation, Ameran Films, Morningside Productions.

Hirschbiegel, O. (2004) *Downfall*. Germany: Constantin Film Produktion, Norddeutscher Rundfunk (NDR), Westdeutscher Rundfunk (WDR).
Hitchcock, A. (1954) *Rear Window*. USA: Paramount Pictures.
Hood, G. (2005) *Tsotsi*. UK, South Africa: UK Film and TV Production Company, Industrial Development Organisation of South Africa, National Film and Video Foundation of South Africa.
Hood, G. (2007) *Rendition*. USA: Anonymous Content, Level 1 Entertainment, MID Foundation.
Hopper, D. (1969) *Easy Rider*. USA: Columbia Pictures Corporation, Pando Company, Raybert Productions.
Jeunet, J. (2001) *Amélie*. France: Claudie Ossard Productions, Union Générale Cinématographique (UGC), Victoires Productions.
Johar, K. (2006) *Kabhi Alvida Naa Kehna*. India: Dharma Productions.
Jones, T. (2005) *The Three Burials of Melquiades Estrada*. USA: Europa Corp, Javelina Film Company, The See.
Jonze, S. (1999) *Being John Malkovich*. USA: Gramercy Pictures, Propaganda Films, Single Cell Pictures.
Jordan, N. (2005) *Breakfast on Pluto*. Ireland, UK: Pathé Pictures International, Bórd Scannán na hÉireann, Northern Ireland Film and Television Commission.
Kieslowski, K. (1993) *Trois couleurs: bleu* (*Three Colours: Blue*). France, Poland, Switzerland: MK2 Productions, CED Productions, France 3 Cinéma.
Kusturica, E. (1993) *Arizona Dream*. USA: Canal+, Constellation, Hachette Premiere.
LaBute, N. (2000) *Nurse Betty*. USA: Gramercy Pictures, Pacifica Film, Propaganda Films.
Landis, J. (1981) *An American Werewolf in London*. UK, USA: PolyGram Filmed Entertainment, Lyncanthrope Films.
Laughton, C. (1955) *The Night of the Hunter*. USA: Paul Gregory Productions.
Leduc, P. (1986). *Frida, naturaleza viva*. Mexico: Clasa Films Mundiales.
Lee, A. (2000) *Crouching Tiger, Hidden Dragon*. Taiwan, Hong Kong, USA: Asia Union Film & Entertainment.
Lee, A. (2003) *Hulk*. USA: Universal Pictures, Marvel Enterprises, Valhalla Motion Pictures.
Lee, A. (2005) *Brokeback Mountain*. USA: Alberta Film Entertainment, Focus Features, Good Machine.
Lee, A. (2007) *Lust, Caution*. USA, China, Hong Kong: Hai Sheng Film Production Company, Focus Features, Haishang Films.
Lozano, A. (2004) *Matando cabos*. Mexico: Instituto Mexicano de Cinematografía (IMCINE), Lemon Films.
Macdonald, K. (2006) *The Last King of Scotland*. UK: Fox Searchlight Pictures, DNA Films, Film4.
Malik, Terrence (2011) *The Tree of Life*. USA: Brace Cove Productions, Cottonwood Pictures, Plan B Entertainment, River Road Entertainment.

Filmography

Meirelles, F. (2002) *Cidade de deus* (*City of God*). Brazil: O2 Filmes, Video-Filmes, Globo Filmes.
Meirelles, F. (2005) *The Constant Gardener*. UK: Focus Features, UK Film Council, Potboiler Productions.
Meirelles, F. (2008) *Blindness*. Canada, Brazil, Japan: Rhombus Media, O2 Filmes, Bee Vine Pictures.
Miller, C. (2011) *Puss in Boots*. USA: Dreamworks Animation.
Miller, F. and Rodriguez, R. (2005) *Sin City*. USA: Dimension Films, Troublemaker Studios.
Minghella, A. (2006) *Breaking and Entering*. UK, USA: Miramax Films, Mirage Enterprises.
Montero, R. (1998) *Cilantro y perejil* (*Recipes to Stay Together*). Mexico: Constelación Films, Fondo de Fomento a la Calidad Cinematográfica.
Morales, G. (2010) *Los ojos de Julia* (*Julia's Eyes*). Spain: Antena 3 Films, Canal+ España, Catalan Film and Television.
Murnau, F. W. (1922) *Nosferatu*. Germany: Jofa-Atelier Berlin-Johannisthal, Prana-Film.
Nixey, T. (2010) *Don't Be Afraid of the Dark*. USA: Central City Studios.
Nolan, C. (2005) *Batman Begins*. USA: Warner Bros Pictures, Syncopy, DC Comics.
Nolan, C. (2008) *The Dark Knight*. USA: Warner Bros Pictures, Legendary Pictures, Syncopy.
Novaro, M. (1991) *Danzón*. Mexico, Spain: Fondo de Fomento a la Calidad Cinematográfica, Gobierno del Estado de Zacatecas, Instituto Mexicano de Cinematografía (IMCINE).
Novaro, M. (1994) *El jardín del Edén* (*The Garden of Eden*). Canada, France, Mexico: Fondo de Fomento a la Calidad Cinematográfica, Instituto de Cinematografía (IMCINE), Macondo Cine Video.
Oplev, N. (2009) *Män som hatar kvinnor* (*The Girl with the Dragon Tattoo*). Sweden: Danmarks Radio (DR), Det Danske Filminstitut, Film i Väst.
Paronnaud, V. and Satrapi, M. (2007) *Persepolis*. France, USA: 2.4.7. Films, France 3 Cinema, Kennedy Marshall Company.
Penn, A. (1967) *Bonnie and Clyde*. USA: Warner Brothers/Seven Arts, Tatira-Hiller Productions.
Penn, S. (2007) *Into the Wild*. USA: Paramount Vantage, Art Linson Productions.
Reeves, M. (2010) *Let Me In*. USA: Overture Films, Exclusive Media Group, Hammer Film Production, SFTI.
Richet, J. (2008a) *L'instinct de mort* (*Mesrine: Killer Instinct*). France: La Petite Reine, Remstar Productions, Novo RPI.
Richet, J. (2008b) *L'ennemi public no. 1* (*Mesrine: Public Enemy No. 1*). France: La Petite Reine, M6 Films, Remstar Productions.
Ripstein, A. (1978) *El lugar sin límites* (*Place Without Limits*). Mexico: Conacite Dos.

Ripstein, A. (1991) *La mujer del puerto* (*The Woman of the Port*). Mexico: Dos Producciones.
Rodríguez, I. (1948a) *Nosotros los pobres* (*We the Poor*). Mexico: Producciones Rodríguez Hermanos.
Rodríguez, I. (1948b) *Ustedes los ricos* (*You the Rich*). Mexico: Producciones Rodríguez Hermanos.
Rodríguez, I. (1953) *Pepe el toro*. Mexico: Producciones Rodríguez Hermanos.
Roeg, N. (1973) *Don't Look Now*. UK, Italy: Casey Productions, Eldorado Films, D. L. N. Ventures Partnership.
Rotberg, D. (1992) *Angel de fuego* (*Angel of Fire*). Mexico: Instituto Mexicano de Cinematografía (IMCINE), Producciones Metropolis, Una Productora Mas.
Rulfo, J. C. (1999) *Del olvido al no me acuerdo* (*Juan, I Forgot I Don't Remember*). Mexico: Producciones X Marca.
Rulfo, J. C. (2006) *En el hoyo* (*In the Pit*). Mexico: La Media Luna Producciones.
Salles, W. (2004) *Diarios de motocicleta* (*The Motorcycle Diaries*). Argentina, USA, Chile: Film4, South Fork Pictures, Tu Vas Voir Productions.
Salles, W. and Thomas, D. (2008) *Linha de passe*. Brazil: Media Rights Capital, Pathé Pictures International, VideoFilmes Producoes Artisticas Ltda.
Sariñana, F. (2007) *Niñas mal*. Mexico: Columbia Pictures Producciones.
Schneider, R. (1995) *Dos crímenes*. Mexico: Cuévano Films, Fondo de Fomento a la Calidad Cinematográfica, Instituto Mexicano de Cinematografía (IMCINE).
Schyfter, G. (1994) *Novia que te vea* (*Like a Bride*). Mexico: Fondo de Fomento a la Calidad Cinematográfica, Instituto Mexicano de Cinematografía (IMCINE), Producciones Arte Nuevo.
Scorsese, M. (1973) *Mean Streets*. USA: Warner Bros Pictures, Taplin–Perry–Scorsese Productions.
Scott, R. (1991) *Thelma and Louise*. USA: Pathé Entertainment, Percy Main, Star Partners III.
Serrano, A. (1998) *Sexo, pudor y lágrimas* (*Sex, Shame and Tears*). Mexico: Argos Producciones, Instituto Mexicano de Cinematografía (IMCINE), Producciones Titán.
Sistach, M. (2001) *Nadie te oye: Perfume de violetas* (*Violet Perfume: Nobody Hears You*). Mexico, Netherlands: Centro de Capacitación Cinematográfica (CCC), Filmoteca de la UNAM.
Soderbergh, S. (2000) *Traffic*. Germany, USA: Bedford Falls Productions, Compulsion, Initial Entertainment Group (IEC).
Soderbergh, S. (2008) *Che Part One* and *Che Part Two*. France, Spain, USA: Wild Bunch, Telecinco, Laura Bickford Productions, Morena Films, Ministerio de Cultura, Estudios Picasso, Guerrilla Films, Section Eight.
Solanas, F. (1992) *El viaje* (*The Voyage*). Argentina: Cinesur, Films A2, Instituto Mexicano de Cinematografía (IMCINE).
Spielberg, S. (1981) *Raiders of the Lost Ark*. USA: Paramount Pictures, Lucasfilm.

Springall, A. (1999) *Santitos.* Mexico, France, Spain: CORE Digital Pictures, Cinematografica Tabasco, Dr José Pinto Mazal.
Stone, O. (1994) *Natural Born Killers.* USA: Warner Bros Pictures.
Tarantino, Q. (1994) *Pulp Fiction.* USA: A Band Apart, Jersey Films, Miramax Films.
Taymor, J. (2002) *Frida.* USA, Canada, Mexico: Handprint Entertainment, Lions Gate Films, Miramax Films.
Tort, G. (2001) *De la calle (Streeters)* Mexico: Instituto Mexicano de Cinematografía (IMCINE), Tiempo y Tono Films, Zimat Consultores.
Tort, G. (2009) *Viaje redondo.* Mexico: Cadereyta Films, Instituto Mexicano de Cinematografía (IMCINE), Fondo para la Producción Cinematográfica de Calidad (FOPROCINE).
Tykwer, T. (1998) *Lola rennt (Run Lola Run).* Germany: X-Filme Creative Pool, Westdeutscher Rundfunk, Arte.
Tykwer, T. (2009) *The International.* USA: Columbia Pictures, Relativity Media, Atlas Entertainment.
Urrutia Lazo, O. (1999) *Rito terminal (Terminal Rite).* Mexico: Instituto Mexicano de Cinematografía (IMCINE), Centro Universitario de Estudios Cinematográficos, Fondo para la Producción Cinematográfica de Calidad (FOPROCINE), Filmoteca de la UNAM.
Van Sant, G. (1991) *My Own Private Idaho.* USA: New Line Cinema.
Vargas, F. (2005) *El violín (The Violin).* Mexico: Camara Carnal, Centro de Capacitación cinematográfica, Fidecine.
Von Donnersmark, F. (2006) *Das Leben der Anderen (The Lives of Others).* Germany: Arte, Bayerischer Rundfunk (BR), Creado Film.
Von Trier, L. (1991) *Europa.* Spain, Denmark, Sweden: Aliceleo, Det Danske Filminstitut.
Wang, W. (1995) *Smoke.* Germany, USA: Miramax Films, Neue Deutsche Filmgesellschaft (NDF), Euro Space.
Wenders, W. (2000) *The Million Dollar Hotel.* Germany, UK, USA: Icon Entertainment International, Kintop Pictures, Road Movies Filmproduktion.
Whale, J. (1931) *Frankenstein.* USA: Universal Pictures.
Winterbottom, M. (2002) *In This World.* UK: The Film Consortium, British Broadcasting Corporation (BBC), Film Council.
Winterbottom, M. (2007) *A Mighty Heart.* UK: Paramount Vantage, Plan B Entertainment, Revolution Films.
Winterbottom, M. and Whitecross, M. (2009) *The Shock Doctrine.* UK: Renegade Pictures, Revolution Films.
Wong, K. W. (1994) *Chungking Express.* Hong Kong: Jet Tone Production.
Yuh, J. (2011) *Kung Fu Panda 2.* USA: Dreamworks Animation.
Zwick, E. (2006) *Blood Diamond.* USA: Warner Bros Pictures, Virtual Studios, Spring Creek Productions.

Bibliography

URLs were verified at the time of writing (2011–12) and updates were made at proof where possible for some of the links no longer functioning.

Acevedo-Muñoz, E. (2004) 'Sex, Class, and Mexico in Alfonso Cuarón's *Y tu mamá también*'. *Film and History: An Interdisciplinary Journal of Film and Television Studies*, 34(1), 39–48.

Albert, A. (2008) 'Mike Mignola Interview, The *Hellboy 2* DVD – *Chapel of Moloch* – The Future of Hellboy'. Retrieved from http://comicbooks.about.com/od/interviews/a/mignoladvd.htm.

Alvaray, L. (2011) 'Hybridity and Genre in Latin American Film Industries'. Paper presented at the Society for Cinema and Media Studies Conference, New Orleans.

Alverson, B. (2010) '*C2E2*: Mike Mignola Spotlight'. Retrieved from www.comicbookresources.com/?page=article&id=25862.

Amaya, H. (2007) '*Amores perros* and Radicalised Masculinities in Contemporary Mexico'. *New Cinemas: Journal of Contemporary Film*, 5(3), 201–216.

Amazon (n.d.) 'Editorial Review: *The Dwelling of the Philosophers*'. Retrieved from www.amazon.com/Dwellings-Philosophers-Fulcanelli/dp/0963521160.

Ancient Mythology (n.d.) 'Kronos/Greek Mythology'. Retrieved from www.ancient-mythology.com/greek/kronos.php.

Andrew, D. (2000) 'Adaptation'. In J. Naremore (ed.), *Film Adaptation* (pp. 28–37). New Brunswick, NJ: Rutgers University Press.

Arroyo, J. (2006) 'Review of *Pan's Labyrinth*'. *Sight and Sound*, 16(12), 66–68.

Atkinson, M. (2006) 'The Village Voice'. Retrieved from www.villagevoice.com/2006-09-12/film/s-lo-con-tu-pareja.

Atkinson, M. (2007) 'Guillermo Del Toro: Finding the Way Through Pan's Labyrinth'. *Film Comment*, 43(1), 50–53.

Atkinson, M. (2008) 'Hellboy II: The Golden Army'. *Sight and Sound*. Retrieved from http://old.bfi.org.uk/sightandsound/review/4453.

Basoli, A. G. (2002) 'Sexual Awakenings and Stark Social Realities: An Interview with Alfonso Cuarón'. *Cineaste*, 27(3), 26–30.
Bell, D. (1992) 'The Coming of the Post-Industrial Society'. In C. Jencks (ed.), *The Post-Modern Reader* (pp. 250–266). London: Academy Editions.
Bergfelder, T., Harris, S. and Street. S. (eds) (2007) *Film Architecture and the Transnational Imagination: Set Design in 1930s European Cinema*. Amsterdam: Amsterdam University Press/University of Chicago Press.
Berra, J. (2008) *Declarations of Independence: American Cinema and the Partiality of Independent Production*. Bristol: Intellect Books.
Berry, C. (2010) 'What is Transnational Cinema? Thinking From the Chinese Situation'. *Transnational Cinemas*, 1(2), 111–127.
Berumen, F. J. G. (1995) *The Chicano/Hispanic Image in American Film*. New York: Vantage Press.
Bordwell, D. (1985) *Narration in the Fiction Film*. London: Routledge.
Bordwell, D. (2002a) 'Intensified Continuity: Visual Style in Contemporary American Film'. *Film Quarterly*, 55(3), 16–28.
Bordwell, D. (2002b) 'The Art Cinema as a Mode of Film Practice'. In C. Fowler (ed.), *The European Cinema Reader* (pp. 94–102). New York: Routledge.
Bordwell, D. (2006) *The Way Hollywood Tells It: Story and Style in Modern Movies*. Berkeley, CA: University of California Press.
Bordwell, D. (2007) 'David Bordwell's Website on Cinema: New Media and Old Story Telling'. Retrieved from www.davidbordwell.net/blog/?p=827.
Bordwell, D. (2008) 'Mutual Friends and Chronologies of Chance'. In D. Bordwell (ed.), *Poetics of Cinema* (pp. 189–252). New York: Routledge.
Borges, J. L. (1970a) 'Three Versions of Judas'. In *Labyrinths* (pp. 125–130). London: Penguin Books. (Originally published as 'Tres versiones de Judas' in *Ficciones*, 1944.)
Borges, J. L. (1970b) 'The Immortal'. In *Labyrinths* (pp. 135–149). London: Penguin Books. (Originally published as 'El inmortal' in *El Aleph*, 1949.)
Boyle, K. (2009) '*Children of Men* and *I Am Legend*: The Disaster–Capitalism Complex Hits Hollywood'. *Jump Cut: A Review of Contemporary Media*, 51. Retrieved from www.ejumpcut.org/archive/onlinessays/index.html.
Brook, T. (2010) 'Talking Movies: Is the Movie Industry Anti-Capitalist?' Retrieved from http://news.bbc.co.uk/1/hi/entertainment/arts_and_culture/8459297.stm.
Brown, S. (2009) 'Q&A: *Hobbit* Director Guillermo del Toro on the Future of Film'. *Wired*. Retrieved from www.wired.com/entertainment/hollywood/magazine/17-06/mf_deltoro?currentPage=2.
Calhoun, J. (2003) 'Heartbreak and Loss'. *American Cinematographer*, 8 (12). Retrieved from www.theasc.com/magazine/deco3/cover/index.html.
Camino, M. (2009) 'Blood of an Innocent: Montxo Armendáriz's *Silencio Roto* (2001) and Guillermo del Toro's *El laberinto del fauno* (2006)'. *Studies in Hispanic Cinemas*, 6(1), 45–64.

Campbell, J. (1968) *The Hero with a Thousand Faces*. Princeton, NJ: Princeton University Press.

Chaudhuri, S. (2005) *Contemporary World Cinema: Europe, the Middle East, East Asia and South Asia*. Edinburgh: Edinburgh University Press.

Childress, D. H. (2000) *Technology of the Gods: The Incredible Sciences of the Ancients*. Kempton, IL: Adventures Unlimited Press.

Chumo, P. (2000) 'Script Review: *Amores perros*'. *Creative Screenwriting*, 8(2), 10–12.

Cohan, S. and Hark, I. (eds) (1997) *The Road Movie Book*. London: Routledge.

Cook, P. (2010) 'Transnational Utopias: Baz Luhrmann and Australian Cinema'. *Transnational Cinemas*, 1(1), 23–36.

Corrigan, T. (1991) 'Genre, Gender, and Hysteria: The Road Movie in Outer Space'. In T. Corrigan, *A Cinema Without Walls: Movies and Culture After Vietnam* (pp. 137–160) New Brunswick, NJ: Rutgers University Press.

Crofts, S. (1998) 'Concepts of National Cinema'. In J. Hill and P. C. Gibson (eds), *The Oxford Guide to Film Studies* (pp. 385–394). Oxford: Oxford University Press.

Cuarón A. (2007) 'Film-Makers Without Borders'. Film Blog, *The Guardian*. Retrieved from www.guardian.co.uk/film/filmblog/2007/feb/05/making movieswithoutborders.

Czyzydlo, K. (2011) 'Transnational Auteurism: Tom Tykwer's and Krzysztof Kieslowski's *Heaven* (2002) Between Political Engagement and Romantic Anti-Capitalism'. *Transnational Cinemas*, 2(1), 37–55.

Dalton, S. (2006) '*Pan's Labyrinth*, When the Biggest Monsters Are Human'. Retrieved from http://entertainment.timesonline.co.uk/tol/arts_and_entertainment/film/article644365.ece.

DasGupta, S. (2010) '(Re)conceiving the Surrogate: Maternity, Race, and Reproductive Technologies in Alfonso Cuarón's *Children of Men*'. In M. Block and A. Laflen (eds), *Gender Scripts in Medicine and Narrative* (pp. 178–213). Newcastle: Cambridge Scholars Publishing.

Davies, A. (2008) 'Guillermo del Toro's *Cronos*: The Vampire as Embodied Heterotopia'. *Quarterly Review of Film and Video*, 25(5), 395–403.

Davies, A. (2012) *Spanish Spaces: Landscape, Space and Place in Contemporary Spanish Culture*. Liverpool: Liverpool University Press.

Dee, J. (2010) 'The Expendables: See It with the Rowdiest Crowd Possible'. *The Guardian*. Retrieved from www.guardian.co.uk/film/filmblog/2010/aug/05/the-expendables-familiar-but-fun.

Deleyto, C. and Azcona, M. (2010) *Alejandro González Iñárritu*. Urbana, IL: University of Illinois Press.

Delgado, M. (2007) *A Life in Pictures: Alfonso Cuarón*. Retrieved from http://guru.bafta.org/alfonso-cuar%C3%B3n-life-pictures-video.

Del Toro, G. (2006) *Guión cinematográfico de Guillermo del Toro: El laberinto del fauno*. Madrid: Ocho y medio.

Del Toro, G. (2008a) 'Transcript from Guillermo del Toro's BD-LIVE Chat!' Retrieved from http://iconsoffright.com/news/2008/11/transcript_from_guillermo_del.html.

Del Toro, G. (2008b) 'How I Made Hellboy in My Image'. *The Observer.* Retrieved from www.guardian.co.uk/film/2008/jul/27/guillermodeltoro.

Del Toro, G. and Hogan, C. (2009) *The Strain.* London: Harper Collins.

Dennison, S. and Lim, S. H. (2006) 'Identity, Culture and Politics in Film: World Cinema as a Theoretical Problem'. In S. Dennison and S. H. Lim (eds), *Remapping World Cinema: Identity, Culture and Politics in Film* (pp. 1–15). London: Wallflower Press.

Desai, J. (2004) *Beyond Bollywood: the Cultural Politics of South Asian Diasporic Film.* London: Routledge.

Díaz, L. M. (n.d.) 'Guillermo del Toro: Terror a la Mexicana'. *Pasadizo: ciencia ficcion, fantasia y terror.* Retrieved from www.pasadizo.com/index.php?option=com_content&view=article&id=1199.

D'Lugo, M. (2003a) 'Authorship, Globalization, and the New Identity of Latin American Cinema: From the Mexican "Ranchera" to Argentinian "Exile"'. In A. Guneratne and W. Dissanayake (eds), *Rethinking Third Cinema* (pp. 103–25). London: Routledge.

D'Lugo, M. (2003b) '*Amores perros/Love's a Bitch*'. In A. Elena and M. Díaz López (eds), *The Cinema of Latin America* (pp. 221–230). London: Wallflower Press.

Ebert, R. (1998) '*Great Expectations*'. Retrieved from http://rogerebert.suntimes.com/apps/pbcs.dll/article?AID=/19980130/REVIEWS/801300306/1023.

Ebert, R. (2006) '*Pan's Labyrinth* (2006)'. Retrieved from http://rogerebert.suntimes.com/apps/pbcs.dll/article?AID=/20061228/REVIEWS/61228001.

Edwards, K. (2008) 'Alice's Little Sister: Exploring *Pan's Labyrinth*'. *Screen Education,* 49, 141–146.

Entelis, J. P. (1989) *Culture and Counterculture in Moroccan Politics.* Boulder, CO: Westview Press.

Ezra, E. and Rowden, T. (eds) (2006) *Transnational Cinema: The Film Reader.* London: Routledge.

Felix (2006) '*Babel* Review'. Retrieved from http://liosliath.com/blog/2006/11/17/babel-review.

Fernández, J. (2001) 'Entrevista con Alfonso Cuarón'. Retrieved from www.canal100.com.mx/telemundo/entrevistas/?id_nota=414.

Finnegan, N. (2007) 'So What's Mexico Really Like?': Framing the Local, Negotiating the Global in Alfonso Cuarón's *Y tu mamá también*'. In D. Shaw (ed.), *Contemporary Latin American Cinema: Breaking into the Global Market* (pp. 29–50). Lanham, MD: Rowman and Littlefield.

Fischer, P. (2002) 'Guillermo del Toro, *Blade 2*. Interviewed by Paul Fischer in *Los Angeles Interview*'. Retrieved from http://dealmemo.com/Interview/Guillermo%20del%20Toro,%20Blade%202.htm.

Fritz, B. (2009) 'Bob Berney Returns With New Independent Film Distributor Apparition'. Retrieved from http://latimesblogs.latimes.com/entertainmentnewsbuzz/2009/08/bob-berney-returns-with-new-indie-film-company-apparition.html.

Fritz, B. (2010) 'Bob Berney Unexpectedly Exits Apparition'. Retrieved from http://latimesblogs.latimes.com/entertainmentnewsbuzz/2010/05/bob-berney-unexpectedly-exits-apparition.html.

Furey, E. (2008) 'Mignola Talks *Hellboy II*'. Retrieved from www.comicbookresources.com/?page=article&id=17166.

Galloway, S. (2007) 'Marketing Movies with VW Vans and Lots of Blood'. *Hollywood Reporter*. Retrieved from www.hollywoodreporter.com/news/marketing-movies-vw-vans-lots 13578a.

Galt, R. and Schoonover, K. (eds) (2010) *Global Art Cinema: New Theories and Histories*. New York: Oxford University Press.

García, R. (2006) 'The Foundations of Babel: A Conversation between Rodrigo García and Alejandro González Iñárritu'. In M. Hagerman (ed.), *Babel, a Film by Alejandro González Iñárritu* (pp. 256–263). London: Taschen.

García Márquez, G. (1978) *One Hundred Years of Solitude*. London: Pan Books. (Originally published as *Cien años de soledad*, 1967.)

García Tsao, L. (2001a) '*Sólo con tu pajero*'. Retrieved from www.jornada.unam.mx/2001/06/22/15an1esp.html.

García Tsao, L. (2001b) '*And Your Mother Too/Y tu mama tambien*'. Retrieved from http://www.variety.com/review/VE1117798363?refcatid=31.

Gardels, N. (2007) '*Babel*'s Alejandro Gonzalez Inarritu: Hollywood Must Portray Point of View of Others'. *Huffington Post*. Retrieved from www.huffingtonpost.com/nathan-gardels/babels-alejandro-gonzalez_1_b_39986.html.

Gibson, S. (2006) 'A Seat With a View: Tourism, (Im)mobility and the Cinematic-Travel Glance'. *Tourist Studies*, 6(2), 157–178.

Gordon, I., Jancovich, M. and McAllister, M. (2007) *Film and Comic Books*. Jackson, MS: University Press of Mississippi.

Grant, C. (2008) 'Auteur Machines? Auteurism and the DVD'. In J. Bennett and T. Brown (eds), *Film and Television After DVD* (pp. 101–115). London: Routledge.

Grant, C. and Kuhn, A. (2006) *Screening World Cinema: A Screen Reader*. London: Routledge.

Graser, M. (2008) 'Del Toro Books Vampire Deal'. *Variety*. Retrieved from www.variety.com/article/VR1117992861.html?categoryid=13&cs=1.

Gray, J. (2010a) *Show Sold Separately: Promos, Spoilers, and Other Media Paratexts*. New York: New York University Press.

Gray, J. (2010b) 'On Anti-fans and Paratexts: An Interview with Jonathan Gray'. Retrieved from http://henryjenkins.org/2010/03/on_anti-fans_and_paratexts_an_1.html.

Bibliography

Guzmán Urrero, P. (2006) '"El laberinto del fauno" (Guillermo del Toro, 2006)'. *Cine y letras*. Retrieved from www.thecult.es/Critica-de-cine/el-laberinto-del-fauno-guillermo-del-toro-2006.html.

Haddu, M. (2005) 'Love on the Run: Re-mapping the Postmetropolis in Alfonso Cuarón's *Sólo con tu pareja*'. *Framework: The Journal of Cinema and Media*, 46(2), 71–89.

Hagerman, M. (2006) 'The Foundations of *Babel*: A Conversation Between Rodrigo García and Alejandro González Iñárritu'. In M. Hagerman (ed.), *Babel: A Film by Alejandro González Iñárritu* (pp. 256–263). Madrid: Taschen.

Hall, J., Weiner, S. and Blake, V. (2008) *The Hellboy Companion*. Milwaukie: Dark Horse Books.

Harkin, J. (2009) 'Losing the Plot.' *Observer Film Quarterly*. Retrieved from www.guardian.co.uk/film/2009/mar/22/21-grams-memento-pulp-fiction.

Hartland, E. S. (1890) *The Science of Fairy Tales: An Inquiry Into Fairy Mythology*. Retrieved from www.gutenberg.org/ebooks/24614.

Harvey, N. (1998) *The Chiapas Rebellion: The Struggle for Land and Democracy*. Durham, NC: Duke University Press.

Hassapopoulou, M. (2008) '*Babel*: Pushing and Reaffirming Mainstream Cinema's Boundaries'. *Jump Cut: A Review of Contemporary Media*, 50. Retrieved from www.ejumpcut.org/archive/jc50.2008/Babel/text.html.

Hershfield, J and Maciel, D. (eds) (1999) *Mexico's Cinema: A Century of Film and Filmmakers*. Wilmington, DE: SR Books.

Higbee, W. and Lim, S. H. (2010) 'Concepts of Transnational Cinema: Towards a Critical Transnationalism in Film Studies'. *Transnational Cinemas*, 1(1), 3–22.

Higson, A. (2000) 'The Limiting Imagination of National Cinema'. In M. Hjort and S. Mackenzie (eds), *Cinema and Nation* (pp. 63–74). London: Routledge.

Hill, J. and Church Gibson, P. (2000) *World Cinema: Critical Approaches*. Oxford: Oxford University Press.

Hillier, J. (2001) *American Independent Cinema: A Sight and Sound Reader*. London: BFI.

Hjort, M. (2009) 'On the Plurality of Cinematic Transnationalism'. In N. Durovicova and K. Newman (eds), *World Cinemas, Transnational Perspectives* (pp. 12–33). New York: Routledge.

Hobson, J. (2008) 'Militarizing Women in Film: Toward a Cinematic Framing of War and Terror'. In B. Sutton, S. Morgen and J. Novkov (eds), *Security Disarmed: Critical Perspectives on Gender, Race and Militarization* (pp. 231–243). Chapel Hill, NC: Rutgers University Press.

Hollywood Jesus (2003) '*21 Grams*. About the Production'. Retrieved from http://hollywoodjesus.com/21_grams_about.htm.

Holmlund, C. (2005) 'From the Margins to the Mainstream'. In C. Holmund and J. Wyatt (eds), *Contemporary American Independent Film* (pp. 1–17). New York: Routledge.

Holmlund, C. and Wyatt, J. (eds) (2005) *Contemporary American Independent Film*. New York: Routledge.

Homer, S. (2001) 'It's the Political Economy Stupid! On Žižek's Marxism'. *Radical Philosophy*, 108, 7–16.

Hubner, L. (2010) '*Pan's Labyrinth*, Fear and the Fairy Tale'. In S. Hessel and M. Huppert (eds), *Fear Itself: Reasoning the Unreasonable* (pp. 45–62). Amsterdam: Rodopi.

Huerta, C. (2006) 'Carlos Rulfo busca nominación a estatuilla'. Retrieved from www2.eluniversal.com.mx/pls/impreso/noticia.html?id_nota=72010&tabla=espectaculos.

Hutcheon, L. (2006) *A Theory of Adaptation*. London: Routledge.

Hyoguchi, P. (n.d.) 'Tim Sexton: Screenwriter. Interviewing Hollywood'. Retrieved from www.interviewinghollywood.com/videos/video-403.php.

IGN Movies (2006) 'Interview: Alejandro Gonzalez Inarritu'. *IGN Movies*. Retrieved from http://uk.movies.ign.com/articles/742/742071p1.html.

Iñárritu, A. G. (n.d.) 'The Similarity of Differences'. Retrieved from www.landmarktheatres.com/mn/babel.html.

Independent Film (2005) 'Focus Features Makes Term Deal With Canana Films'. Retrieved from www.independentfilm.com/resources/focus-features-makes-term.shtml.

Insdorf, A. (2005) 'Ordinary People, European-Style or How to Spot an Independent Feature'. In C. Holmund and J. Wyatt (eds), *Contemporary American Independent Film* (pp. 23–39). New York: Routledge.

Jameson, F. (1990) 'Cognitive Mapping'. In C. Nelson and L. Grossberg (eds), *Marxism and the Interpretation of Culture* (pp. 347–357). Urbana, IL: University of Illinois Press.

Jameson, F. (1991) *Postmodernism, or, The Cultural Logic of Late Capitalism*. Durham, NC: Duke University Press.

Jenkins, D. (2006) 'Guillermo del Toro: Interview'. Retrieved from www.timeout.com/film/features/show-feature/4157/Guillermo_del_Toro-interview.html.

Jenkins, H. (1992) *Textual Poachers: Television Fans and Participatory Culture*. New York: Routledge.

Kantaris, G. (1998) 'Between Dolls, Vampires, and Cyborgs: Recursive Bodies in Mexican Urban Cinema'. Retrieved from www.latin-american.cam.ac.uk/culture/vampires.

Kantaris, G. (2006) 'Cinema and Urbanías: Translocal Identities in Contemporary Mexican Film'. *Bulletin of Latin American Research*, 25(4), 517–527.

Kaufman, D. (2006) 'D. P. Rodrigo Prieto on Shooting *Babel*: Mixed Formats, Anamorphic Lenses, and Three Shades of Red'. *Film and Video*.

Retrieved from www.studiodaily.com/main/searchlist/D-P-Rodrigo-Prieto-on-Shooting-Babel_6630.html.
Kermode, M. (2006) 'Girl Interrupted'. *Sight and Sound*, 16(12), 20–24.
Kerouac, J. (1957) *On the Road*. New York: Viking Press.
Kerr, P. (2010) '*Babel*'s Network Narrative: Packaging a Globalized Art Cinema'. *Transnational Cinemas*, 1(1), 37–51.
Kilday, G. (2010) 'King's Film District Taps Bob Berney'. *Hollywood Reporter*. Retrieved from www.hollywoodreporter.com/news/kings-filmdistrict-taps-bob-berney-28391.
King, G. (2004) 'Notes from Weighing Up the Qualities of Independence: *21 Grams* in Focus'. *Film Studies*, 5, 80–91.
King, G. (2005) *American Independent Cinema*. London: I. B. Taurus.
King, G. (2009) *Indiewood, USA: Where Hollywood Meets Independent Cinema*. London: I. B. Tauris.
Klein, N. (2000) *No Logo*. London: Flamingo.
Klein, N. (2007) *The Shock Doctrine: The Rise of Disaster Capitalism*. New York: Metropolitan.
K-punk (2010) 'They Killed Their Mother: *Avatar* as Ideological Symptom'. Retrieved from http://k-punk.abstractdynamics.org/archives/011437.html.
Kraniauskas, J. (1998) '*Cronos* and the Political Economy of Vampirism: Notes on a Historic Constellation'. In F. Barker, P. Hulme and M. Iversen (eds), *Cannibalism and the Colonial World* (pp. 142–157). Cambridge: Cambridge University Press.
Krassakopoulos, G. (2007) 'Masterclass: Alfonso Cuarón'. In *48th Thessaloniki International Film Festival* (pp. 16–25). Retrieved from http://tiff.filmfestival.gr/inst/Festival/gallery/FilmFestival/48/Masterclasses/Cuaron_Masterclass.pdf.
La Crónica de Hoy (2007) 'Del Toro, Cuarón e Iñárritu Presentan Sus Propuestas a las Autoridades'. Retrieved from www.cronica.com.mx/nota.php?id_nota=291588.
Laderman, D. (2002) *Driving Visions: Exploring the Road Movie*. Austin, TX: University of Texas Press.
Lambie, R. (2011) 'Guillermo del Toro Interview: The Director's Cut of *Mimic*, HP Lovecraft and More'. Retrieved from www.denofgeek.com/movies/1102851/guillermo_del_toro_interview_the_directors_cut_of_mimic_hp_lovecraft_and_more.html.
La Nación (2007) 'Tres Mosqueteros al Ataque'. Retrieved from www.lanacion.com.ar/893663-tres-mosqueteros-al-ataque.
Landis, J. (n.d.) Tribute to Ray Harryhausen on the Official Ray Harryhausen website. Retrieved from www.rayharryhausen.com/tributes.php.
Lang, R. (1997) '*My Own Private Idaho* and the New Queer Road Movies'. In S. Cohan and I. Hark (eds), *The Road Movie Book* (pp. 330–348). London: Routledge.

Langford, B. (2005) *Film Genre: Hollywood and Beyond*. Edinburgh: Edinburgh University Press.
Lawrenson, E. (2002) 'Interview'. *Sight and Sound*. Retrieved from http://old.bfi.org.uk/sightandsound/feature/367.
Lawrenson, E. and Pérez Soler, B. (2001) 'Pup Fiction'. *Sight and Sound*, 11(5). Retrieved from www.bfi.org.uk/sightandsound/feature/78.
Lázaro-Reboll, A. (2007) 'The Transnational Reception of *El espinazo del diablo*'. *Hispanic Research Journal*, 8(1), 39–51.
Leitch, T. (2003) 'Twelve Fallacies in Contemporary Adaptation Theory'. *Criticism*, 45(2), 149–171.
Leitch, T. (2007) *Film Adaptation and Its Discontents: From* Gone with the Wind *to* The Passion of the Christ. Baltimore, MD: Johns Hopkins University Press.
Levy, E. (1999) *Cinema of Outsiders: The Rise of American Independent Film*. New York: New York University Press.
Levy, E. (2006) '*Pan's Labyrinth*: Brilliant Del Toro'. Emanuel Levy Cinema 24/7. Retrieved from www.emanuellevy.com/interview/pans-labyrinth-brilliant-del-toro-1.
Lomnitz, C. (2005) *Death and the Idea of Mexico*. New York: Zone Books.
Lu, S. H. (ed.) (1997) *Transnational Chinese Cinemas: Identity, Nationhood, Gender*. Honolulu, HI: University of Hawaii Press.
Lyotard, J. (1984) *The Postmodern Condition: A Report on Knowledge* (G. Bennington and B. Massumi, trans.). Minneapolis, MN: University of Minnesota Press. (Originally published 1979.)
Maciel, D. (1999) 'Cinema and the State in Contemporary Mexico, 1970–1999'. In J. Hershfield and D. Maciel (eds), *Mexico's Cinema: A Century of Film and Filmmakers* (pp. 197–232). Wilmington, DE: SR Books.
M&C News (2008) 'In Photos: New York Comic Con 2008 – Hellboy II: The Golden Army Preview'. Retrieved from www.monstersandcritics.com/movies/features/article_1401047.php/In_photos_New_York_Comic_Con_2008_-_Hellboy_II_The_Golden_Army_Preview?page=4.
Marks, L. (2000) *The Skin of the Film: Intercultural Cinema, Embodiment, and the Senses*. Durham, NC: Duke University Press.
Maslin, J. (1998) 'The Tale of Two Stories, This One With a Ms'. *New York Times*. Retrieved from http://movies.nytimes.com/movie/review?res=9402E7DB143AF933A05752C0A96E958260.
McCarthy, T. (2003) '*Hulk* Film Review'. *Variety*. Retrieved from www.variety.com/review/VE1117920999.html?categoryid=31&cs=1&p=0.
Menne, J. (2007) 'A Mexican Nouvelle Vague: The Logic of New Waves Under Globalization'. *Cinema Journal*, 47(1), 70–92.
Merritt, G. (1999) *Celluloid Mavericks: A History of American Independent Film*. New York: Thunder's Mouth Press.
Miller, S., Ertegun, A. and Curtis, E. (2004) 'The Joker' [recorded by Fatboy Slim and Bootsy Collins]. On *Palookaville* [CD]. Brighton: Skint Records.

Miller, T., Schiwy, F. and Hernández-Salván, M. (2012) 'Distribution, the Forgotten Element in Transnational Cinema'. *Transnational Cinemas*, 3(1), 197–214.
Minns, A. (2001) 'Icon Take UK Rights to *Y tu mama tambien* in the UK'. *Screen Daily*. Retrieved from www.screendaily.com/icon-takes-uk-rights-on-y-tu-mama-tambien/407295.article.
Mitchell, E. (2006) 'Alejandro Gonzalez Inarritu: How the Fearless Director Captured All the Anxiety, Xenophobia, Violence, and Globalism of the World Today Into His New Film Babel. Interview'. Retrieved November from www.encyclopedia.com/doc/1G1-153707782.html.
Mohr, I. (2007) 'Pan's Breaks Out of Art Niche'. *Variety*, 206(2). Retrieved from www.variety.com/article/VR1117960060?refCatId=13.
Molina Ramírez, T. (2007) 'Del Toro trascendió el gueto del cine fantástico, dice García Tsao'. *La Jornada*. Retrieved from www.jornada.unam.mx/2007/03/20/index.php?section=espectaculos&article=a08n1esp.
Murphy, J. J. (2007) *Me and You and Memento and Fargo: How Independent Screenplays Work*. London: Continuum.
Murray, R. (n.d.) 'Director Alfonso Cuaron Discusses "Children of Men"'. Retrieved from http://movies.about.com/od/childrenofmen/a/childac122006.htm.
Naficy, H. (2001) *An Accented Cinema: Exilic and Diasporic Filmmaking*. Princeton, NJ: Princeton University Press.
Nafus, C. (1998) 'Vampire in a Box'. *Weekly Wire*. Retrieved from http://weeklywire.com/ww/10-19-98/austin_screens_feature2.html.
Naremore, J. (2000) 'Introduction: Film and the Reign of Adaptation'. In J. Naremore (ed.), *Film Adaptation* (pp. 1–16). New Brunswick, NJ: Rutgers University Press.
Neale, S. (2002) 'Art Cinema as Institution'. In C. Fowler (ed.), *The European Cinema Reader* (pp. 103–120). New York: Routledge.
Newman, M. Z. (2006) 'Character and Complexity in American Independent Cinema: *21 Grams* and *Passion Fish*'. *Film Criticism*, 31(1/2), 89–106.
Noble, A. (2005) *Mexican National Cinema*. London: Routledge.
Nowell-Smith, G. (2000) *Oxford History of World Cinema*. Oxford: Oxford University Press.
Oppenheimer, J. (2001) 'A Dog's Life'. *American Photographer* (30April), 21–27.
Ordóñez, M. A. and Nieto, P. (2007) 'Entrevista con Gustavo Santaolalla'. *Score Magazine*. Retrieved from www.scoremagacine.com/Entrevistas_det.php?Codigo=38.
Parsa, A. (2006) 'Exclusive – Political References in New Film "Children of Men" Examined'. Retrieved from www.thedailybackground.com/2006/12/31/exclusive-political-references-in-new-film-children-of-men-examined-illustrated/.
Patterson, J. (2001) 'Aztec Camera'. *The Guardian*. Retrieved from www.guardian.co.uk/film/2001/may/18/culture.features2.

Paz, O. (1967) *The Labyrinth of Solitude: Life and Thought in Mexico* (L. Kemp, trans.). London: Penguin. (Originally published as *El laberinto de soledad*, 1959.)
Pérez Soler, B. (2001) 'Amores perros'. *Fade*, 6(3), 19.
Podalsky, L. (2003) 'Affecting Legacies: Historical Memory and Contemporary Structures of Feeling in *Madagascar* and *Amores perros*'. *Screen*, 44(3), 277–294.
Podalsky, L. (2011) 'Migrant Feelings: Melodrama, *Babel*, and Affective Communities'. *Journal of Hispanic Cinemas*, 7(2), 47–58.
Preston, P. (1990) *The Politics of Revenge: Fascism and the Military in Twentieth-Century Spain*. London: Routledge.
Priego, E. (2002) 'Long on Allegory, Short on Critique: *Y tu mamá también*'. Retrieved from www.cinematropical.com/newsletter/200202/ytumama.html.
Propp, V. (1968) *Morphology of the Folktale* (L. Scott, trans.). Austin, TX: University of Texas Press. (Originally published 1928.)
Rae, N. and Gray, J. (2007) 'When Gen-X Met the X-Men'. In I. Gordon, M. Jancovich and M. McAllister (eds), *Film and Comic Books* (pp. 86–100). Jackson, MS: University Press of Mississippi.
Ramírez Berg, C. (1990) 'Stereotyping in Films in General and of the Hispanic in Particular'. *Howard Journal of Communications*, 2(3), 286–300.
Ramírez Berg, C. (2002) *Latino Images in Film: Stereotypes, Subversion, Resistance*. Austin, TX: University of Texas Press.
Rashkin, E. (2001) *Women Filmmakers in Mexico: The Country in Which We Dream*. Austin, TX: University of Texas Press.
Richard, A. (1994) *Contemporary Hollywood's Negative Hispanic Image: An Interpretative Filmography, 1956–93*. Westport, CT: Greenwood Press.
Riviere, P. (2006) *Fulcanelli: His True Identity Revealed*. Grande Prairie, Alberta: Red Pill Press.
Roary, M. (2010) 'Tails Float Out From Cuaron's *Gravity*'. Retrieved from www.screened.com/news/details-float-out-from-cuarons-gravity/225.
Roberts, S. (2008) 'Guillermo del Toro Interview, *Hellboy 2*'. Retrieved from www.moviesonline.ca/movienews_14974.html.
Rombes, N. (2005) 'The Rebirth of the Author'. *CTheory* (June). Retrieved from www.ctheory.net/articles.aspx?id=480.
Romney, J. (2004) 'Emotional Order Interview with Alejandro González Iñárritu'. *Sight and Sound*, 14(3), 12–16.
Romney, J. (2006) 'Of Raw Hides and Hot Mamas'. Retrieved from www.independent.co.uk/arts-entertainment/films/reviews/jonathan-romney-of-raw-hides-and-hot-mamas-430354.html.
Ross, M. (2010) *South American Cinematic Culture: Policy, Production, Distribution and Exhibition*. Newcastle upon Tyne: Cambridge Scholars.
Said, E. (1979) *Orientalism*. New York: Vintage Books.

Samardzija, Z. (2010) 'DavidLynch.com: Auteurship in the Age of the Internet and Digital Cinema'. Retrieved from www.scope.nottingham.ac.uk/article.php?issue=16&id=1171.
Sánchez Prado, I. (2010) 'El blog de Ignacio Sanchez Prado'. Retrieved from http://ignaciosanchezprado.blogspot.com/2010/10/publicistas-enamorados.html.
Sandoval, S. and Velasco, F. (2008) *Hellboy II: Art of the Movie*. Milwaukie, OR: Dark Horse Books.
Schivelbusch, W. (1986) *The Railway Journey*. Berkeley, CA: University of California Press.
Sciolino, E. and Daly, E. (2002) 'Spaniards at Last Confront the Ghost of Franco'. *New York Times Online*. Retrieved from www.nytimes.com/2002/11/11/world/spaniards-at-last-confront-the-ghost-of-franco.html?pagewanted=all&src=pm.
Sciretta, P. (2007) 'Academy Award Winners 2007. Slash Film'. Retrieved from www.slashfilm.com/2007/02/25/2007-academy-awards-winners.
Scott, A. O. (2003) 'Tall Green, But No Ho Ho Ho'. *New York Times*, 20 September. Retrieved from http://movies.nytimes.com/movie/review?res=9404E0DF1E38F933A15755C0A9659C8B63.
Scott, A. O. (2006) 'Movie Review: *Solo con tu pareja*, A Bedroom Farce With Mortality Hiding in the Closet'. *New York Times*. Retrieved from http://movies.nytimes.com/2006/09/20/movies/20solo.html.
Segerstrom, P. S. (2010) 'Naomi Klein and the Anti-Globalization Movement'. Retrieved from www2.hhs.se/personal/segerstrom/naomiklein.pdf.
Seymour, M. (2007) 'Hard Core Seamless vfx'. Retrieved from www.fxguide.com/featured/Children_of_Men_-_Hard_Core_Seamless_vfx.
Shaw, D. (2003) *Contemporary Latin American Cinema: Ten Key Films*. London: Continuum Publishers.
Shaw, D. (2004) 'The Figure of the Absent Father in Recent Latin American Films'. *Studies in Hispanic Cinemas*, 1(2), 85–102.
Shaw, D. (2005) '"You Are Alright But...": Individual and Collective Representations of Mexicans, Latinos, Anglo-Americans and African-Americans in *Traffic*'. *Quarterly Review of Film and Video*, 22(3), 211–224.
Shaw, D. (2007) '*Blow*: How a Film Created a Hero From a Top-level Drug Trafficker and Blamed the "Colombians" For His Downfall'. *Quarterly Review of Film and Video*, 24(1), 31–40.
Shaw, D. (2013, forthcoming) 'Deconstructing and Reconstructing "Transnational Cinema"'. In S. Dennison (ed.), *Contemporary Hispanic Cinema: Interrogating Transnationalism in Spanish and Latin American Film*. Woodbridge: Tamesis.
Shoard, C. (2010) 'Government to Axe UK Film Council'. *The Guardian*. Retrieved from www.guardian.co.uk/film/2010/jul/26/uk-film-council.
Smith, P. J. (2003a) *Amores Perros*. London: British Film Institute.

Smith, P. J. (2003b) 'Transatlantic Traffic in Recent Mexican Films'. *Journal of Latin American Cultural Studies*, 12, 389–400.

Smith, P. J. (2007) '*Pan's Labyrinth* (*El laberinto del fauno*)'. *Film Quarterly*, 60(4), 4–9.

Sneider, J. (2007) 'Rodrigo Prieto, *Babel*'. Retrieved from www.variety.com/article/VR1117956612.html.

Staiger, J. (2003) 'Hybrid or Inbred: The Purity Hypothesis and Hollywood Genre History'. In B. K. Grant (ed.), *Film Genre Reader III* (pp. 185–199). Austin, TX: University of Texas Press.

Stewart, M. (2007) 'Irresistible Death: *21 Grams* as Melodrama'. *Cinema Journal*, 47(1), 49–69.

Stock, A. (1999) 'Authentically Mexican? *Mi Querido Tom Mix* and *Cronos* Reframe Critical Questions'. In J. Hershfield and D. Maciel (eds), *Mexico's Cinema: A Century of Film and Filmmakers* (pp. 269–280). Wilmington, DE: SR Books.

Strain, E. (2003) *Public Places, Private Journeys: Ethnography, Entertainment, and the Tourist Gaze*. New Brunswick, NJ: Rutgers University Press.

Stringer, J. (1997) 'Exposing Intimacy in Russ Meyer's *MotorPsycho!* and *Faster Pussycat! Kill! Kill!*'. In S. Cohan and I. Hark (eds), *The Road Movie Book* (pp.165–178). London: Routledge.

Tallerico, B. (2008) 'Exclusive: Guillermo del Toro Interview by Brian Tallerico, UGO Entertainment'. Retrieved from www.ugo.com/ugo/html/article/?id=16348.

Taylor, J. (1983) *Strangers in Paradise: The Hollywood Émigrés, 1933–1950*. London: Faber and Faber.

Thanouli, E. (2006) 'Post-Classical Narration: A New Paradigm in Contemporary Cinema'. *New Review of Film and Television Studies*, 4(3), 183–196.

Thanouli, E. (2008) 'Narration in World Cinema: Mapping the Flows of Formal Exchange in the Era of Globalization'. *New Cinemas: Journal of Contemporary Film*, 6(1), 5–15.

Thomas, H. (1998) *The Spanish Civil War*. London: Penguin Books. (Originally published 1961.)

Tierney, D. (2009) 'Alejandro González Iñárritu: Director Without Borders'. *New Cinemas: Journal of Contemporary Film*, 7(2), 101–117.

Tovar, L. (2007) 'Sin sorpresas o casi'. *La Jornada*, 632. Retrieved from www.jornada.unam.mx/2007/04/15/sem-tovar.html.

Triana-Toribio, N. (2003) *Spanish National Cinema*. London: Routledge.

Triana-Toribio, N. (2008) 'Auteurism and Commerce in Contemporary Spanish Cinema: *Directores Mediáticos*'. *Screen*, 49(3), 259–276.

Tzioumakis, Y. (2006) *American Independent Cinema: An Introduction*. Edinburgh: Edinburgh University Press.

Udden, J. (2009) 'Child of the Long Take: Alfonso Cuaron's Film Aesthetics in the Shadow of Globalization'. *Style*, 43(1), 26–44.

UK Film Council (2007) *Statistical Yearbook 2006/07*. Retrieved from www.bfi.org.uk/sites/bfi.org.uk/files/downloads/uk-film-council-statistical yearbook2006-2007.
Urry, J. (2002) *The Tourist Gaze*. London: Sage.
Vargas, J. C. (2002) 'Mexican Post-Industrial Cinema (1990–2002)'. Retrieved from www.slideshare.net/Uskidz/artico2.
Verkaik, R. (2010) 'Immigrants Should Not Be in Jail, Says Prisons Watchdog'. *Home Affairs Editor*. Retrieved from www.independent.co.uk/news/uk/home-news/immigrants-should-not-be-in-jail-says-prisons-watchdog-2025990.html.
Vigil, D. and López, F. (2004) 'Race and Ethnic Relations in Mexico'. *Journal of Latino-Latin American Studies*, 1(2), 49–74.
Visual Hollywood (2006a) '*Children of Men* (2006). About the Production'. Retrieved from www.visualhollywood.com/movies/children-of-men/about2.php.
Visual Hollywood (2006b) '*Children of Men* (2006). Casting the Children of the Future'. Retrieved from www.visualhollywood.com/movies/children-of-men/about3.php.
Visual Hollywood (2006c) '*Children of Men* (2006). Synopsis'. Retrieved from http://www.visualhollywood.com/movies/children-of-men/news.php.
Vogler, C. (1998) *The Writer's Journey: Mythic Structure for Writers* (second edition). Studio City, CA: Michael Wiese Productions.
Von Busack, R. (2007) 'Making the Future: Richard von Busack Talks to Alfonso Cuarón About Filming *Children of Men*'. Retrieved from www.metroactive.com/metro/01.10.07/alfonso-cuaron-0702.html.
Voynar, K. (2006) 'Interview: *Children of Men* Director Alfonso Cuaron' (25 December). Retrieved from www.cinematical.com/2006/12/25/interview-children-ofmen-director-alfonso-cuaron/.
Wagner, A. (2006) 'Politics, Bible Stories and Hope: An Interview with Alfonso Cuarón'. *The Stranger*. Retrieved from www.thestranger.com/seattle/Content?oid=128363.
Wells, P. (2002) *Animation: Genre and Authorship*. London: Wallflower Press.
Williams, H. (2011) 'Mexico's B-Movie Boom: "Narco Cinema" Inspired by Real-Life Crime Is on a High'. *The Independent*. Retrieved from www.independent.co.uk/arts-entertainment/films/features/mexicos-bmovie-boom-narco-cinema-inspired-by-reallife-crime-is-on-a-high-2209472.html.
Woll, A. (1980) *The Latin Image in American Film*. Los Angeles, CA: UCLA Latin American Center Publications.
Wood, J. (2006) *The Faber Book of Mexican Cinema*. London: Faber and Faber.
Wood, J. (2008) 'A Life in Pictures: Guillermo Del Toro'. Retrieved from www.bafta.org/access-all-areas/videos/a-life-in-pictures-guillermo-del-toro,466,BA.html.
Wood, J. (2011) 'Specialty Cinema – Distribution and Exhibition'. Paper presented at the Screen Industries Seminar, University of Portsmouth.

York, J. (2007) '*Babel* Babble'. Retrieved from http://inthefray.org/content/view/2118/142.

Zaniello, T. (2007) *The Cinema of Globalization: A Guide to Films About the New Economic Order*. Ithaca, NY: Cornell University Press.

Zavala, L. (2011) 'Tendencias Temáticas y Formales en las Óperas Primas del Cine Mexicano, 1988–2004'. Retrieved from www.elojoquepiensa.net/elojoquepiensa/index.php/articulos/154.

Zipes, J. (1999) *When Dreams Came True: Classic Fairy Tales and Their Tradition*. New York: Routledge.

Žižek, S. (2006) 'The Clash of Civilizations at the End of History'. Retrieved from www.scribd.com/doc/19133296/Zizek-The-Clash-of-Civilizations-at-the-End-of-History.

Žižek, S. (2007) 'Slavoj Zizek Reacts to *Children of Men*'. Retrieved from www.continental-philosophy.org/2007/01/01/slavoj-zizek-reacts-to-children-of-men.

Index

ABC Disney 116
Abraham, Marc 203
Acevedo-Muñoz, Ernesto 193, 195, 196
Aguilera, Jorge 107
AIDS 161, 164–5, 167
alchemy 26–9
Alfredson, Tomas 73
Almodóvar, Pedro 11, 77, 79, 167
Altavista 96–7
Althusser, Louis 221
Altman, Robert 103, 120, 207
Alvaray, Luisela 183
Alvarez, Javier 32
Amenábar, Alejandro, *Abre los ojos* 72, 73
amigos 3, 228
Andersen, Hans Christian 83
Anderson, Paul Thomas 98, 116, 178–9
Angeles, Pablo 51
Anhelo Producciones 4, 180
Anonymous Content 140
Antonioni, Michelangelo 178, 206–7
Araki, Gregg 184
Arau, Alfonso, *Como agua para chocolate* 97, 159, 169
Argento, Dario 36
Armenábar, Alejandro 11
Aronofsky, Darren 98
Arriaga, Guillermo 5, 95, 102, 103, 104–5, 110, 111, 114, 121, 135, 142
Art Linson Productions 6, 170
Ashby, Hal 186
Ashitey, Claire-Hope 205
Atkinson, Michael 69, 169
Atwood, Margaret 88

Audiard, Jacques 73
Auster, Paul 102
auteurism, meaning 7–8
Azcona, M. 95, 100, 103, 114
Aztecs 27, 32

Balagueró, Jaume 73
Balkans 209
Bancroft, Anne 170
Baquero, Ivana 78
Bardem, Javier 6, 226
Barlowe, Wayne 50
Barraza, Adriana 138
Bauche, Vanessa 104
Bava, Mario 36
Bayona, Juan Antonio 3, 73
Bazin, André 178
Bell, Daniel 217
Benet, Isabel 162
Bergman, Ingmar 71
Bernal, Gael García 101, 104, 139, 176, 181, 182, 185, 228
Berney, Bob 77–8, 182
Berry, Chris 9
Big Bad Wolf 85
Blanchett, Cate 138, 139, 140
Blatty, William Peter 36
Böcklin, Arnold 59, 76–7
Bolivia 222
Bolt, Gary 52
Bond films 70
Bordwell, David 57, 71, 72, 98–100, 103, 104, 108, 124, 125, 206
Borges, Jorge Luis 30

Bosch, Hieronymus 59
Boyle, Danny 98
Boyle, Kirk 217
BPRD 54, 60
Bravo 182
Brazil 222
Broch, Brigitte 5, 95, 114, 121, 125, 147
Brody, Jackson 53–4
Brook, Claudio 22, 25
Browning, Tod 37
Bruegel. Pieter 59
Buñuel, Luis 109
Burton, Tim 63
Bush, George W. 140, 146, 229

Caballero, Eugenio 79
Cablevision 182
Caine, Michael 205
Calderón, Felipe 3
Campbell, Gerardo 107
Campbell, Joseph 84, 87
Canada Films 228
Cann, Benjamin 103
Cannes Film Festival 21, 35, 78, 97
Carrera, Carlos 227
Carroll, Lewis 68, 83
Carter, Angela 88
Castro, Oliver 107
Cazals, Felipe 102
Central Films 140
Cha Cha Cha 2, 181, 228
Chávez, Hugo 222
Chernobyl 209
CIE 96–7
Cinema du Look 99
Cinemark 160
climate change 219, 220
Coen Brothers 116
Cohan, S. 184
colonialism 24, 27, 142, 146, 202
Columbus, Chris, *Harry Potter and the Chamber of Secrets* 82–3
Control Machete 107
Cook, Pam 35
Correa, Rafael 222
Corrigan, Tim 120
Cortés, Busi 226
Criterion 22, 169

Cronenberg, David 35
Crowe, Cameron 73
Cruz, Pablo 228
Cuarón, Alfonso
  auteurism 1–2, 14, 171–2
  career 1–3, 159, 197–8
  Children of Men 1, 10, 12
    auteurism 173, 212, 214, 228
    collaborators 203–4, 228
    creative control 7
    critical success 203
    distribution 228
    filmography 237–8
    illustrations 209, 210
    Iñárritu and 209, 228
    international success 170, 201
    nominations 201, 203
    overview 201–23
    plot 204–5
    political vision 212–17, 229
    Possibility of Hope and 217–23
    publicity 179
    techniques 165, 178, 201, 206–8
    transnationalism 202–12
    world cinema 137, 204
  colours 171–2
  creative control 7
  Gravity 179
  Great Expectations 1, 6, 169
    auteurism 170
    cast 170
    creative control 170
    'failed' text 14, 173
    filmography 236–7
    'green period' 167
    Hollywood film 170–1, 177, 178, 226
  'green period' 167
  Harry Potter and the Prisoner of Azkaban 7, 14, 169, 178, 197, 203, 226, 237
    Hollywood period 170–3
    introduction 6–7
  A Little Princess 1, 169, 226
    filmography 236
    'green period' 6, 167
    Hollywood film 170, 171, 177, 178
    illustration 172
    Mexican identity 2–3, 226–7

Index

Possibility of Hope 202, 215
  political vision 217–23
  production companies 68, 70–1, 180, 181, 218
  productions 238
Sólo con tu pareja (Love in a Time of Hysteria) 1, 6
  AIDS 161, 164–5, 167
  creative control 176
  décors 171
  distribution 169
  effect 226
  'failed' text 14, 169
  filmography 236
  funding 168
  'green period' 167, 172–3
  illustrations 162, 166
  Japanese characters 165, 167
  lessons 176
  Mexican middle-class success 159–69
  music 165
  screwball comedy 161
  transnationalism 167–8
  urban images 165–6
  women 163–4, 229
  television works 175n13
Y tu mamá también 4, 10, 12, 169
  anti-globalisation 181, 191, 193
  auteurism 7, 172–3, 176–98, 207
  budget 180
  cast 181
  class 173
  creative control 6–7
  distribution 97, 169
  effect 203, 226
  feminism 163, 195–7
  filmography 237
  funding 21, 180–1, 193
  global Mexican film 179–83
  homosexuality 197
  illustrations 189, 192, 194
  international success 170, 176, 177, 181–2
  marketing 180
  Mexico 176, 177–9, 184, 186–95
  national success 180
  politics 229
  return to Mexico 159, 177–9
  road movie 183–6
  slang 161
  techniques 165, 178–9, 191, 195
  transnationalism 159, 179–83
Cuarón, Carlos 3, 161, 170, 176, 177, 180, 185
Cuarón, Jonás 221
Culture Publishers 79
cyberrealism 124

Dadaists 59
Dali, Salvador 59
DasGupta, Sayantani 213
D'Aurillac, Gilbert 27
Davies, Ann 19–20, 24, 25, 27, 80
De Niro, Robert 170
de Palma, Brian 140
del Toro *see* Toro, Guillermo del
Deleyto, Celestino 95, 100, 103, 114
Delgado, María 188
Dennison, Stephanie 136–7, 138–9
Desai, Jigna 183
Deseo, El 4
Dickens, Charles 173
Disney 88, 116
D'Lugo, Marvin 8, 101, 109
Dotrice, Roy 63
Dracula 20, 36, 37, 38
DreamWorks 119

Ebert, Roger 170–1
Echevarria, Emilio 102, 104
Ecuador 222
Edwards, Blake 161, 167
Edwards, Kim 88
Egoyan, Atom 103
Eimbcke, Fernando 227
Ejiofor, Chiwetel 205
El Caid, Boubker Ait 138
Elfman, Danny 57, 58
Erice, Victor 11, 35, 81
Esperanto Filmoj 70, 71, 218
Estudio México 96–7
Eva, Fabrizio 218
Ezra, E 183, 204

fairy tales 68, 76, 83–9, 229
Fassbinder, Rainer Werner 99

Faulkner, William 102
feminism
    El laberinto del fauno 88–9
    Mexico 163
    Y tu mamá también 195–7
Ferris, Pam 207
Finnegan, Nuala 187
Fisher, Terence 20, 35, 36, 37
Focus Features 6, 7, 118–19, 173, 181, 227–8
Fons, Jorge 103
Fox, Vicente 199n16
France 71, 146
Franco, Francisco 63
Frankenstein 20, 35, 36, 37–8
Frears, Stephen 137
Friedman, Milton 222
Fulcanelli 28

Gaghan, Stephen 137, 140
Gainsbourg, Charlotte 115
Galt, Rosalind 71, 72
García, José 121
García Márquez, Gabriel 28, 29, 186
García Tsao, Leonardo 180, 189
Genette, Gérard 46
Giménez Cacho, Daniel 32–3, 159, 187
Glatzer, Richard 116
Glazer, Mitch 171
globalisation 9, 10, 137, 139, 181, 191, 193, 204, 222
global warming 219, 220
Godard, Jean-Luc 186
Goldin, Nan 102
Gómez Reja, Alfonso 121
Good Machine International 181, 182, 227–8
Gordon, I. 51
Goya, Francisco 76
Grant, Catherine 46, 56, 136, 137
Grau, Jorge Michel 33, 227
Gray, John 219, 220
Gray, Jonathan 46
Grimm Brothers 76
GrupoOmnilife 180
Guantanamo Bay 205
Guerra, Ely 107
Guerrrero, Alvaro 104
Gutiérrez, Tomás 8

Hadad, Astrid 166
Haddu, Miriam 160, 163, 165, 166, 167
Haggis, Paul 140
Hammer Film Productions 35, 36
Haneke, Michael 11, 73, 103, 207
Hark, I. 184
Hark, Tsui 99
Harkin, James 123–4
Harryhausen, Ray 11, 57–8
Hartland, Edward Sidney 83–7, 92n24
Hawke, Ethan 170
Hayek, Salma 182
Haynes, Todd 120
Hegel, Georg 219
Hermann, Bernard 57, 58
Hermosillo, Jaime Humberto 102, 161
Hernández, Julián 227
Hernández, Martin 121
Herzog, Werner 99
Hezbollah 222
Higbee, W. 9, 202, 204
Hirschbiegel, Oliver 214
Hit and Run Productions 202
Hitchcock, Alfred 11, 35, 44n15, 48, 55
Hjort, Mette 212
Hobson, Janell 88
Hollywood
    art cinema and 60, 122
    box office returns 117
    Cuarón 6, 12, 170–3, 177–8, 183
    del Toro and 4, 8, 23, 35, 37, 39, 80
    Hellboy II 45, 47, 49, 50, 52, 65, 69, 70
    fantasy films 70, 74
    genres 39, 67
    hegemonic practices 115
    heroes 41
    Latin American stereotypes 23–4
    narrative practices 71–2, 74, 84–5
    network narratives 99–100, 102, 103, 104, 106, 111
    post-classicism 98–9
    road movies 184, 195–6
    teen sex comedies 191
    world cinema and 136–7, 138–41, 154
    see also independent cinema
Holmlund, Chris 117, 211
Holocaust 209

Index

Hood, Gavin 77, 140
Hope, Ted 181, 227
Hopper, Dennis 184
Hubner, Laura 88
Hughes, Howard 33
Hurricane Katrina 222
Hutcheon, Linda 52

Icaza, Luis de 188
Icon 182
IFC Films 169, 182
IMCINE 4, 21, 42, 160, 168–9, 180
Iñárritu, Alejandro Gonzáles
  21 Grams 1, 5
    collaborators 121–2, 125
    colours 5, 125–32
    critiques 151
    disruption of chronology 105
    distribution 173, 228
    filmography 234–5
    illustrations 128, 130, 131, 132
    independence and auteurism 119–22
    independence and studios 118–19
    independent art film 122–32
    international cast 115, 120
    Mexico 114
    overview 114–33
    production company 181–2
  Amores perros 1, 5, 10, 21
    collaborators 95, 228
    critiques 151
    distribution 96–8
    filmography 234
    funding 101
    illustrations 101, 102
    international success 177
    Mexican film 114
    new international style 98–109
    overview 95–111
    techniques 5, 99–109, 126, 206
    transnationalism 96–8, 137, 159, 179
    transnational Mexico 109–11, 114
    youth market 107–8
  auteurism 5, 96
  Babel 10, 12, 95
    ambition 5
    auteurism 124, 228
    cast 153
    collaborators 121
    critique 103
    distribution 140
    film languages 135
    filmography 235
    globalisation 137–8
    Hollywood world cinema 138–41, 148–51, 154, 225
    illustrations 144, 150
    music 140–1
    nominations 140
    overview 135–54
    ownership 6
    politics 151–4, 229
    storylines 138
    suffering 141–2
    suffering and world cinema gaze 148–51
    tourist gaze 141–8, 154
  Biutiful 5–6, 95, 103, 112n2, 225–6, 228, 235
  career 1–3, 159, 225
  Children of Men and 209, 228
  co-productions 236
  creative control 2, 7, 118, 121
  international status 173
  introduction 5–6
  Mexican identity 177, 226–7
  production companies 140, 181
  transnationalism 11–12
  trilogy 96
independent cinema
  21 Grams 114–33
  art cinema 122–32
  auteurism 119–22
  studios 118–19
  creative control 118, 121
  meaning 116–18
  United States 105, 182–3
Independent Film Channel 182
Indiana Jones 70
Iraq 205, 208–9, 210
Isabel, Margarita 25
Islamophobia 146

James, P. D. 7, 202–3, 204
Jameson, Frederic 151–2

Japan 79, 146, 147
Jarmusch, Jim 120
Jenkins, Henry 51
Jeunet, Jean-Pierre 98
Jones, Tommy Lee 116
Jordan, Neil 99, 116
Jung, Carl 84

Kantaris, Geoffrey 24, 35, 111
Kees_L 54
Kermode, Mark 30–1, 37
Kerouac, Jack 184
Kerr, Paul 103, 146
Kidfromhell 53
Kieslowski, Krzysztof 100, 126–7
Kikuchi, Rinko 138
King, Geoff 116, 118, 122–3
Klein, Naomi 213, 217, 218, 219–23
Kraniauskas, J. 19
Krassakopoulos, George 170
Kuhn, Annette 136, 137
Kurosawa, Akira 71
Kusturica, Emir 98

Lacan, Jacques 221
Laderman, David 184
Landis, John 57
Langford, Barry 39
Laughton, Charles 35
Lázaro-Reboll, A. 21
Lebanon 222
Lee, Ang 11, 59, 63, 97
Lee, Christopher 37
Lee, Spike 120
Leitch, Thomas 48, 55
Leone, Sergio 36
Lewis, C.S. 83
Lim, Song 9, 136–7, 138–9, 202, 204
Linde, David 118, 119, 181, 227
Lion's Gate 97
Llosa, Claudia 9
Lomnitz, Claudio 30
Lovelock, James 218, 219–20
Lubezki, Emmanuel 6, 12, 165, 170, 171, 172, 178, 179, 185, 188, 201, 203, 226
Lubitsch, Ernst 161, 167
Lucas, George 120

Lugosi, Bela 37
Luhrmann, Baz 11, 35
Lula Da Silva, Luix Inácio 222
Luna, Diego 176, 181, 182, 185, 228
Luppi, Frederico 22, 25, 30, 40, 63
Lynch, David 120

Macdonald, Kevin 214
Manilow, Barry 60
Marcos, Subcomandante 110
Margolyes, Miriam 82
Marks, L. 9
Marsan, Eddie 115
Martel, Lucrecia 9, 11
Marxism 216–17, 221
Maslin, Janet 171
Matthews, Liesel 172
McCarthy, Todd 59
Media Rights Capital 140
Meirelles, Fernando 8, 11, 98, 116, 137
Merritt, Greg 116
Mexico
 21 Grams 114
 AIDS 164
 Amores perros 109–11, 114
 cinema 102–3
 death theme 30–1
 ethnicity 161, 176, 229
 feminism 163
 Film Academy 79
 film funding 1, 3, 8, 19, 21
  see also IMCINE
 immigration to US 139
 Laberinto del fauno, El 78–83
 machismo 176
 Mexican identity 2–3, 177, 226–7
 Mexico City 165–6
 middle-class audience 159–69
 prostitutes 163
 United States and 229–30
 Y tu mamá también 176, 177–9, 184, 186–95
Midsummer Day 86
Mignola, Mike 8, 45, 47–51, 52, 54–5
migration 110, 138, 153, 201–5, 213–20, 226, 229
Miller, Chris 3
Miller, T. 182

Index

Minghella, Anthony 116
Miramax 116, 119, 168
Mirrione, Stephen 112n1, 122, 127
Mizoguchi, Kenji 207
Monge, Raul 51
Montero, Rafael 103
Moore, Julianne 202, 203, 205, 212, 215
Morales, Esai 3, 73
Morales, Eva 222
Moreau, Gustave 36
Morocco 146, 147–8, 153
Mozart, Wolfgang Amadeus 165, 167
Murnau, Friedrich Wilhelm 35, 37
Murphy, J.J. 117, 122
Murray, Rodrigo 110

Nacha Pop 107
Naficy, H. 9
NAFTA 3, 24, 39
Napoli, Donna Jo 88
National Lottery 77
Navarro, Guillermo 4, 51, 61, 78, 79, 227
Neale, Stephen 71–2, 77
neo-liberal economics 161, 181, 219, 221–2
network narratives 99–100, 101, 102, 103, 104, 106, 111
Newman, Michael Z. 122–3
New Wave 71
Nicaragua 222
Nixey, Troy 3
Noble, Andrea 163
Nolan, Christopher 63
Northern Ireland 209
Novaro, Maria 103, 184, 195, 227
Nu Visión 97

Omnilife de Mexico 180, 181
Oplev, Niels Arden 73
Optimum Home Entertainment 79, 97
Orientalism 146, 147
Ortega, Daniel 222
Owen, Clive 202, 204, 211

Paltrow, Gwyneth 170
Paramount Vantage 138, 140
Paronnaud, Vincent 116
Parsa, Arlen 210

Partido Revolucionario Institucional (PRI) 109, 188
Paz, Octavio 31, 34
Penn, Arthur 184
Penn, Sean 1, 115, 120, 122, 124
Perlman, Ron 22, 25
Picasso, Pablo 172
Picturehouse 68, 77, 79, 230
Pinochet, Augusto 222
Pitt, Brad 138, 139, 140, 153
Plaza, Paco 73
Pollack, Sydney 169
post-classicism 98–9
PRI (Partido Revolucionario Institucional) 109, 188
Priego, Ernesto 180, 189, 199n15
Prieto, Rodrigo 5, 95, 107, 114, 121, 122, 125, 129, 131, 134n15, 143–5, 147, 149–51, 219, 226
Propp, Vladimir 84, 87
Pyramide Distribution 97

Rackham, Arthur 76
Ramírez, Claudia 162
Ramírez Berg, Charles 110
Rashidi, Mustapha 153
Reagan, Ronald 222
Red Riding Hood 85
Regency Enterprises 119
Reygadas, Carlos 9, 227
Richet, Jean-François 73
Ripstein, Arturo 8, 102, 103, 109, 161
Ritchie, Guy 99
road movies 183–6, 195–6
Roeg, Nicolas 35
Rombes, Nicholas 56
Romney, Jonathan 118, 206
Ross, Miriam 160
Rotberg, Dana 195, 227
Rowden, T. 183, 204
Ruela, Julio 36
Rulfo, Juan Carlos 227

Said, Edward 146, 147
Sakamoto, Ryuichi 141
Salerno, Robert 122
Salles, Walter 8, 11, 183
Sánchez Parra, Gustavo 107

Sánchez Prado, Ignacio 161
Santoalla, Gustavo 5, 95, 106, 114, 121, 125, 129, 140–1, 145
Sarris, Andrew 39
Sassen, Saskia 218, 219
Satrapi, Marjane 116
Sayles, John 120
Schamus, James 118, 119, 181, 227
Schoonover, Karl 71, 72
Schwabe, Carlos 36, 77
Schyfter, Guita 195, 227
Scorcese, Martin 120
Scott, Ridley 184
screwball comedies 159, 161, 167
Sefami, José 110
Serrano, Antonio 159
Sexton, Tim 203
Seymour, M. 208
Shanath, Tamara 22
Shor, Hilary 202–3, 212
Shrek films 88
Silvester II, Pope 27
Sinbad films 57
Sistach, Marisa 195, 227
Smith, Dick 37, 58
Smith, Kevin 120
Smith, Paul Juilian 76, 78, 81, 96–7, 110
Soderbergh, Steven 120, 127, 134n7
Sokurov, Alexander 206–7
Solanas, Fernando 8, 137
Somalia 209
Sony Columbia 116
Sony Picture Classics 116
Sosa, Martha 97
Spain
 Civil War 69, 81
 Francoism 63, 81, 229
 Laberinto del fauno, El 78–83
 post-Civil War 68, 80
Springall. Alejandro 32
Sri Lanka 208–9
Staiger, Janet 39
Stock, Anne Marie 19, 35, 42
Stone, Oliver 98
Strain, Ellen 142, 143
Strike Entertainment 203
structuralism 84–5
Sulichin, Fernando 140

surrealists 59
Sylvian, David 141
symbolists 59, 76–7

Tallerico, Brian 83
Tarantino, Quentin 102, 103
Tarchani, Said 138
Tarkovsky, Andrei 100, 206–7
Tennyson, Alfred 60
Tequila Gang 4
terrorism 138, 139, 146, 153, 205, 214, 215
Thanouli, Eleftheria 98, 99–100, 104, 108, 124
Thatcher, Margaret 222
theoretical approaches 7–12
This Is That Productions 118, 119
Tierney, Dolores 103, 105, 114, 151
Todorov, Tzvetan 218, 220
Toledo, Goya 104
Toro, Benicio del 1, 115, 119, 120, 122, 124
Toro, Guillermo del
 actor 134n7
 auteurism 20
 Blade 4
 Blade II 37, 78, 225, 232
 borrowings 11
 career 1–2, 159
 collaborations 3, 228
 co-productions 234
 creative control 7
 Cronos 1, 10
  alchemy 26–9
  awards 21, 35
  budget 67
  commercial shift 159
  death 29–34
  fans 78
  filmmaker as alchemist 34–8
  filmography 231
  funding 21
  influences 35–6
  key to cinematic universe 38–42
  objects and symbols 41–2
  overview 19–43
  plot 22
  Spanish language 3
  transnationalism 19–26, 137

Index

vampire genre 19, 24, 26–32, 34, 37, 70
visual motifs 63
El Espinazo del diablo (Devil's Backbone)
  children 40
  fans 78
  filmography 232
  funding 21
  genre boundaries 22, 39, 70
  Spanish language 4
genres 3
Hellboy 4, 8, 39, 42, 78, 233
Hellboy II
  auteurism 45–7, 50, 55–60
  collaborators 50–1
  fans and auteurism 51–5
  filmography 233–4
  funding 45, 47
  genres 39
  illustrations 62, 64
  Laberinto del fauno, El and 60–5, 69–71
  magic 41–2
  Mignola's role 47–51
  monsters 38
  overview 45–65
  producer 228
  references 57, 59–60
  Spanish language 4
  stylistic markers 225
on Hollywood blockbusters 8
introduction 3–5
Laberinto del fauno, El (Pan's Labyrinth) 1
  art and genre cinema 71–8
  auteurism 46, 67, 228
  children 40
  collaborators 51, 228
  creative control 70–1
  distribution 68, 77, 79, 230
  fairy tale 83–8, 229
  filmography 233
  funding 68, 77
  gender 88–9, 195
  genre boundaries 22, 39, 47, 48, 67–90
  Hellboy II and 60–5, 69–71
  illustrations 62, 64, 75, 76, 82
  marketing 68, 183
  monsters 38
  national identities 10, 78–83, 227
  nominations 78–9
  overview 67–90
  politics 199n20
  references 60, 75–7, 81–3
  social vision 12
  Spanish language 4
  techniques 31
  visual motifs 41–2
Mexican funding and 180
Mexican identity 177, 226–7
Mimic 1, 4, 225, 232
on NAFTA 3
production companies 68, 70–1, 181
productions 3, 73
The Strain (novel) 34, 37
transnationalism 183
Torreblanco, Frida 71
Torrent, Ana 35, 81
tourist gaze 141–8, 154, 189
transnationalism
  Amores perros 96–109, 114, 137, 159, 179
  Children of Men 202–12
  Cronos 19–26, 137
  Sólo con tu pareja 167–8
  theory 8–12
  Y tu mamá también 159, 179–83
Triana-Toribio, Núria 120, 167
Trier, Lars von 11, 98
Twentieth Century Fox 6, 170, 182
Tykwer, Tom 98, 99, 137
Tzioumakis, Yannis 116, 117

Udden, James 178, 190, 203, 207, 211
UK Film Council 77
United Kingdom, colonialism 146
United States
  cultural misunderstandings 152
  foreign relations 140
  Hispanic population 182
  Hollywood *see* Hollywood
  Hurricane Katrina 222
  independent cinema *see* independent cinema

Mexico and 139, 229–30
NAFTA and 39
neo-colonialism 24, 27
power structures 154
war on terror 139, 153, 229
Universal Pictures 7, 32, 35, 45, 71, 118, 179, 202–3, 207, 211, 227–8
Universal Studios 223, 227
Urry, John 143, 146

vampire genre 19, 24, 26–32, 34, 37, 70
Van Sant Gus 120, 179, 184
Vargas, Francisco 110, 227
Vargas, Juan Carlos 160
Velasco, Francisco Ruiz 50, 51
Velásquez, Diego 76, 81
Venegas, Julieta 107
Venezuela 222
Verdú, Maribel 176, 181, 195, 196
Vergara, Jorge 180–1
Vilaplana, Bernat 51, 61, 78
Villares, Raul 51
Vogler, Christopher 84, 87

Wang, Wayne 102
Warner, Marina 88
Warner Brothers 6, 7, 79, 198n7
Warner Home Video 97, 98
Watts, Naomi 1, 115, 120, 122, 124
Welles, Orson 207

Wenders, Wim 98, 100
Westmoreland, Wash 116
Whale, James 20, 35, 36
Wild Bunch 78
Winterbottom, Michael 137
Wizard of Oz 68, 75, 83
Wong-Kar-Wai, Raymond 98, 100, 103
Woo, John 99
Wood, Jason 23, 118, 121
world cinema
  Babel
    Hollywood world cinema 138–41, 154
    suffering 148–51
    tourist gaze 141–8
  Children of Men 137, 204
  meaning 136–8
Wormwood, J.R. 53

Yakusho, Kôji 152
Yuh, Jennifer 3

Zaniello, Tom 10
Zapatistas 110, 192
Zavala, Lauro 160
Zeta film 140
Zipes, Jack 88
Žižek, Slavoj 205–6, 218, 219–23
Zwick, Edward 137